D0930944

HARVARD HISTORICAL MONOGRAPHS

XLIX

Published under the direction of the Department of History
from the income of The Robert Louis Stroock Fund

G.Vertue.

R.Graves sculp

BISHOP JEWEL.

JOHN JEWEL

AND THE PROBLEM OF
DOCTRINAL AUTHORITY

W. M. SOUTHGATE

HARVARD UNIVERSITY PRESS
Cambridge, Massachusetts
1962

Distributed in Great Britain by Oxford University Press, London

Library of Congress Catalog Card Number 62–9430

Printed in the United States of America

To

J. R. S.

Preface

The problem of the authority for Christian doctrine is the central problem of the Reformation. Only when the reformers came finally to reject the old accepted authority for doctrine did the movement for reform become a revolution, the religious revolution that we call the Reformation. It was the question of the ultimate sanction for doctrine rather than a divergence over particular doctrines themselves which in the end proved insoluble and irrevocably divided the reformed Churches from the Church of Rome.

Although the problem was fundamental, it was not causative. It emerged only as the pressure of more immediate issues drove men to it. Not until the teachings professed by the reformers were officially rejected by the Church was it recognized as a central issue. So long as there was a measure of indefiniteness concerning doctrinal orthodoxy there was no real problem. But as soon as the older conventional authority of the institutional Church was cited against doctrines which the reformers believed essential, they had no choice but to reject that authority and to cite in its place authority of greater validity. In the end every man and every communion had to face the question and answer satisfactorily: not merely *what do I believe,* but *by what authority do I believe it?*

With the signal exception of the Church of England, the Churches that repudiated the doctrinal authority of Rome replaced institutional authority with a sanction at once independent of tradition and highly individualistic. The English Church, at one with the continental Churches in its rejection of Rome, moved positively in a different direction. The Anglican solution was later in attaining final formulation, as a result of the erratic course of the Reformation under the early Tudors. The task of constructing a theory of doctrinal authority independent of the institutional control of the Roman Church and yet at the same time both traditional and Catholic was only completed toward the end of the century when Richard Hooker wrote his *Laws of Ecclesiastical Polity*. Hooker's work, however, was not the first effort made to solve the problem. It was rather the culmination of a series of attempts extending back half a century, of which the most successful was that of John Jewel in the early years of Elizabeth's reign.

Bishop Jewel was an apologist and a controversialist rather than a systematic thinker. Even his *Apology of the Church of England* is primarily a defense of the English Church against Rome and only secondarily a statement of English teachings. As a result, his extremely voluminous and unsystematic work, unlike the beautifully ordered treatise of Hooker, does not attract the modern reader. Yet during Elizabeth's reign and well into the seventeenth century, Jewel's works were highly valued and even popular, an essential part of the education of the Anglican churchman. Early in the reign it was ordered that they be placed in every church for the layman to read and they played a vital role in the process whereby the majority of Englishmen, during the course of the century, became good Anglicans. The importance of Jewel's works in the strengthening of the Church of England warrants a close and detailed examination.

Jewel himself has a very strong claim to the attention of the historian. His preeminence in learning and literary ability among contemporary churchmen was unquestioned. At the same time he was a practical churchman, highly successful in the administration of one of the more important dioceses of the Church. His experience as apologist and as bishop during the formative and crucial first decade of the reign presents a significant and extremely valuable case study of Anglicanism.

Except for an article in the *Dictionary of National Biography,* Jewel has received no adequate biographical treatment. Shortly after his death his friend, Laurence Humphrey, the president of Magdalen, wrote a brief Latin life. Unfortunately, while this was not of sufficient distinction to warrant either a translation or a second edition, it was just good enough to discourage later potential biographers and antiquarians like John Strype. Humphrey's concept of biography was rudimentary. He padded his work with speeches of others and with digressions on the Reformation while at the same time he omitted much essential information concerning Jewel which he must have known. Furthermore, Humphrey's sympathies were strongly Puritan. Although he conformed to the order of the Establishment after playing a central role in the early stages of the vestments controversy of the sixties, his position continued to be to the left of Jewel in terms of Elizabethan Anglicanism. His portrayal of Jewel was naturally colored by his Puritan bias and as a result the Bishop is made to appear far more the Puritan than was actually the case.

When Jewel's works were collected and published in 1609 a short English life by Daniel Featley was appended. Featley noted in another sketch which he wrote later for inclusion in Thomas Fuller's *Abel Redivivus,* that this early memoir was no more than an abstract of Humphrey. Then in the early nineteenth century Charles Webb Le Bas wrote a readable but wholly uncritical biography of the Bishop. He incorporated most of Humphrey's work in his, together with Humphrey's point of view and his use of Featley suggests that he was unaware of the relation between the latter's work and that of Humphrey. He made use of Strype's various collections and several of the short sketches of Jewel which had appeared in such collections as Fuller's *Worthies,* all based upon the Humphrey *vita.* This process of repetition was continued by several nineteenth-century editors of the *Apology* in memoirs affixed to their editions. John Ayre, the scholarly editor of the Parker Society edition of Jewel, wrote the best of these, making use for the first time of Jewel's letters in the Zurich collection.

Bishop Mandell Creighton's life of Jewel in the *Dictionary of National Biography* is the work of a trained historian. He used the obvious documentary material available and presents an adequate summary of the events of Jewel's life. But Creighton, thoroughly unsympathetic to the early Elizabethan churchmen and their problems, generally accepted Humphrey's earlier interpretation of Jewel. As a result, the conventional characterization with which we are presented is that of a churchman deeply sympathetic to Puritanism but forced by the pressure of administrative responsibility and political reality to a half-hearted acceptance of Anglicanism. We have only to examine Jewel's formal writings to realize the essential unsoundness of such a view. Furthermore, once we are rid of this misconception and turn to a reexamination of Jewel's career, in its early stages at Oxford and abroad, and later during the reign of Elizabeth, we recognize how wide in fact was the gulf that separated him from the Puritans on fundamental issues. John Jewel was an Anglican, after Archbishop Parker the most important of the first generation of Elizabethan churchmen, the heir of the Christian humanists and of Cranmer, and the progenitor of Richard Hooker.

In a biographical study the works of the author are usually considered at the time of their appearance and in relation to the events which preceded and followed them. With Jewel such a procedure is desirable only in regard to his one systematic work, his *Apology for the Church of England*. His longer works, *The Defence of the Apology* and *The Reply to Harding,* do not invite such treatment. The *Defence* is a vast expansion of the *Apology* itself and the *Reply* a controversial work limited to specific points most of which are treated in both the *Apology* and the *Defence*. Furthermore all these works were completed and published within a short space of time. They do not reflect a development or a change in Jewel's ideas but, taken together, represent a point of view fully developed during the author's earlier years. Hence it has seemed advisable to separate the analysis of Jewel's ideas from the treatment of his life, especially since the analysis is concerned with one aspect of his thought rather than with his theology as a whole. The following biography and analysis are therefore presented as separate though complementary essays; the facts of his life, an essential preface to his treatment of the problem of doctrinal authority: his treatment of the problem of doctrinal authority essential to the understanding of his place as one of the fathers of Anglicanism.

To the scholars of the Continental Reformation and of Tudor England who have made such valuable contributions in recent years to the background of the Elizabethan settlement my debt is far greater than the mere citations of their works in footnotes can possibly indicate. In common with all who have studied the England of Elizabeth, I must note my special debt to the dean of Elizabethan

historians, Sir John Neale. To students of the reign such a debt will
be obvious and regarded as a matter of course. I would note it
especially, however, since it extends well beyond his written work.
His personal encouragement at a crucial stage in my own work on
Jewel was a major factor in my carrying it on to its conclusion.
Canon E. T. Davies has read portions of the manuscript and the
Reverend Harvey Guthrie the entire manuscript. Both churchmen,
one British and one American, by their frank and detailed criticisms
have saved me from many of the pitfalls which beset the student of
church history. I am deeply indebted to Professor John T. McNeill
for his careful reading of the manuscript, for his generous criticism,
and especially for his invaluable suggestions concerning the continental background of Jewel's thought. From the beginning of my
study of Jewel I have had the advice and criticism of Professor
W. K. Jordan who with infinite patience has read the manuscript
both in its several preliminary stages and in its final form. While
he cannot be held responsible for the views I have expressed, he must
accept the credit, for good or for ill, that this study was begun and,
more important, that it was finally completed.

For their generous aid and counsel during a long and often
unrewarding search for new materials on Bishop Jewel, I would like
to express my gratitude to Professor Norman Sykes, Miss Kathleen
Major, Mr. Gordon Blackman, Miss Joyce Youings, Miss Kathleen
Edwards, Miss Phyllis Hembry, Mrs. Marjorie Bindoff, Mr. Neil
Ker, Miss Margaret Whiteman, Mr. R. B. Pugh, and, most particularly, to Professor Edwards, Mr. Taylor Milne, and the staff of the
Institute of Historical Research. The librarians of the British
Museum, the Bodleian, and of the colleges at Oxford and Cambridge
have been extremely generous as have the librarians and archivists
of the great private collections, especially Miss Dorothy Coates of
Longleat. For her continuing interest and invaluable assistance
through the years I especially wish to thank Miss Doris Coates of
the National Register of Archives. My colleagues on the staff of the
Doane Library at Denison and the staffs of the libraries at the Ohio
State University and Bexley Hall, Kenyon College, have shown
endless patience with a point of view which all too frequently

assumed, I fear, the priority of the claims of my own researches.

Finally I wish to acknowledge my gratitude to the American Philosophical Society for making possible a period of research in England; to the Denison University Research Foundation for providing technical assistance; and to the History Department of Harvard University for its aid towards the expenses of publication.

Granville, Ohio   W. M. Southgate
July, 1961

CONTENTS

Part One

THE LIFE OF JEWEL

Chapter I

Early Years

Devon and Oxford

J OHN JEWEL was born May 24, 1522, on a farm in north Devon not far from the village of Berrynarbor. The farmhouse still stands in excellent condition, on the slope of a little coomb that leads north to the sea. From its extensive barns and outbuildings one can glimpse the Bristol Channel, a broad wedge of blue between the hills that dominate the coast from Somerset to Cornwall. The family of Jewel, though not wealthy, was well established, of good yeoman stock, solid and substantial like their stone house and barns and of excellent reputation in the parish where they had lived for over two hundred years.[1]

Jewel owed his schooling to the interest of his mother's brother, the rector of a nearby parish, who very early recognized the boy's exceptional ability and undertook to tutor him. Later he arranged for the boy to continue his education with a fellow cleric at Braunton, some eight miles over the moors from Berrynarbor, and then to attend a small school established by Walter Bowen at Barnstaple.

So well did Jewel acquit himself at Barnstaple that his masters marked him out for further study. In 1535, with their help, he entered Oxford as a student of Merton College. Initially he was assigned to Peter Burry, a quite undistinguished and conservative fellow of the college. Burry, however, was unable to accept him as

[1] Except when otherwise specified, the Latin life of Jewel by Laurence Humphrey (*J. Juelli, Episcopi Sarisburiensis, vita*, London, 1573) is the source of information for the years before Oxford and a major source for the years which followed.

a scholar and he was assigned instead to a younger fellow, John Parkhurst, who had only recently come to Merton from Magdalen. At Magdalen, Parkhurst had become thoroughly imbued with the humanistic approach to biblical criticism and the distrust of scholastic methods that had taken hold there since Tyndale's day.[2] The association of Jewel and Parkhurst, begun so fortuitously, was to prove vital for Jewel and of great import for the future of the English Church. In conservative Oxford he had as his tutor one of the few vigorous proponents of the New Learning in the university. For the most formative period of his life, from his thirteenth to his seventeenth year, Jewel was exposed to the novel and indeed radical ideas and methods of the humanists. The direction of Parkhurst's interests and the nature of his influence upon Jewel is well illustrated by a major project that Jewel undertook under his supervision, a careful comparison of Tyndale's translation of the New Testament with the recently imported version of Miles Coverdale, a radical project indeed, in view of the government's rigorous repression of unauthorized translations. While Parkhurst disagreed with Burry on many basic questions they remained good friends and not the least of Jewel's valuable experiences at Merton was the enjoyment of the long and vigorous arguments between the two dons over the validity of the new approach to classical and biblical scholarship.

In 1539 Parkhurst with Burry's cooperation procured a scholarship for Jewel in the neighboring and much richer foundation of Corpus Christi. Parkhurst's desire to establish Jewel at Corpus, though influenced by his protégé's financial needs and the wealth of Corpus, also reflected his appreciation of the attractive features of the newer foundation. Corpus Christi, as a result of the wise beneficence of Bishop Richard Foxe, was one of the most forward-looking of the Oxford colleges, admirably suited to the humanistic studies which Jewel had begun at Merton. Foxe had radically altered the traditional Oxford curriculum. Theology was no longer the mere study of the medieval schoolmen but rather the investigation of the

[2] C. E. Mallet, *A History of the University of Oxford*, 3 vols. (London, 1924–1927), I, 441.

fathers of the Church, in particular those whose works had been recently made so easily available by Erasmus' editorial labors: Jerome, Augustine, Ambrose, and Origen. At the same time, humane learning had been given prominence far beyond the medieval collegiate tradition, since lectures in both the Latin and the Greek classics were attached to the foundation. The college, as Foxe founded it and as it continued under John Claymond and Robert Morwen, his own appointees to the presidency, was a great center of classical studies, a veritable beehive of humanistic learning.[3]

Jewel took full advantage of the rich opportunities offered by Corpus. Although he continued his theological studies, his primary interest was the mastery of the Latin and Greek classics and the works of Erasmus, especially the *Adages* and the *Epistles*. His literary taste was broadly catholic and his reading during his long residence at Oxford was limited only by the availability of materials. Greek philosophers, Roman poets and historians, ancient and modern theologians, all were read and remembered, a vast storehouse to which he could return in later years.

So seriously did Jewel take his humane studies that a mere reading of the classic orators was not enough. They must be dramatized. Jewel, however, was either more diffident than the modern student— or more considerate of his fellows. In the woods at Shotover, several miles from the university, he would walk for hours declaiming the Latin periods of Cicero and the Greek of Demosthenes, memorized and delivered as if he were the orator himself. He was blessed with an extraordinary memory, the sort which would reduce most minds to mere encyclopedias of cluttered detail. Once, later in his career, when challenged by Bishop Hooper, he committed to memory in a few minutes a list of forty words in languages strange to him. Again, at Sir Nicholas Bacon's, he memorized in a few moments ten lines from Erasmus' *Paraphrases* and repeated them both forward and backwards.[4] Such achievements were but parlor tricks, but the

[3] *Ibid.*, II, 21–23.
[4] John Ayre, "Memoir," in John Jewel, *Works*, 4 vols. (Cambridge, 1845–1850), IV, xxiv. The text of this Parker Society edition was used throughout this essay after it had been compared with the available sixteenth-century texts. It is a model of careful scholarship and represents a collation of all the early editions up to and

photographic memory which made them possible was to prove of enormous value to Jewel in his later work.

In 1540 Jewel proceeded Bachelor of Arts.[5] Although only eighteen and not yet a fellow of the college, so great was his reputation for learning that he attracted a considerable number of students. His erstwhile tutor, John Parkhurst, in the meanwhile had entered the great world of the court, first as chaplain to the King's brother-in-law, Charles Brandon, Duke of Suffolk, and then in 1543 as chaplain to Queen Catherine Parr herself. His advancement was much to Jewel's advantage since it meant the acquisition of a patron. Parkhurst proved a generous friend, defraying the cost of the master's degree to which Jewel proceeded in 1544. Jewel had become a probationary fellow of Corpus in 1542[6] and with his master's degree, became a perpetual fellow. As the Henrician reformation followed its uncertain course the divisions at court between conservatives and reformers, with first one and then the other in apparent favor with the King, were reflected in the universities. At Cambridge the reform group was the more prominent, though by no means in full control. But at Oxford the reformers were very much in the minority. Jewel, as a result of his association with Parkhurst, became identified quite early with the radical minority, especially in his own college. According to Humphrey, Robert Morwen, the president of Corpus, once declared to Jewel: "Amarem te Iuelle, si non esses Zwinglianus: Et, Haereticus fide, vita certe videris Angelus: Et, Honestus es, at Lutheranus,"[7] a remark of more credit to the tolerance of the man than to his understanding of the differences between the continental reformers.

The death of Henry VIII and the accession of the young Edward brought change to Corpus. Morwen managed to keep his presidency by accepting the Edwardian innovations, but preserved the rich

including the 1611 edition of the *Works.* Ayre has followed the text in the 1611 edition but has noted each case wherein the 1611 edition differs from earlier editions of the various separate works.

[5] Anthony À Wood, *Athenae Oxonienses,* 4 vols. (London, 1813–1820), II, 111; *J. Juelli,* p. 23.

[6] Thomas Fowler, *The History of Corpus Christi College* (Oxford, 1893), p. 91.

[7] *J. Juelli,* p. 25.

vestments and chapel ornaments of Corpus against the possibility of future change. Parkhurst, through the patronage of Thomas Seymour, received the rich living of Bishop's Cleeve, not far from Sudeley Castle, the home of the Lord Admiral and his bride, Queen Catherine. Cleeve was just far enough from Oxford to prevent Parkhurst from continuing his duties at Merton and yet near enough to allow his Oxford friends to visit him with ease. Jewel frequently made the journey across the Cotswolds and came to regard Cleeve as a second home.

Jewel was elected to the post of Reader in Humanity and Rhetoric in 1548. This chair was a public lectureship attached to Corpus but open to all students of the university, having remained, as its founder intended, "of the nature of a University Professorship rather than a college lectureship." The humanist, Ludovic Vives, had probably been one of its earlier occupants. Jewel's declamatory walks in the woods of Shotover evidently stood him in good stead, for he became a highly successful lecturer. He lectured with such "diligence and facilitie," wrote Featley, paraphrasing Humphrey, "that many came from divers other colledges to behold Rhetorik so richlie set forth, with her owne costlie apparel, and furniture, by the dexteritie of his wit and learning." [8] Parkhurst often came over from Cleeve to hear him, on one such occasion producing the distich:

> Olim discipulus mihi, chare Iuelle, fuisti,
> Nunc ero discipulus, te renuente, tuus. [9]

The only addresses of Jewel's that have been preserved are a commemorative address on Richard Foxe and the *Oratio Contra Rhetoricam*. [10] In the first Jewel lamented the decay of learning at Corpus and at Oxford since the days of Bishop Foxe, concluding with a vigorous exhortation to the students that they recover the ancient classical virtues and so become students in the full sense of the word. The *Oratio Contra Rhetoricam* is a thoroughly Erasmian attack on mere eloquence and the Ciceronians. Both orations are the work

[8] Daniel Featley in *The Works of J. Jewell; and a briefe discourse of his life* [by D. Featley] (London, 1609, 1611), par. 6; *J. Juelli*, p. 29.

[9] *J. Juelli*, p. 29.

[10] Jewel, *Works*, IV, 1304–1305, 1283–1291.

of a humanist, of a man primarily the Reader in Humanity and in no sense the preachings of a militant religious reformer.

During his early years at Oxford the most compelling influence on Jewel was that of John Parkhurst. To him must go the credit for giving initial direction to the interests and labors of the young scholar. As the years went by, however, Jewel tended to go his own way and, as Parkhurst frankly admitted, far outstripped the older man in learning. After 1540 the relation between the two was the friendly relation of equals, not that of master and scholar. Parkhurst, to judge from his letters, his poetry—if we can call his distichs poetry—and his subsequent career as bishop, was a forthright, honest figure, a thoroughly good man, but without the fineness of mind of his pupil. He was a bluff, rather lovable and impractical person, most happy, as Jewel later wrote of him, to be in his kingdom at Cleeve. Indeed, the years spent there were the happiest of his life. As Bishop of Norwich under Elizabeth he was a failure and realized it. He was a poor administrator with no head for finances and altogether unsuccessful in his half-hearted attempts to reconcile the policies of the Archbishop and the government with the problems posed by Puritanism in his diocese. There is perhaps no better illustration of the difference in character and in point of view between Parkhurst and Jewel than the contrast between their subsequent careers as bishops.

For Jewel's future neither his nor Parkhurst's new honors could compare in importance with the appointment in 1548 of the new Regius Professor of Divinity, Peter Martyr Vermigli. Martyr, together with his friend Martin Bucer, who became Regius Professor at Cambridge, were the most distinguished of the continental reformers whom Cranmer was instrumental in bringing to England to further the cause of the Reformation and aid in his project for Protestant union. Martyr had been an Augustinian monk, prior of S. Fredonia at Lucca and friend of the humanist cardinals Contarini and Pole. His interest in reform doctrines finally caused him in 1542 to flee from Italy to Switzerland and then to Strasbourg where he became a professor of theology at the invitation of Bucer. Martyr was not only an able theologian but an excellent classicist with a profound knowledge of Greek literature from Homer to Aristotle, a master of Hebrew, and a preeminent authority on the Greek and Latin fathers of the Church.[11]

Jewel's reaction to the advent of Martyr was probably not unlike that of the young graduate student of today when his university announces the appointment of a brilliant and recognized leader in his chosen field. As one of the very small minority of fellows who welcomed the religious changes now in full swing, he was immediately attracted to Martyr and soon came to serve him as a secretarial assistant, transcribing his lectures and later acting as notary in the formal disputation over the sacrament of the Eucharist between Martyr and the conservatives, Tresham and Chedsey. Humphrey, who was a student at Magdalen at the time, describes Martyr as Jewel's spiritual father and Jewel as Martyr's disciple. The combination of reformer and learned classical scholar in Martyr admirably supplemented Jewel's own interests. Temperamentally Martyr was not unlike Jewel. Despite the air of controversy which pervades his years at Oxford, Martyr, like Bucer and Archbishop Cranmer himself, had little of the arrogance and self-righteousness that characterized so many of the contemporary religious leaders on both sides. His theological work is characterized by a quality of tentativeness, understandable when we remember that his final break with the Roman Church had come in his mature years after a long and prominent career in the Augustinian order. Small wonder that his contemporaries, impressed by his reputation and fully cognizant of his learning, were puzzled, and that scholars since his time have disagreed concerning his views just as they have concerning the views of Bucer and Cranmer.

In the dramatic events which disturbed Edwardian Oxford, Jewel played only a minor role. His relation to Martyr and hence to Richard Cox, dean of Christ Church and vice-chancellor, who was Martyr's chief protector in the university, brought him some prominence, at least enough to cause trouble later, but he was still pri-

---

[11] C. H. Smyth, *Cranmer and the Reformation under Edward VI* (Cambridge, 1926), p. 112; J. C. McLelland, *The Visible Words of God* (Grand Rapids, 1957), pp. 267–271.

marily the student. In December 1551, he received a license to preach,[12] presumably having completed his Bachelor of Divinity degree and having been ordained during the preceding year.[13] At the same time he received his first preferment, the rectory of Sunningwell just south of Oxford. The parish still gratefully remembers Jewel for the unusual octagonal porch which was added to the front of the church during his incumbency. In his college, where he was one of the more junior of the fellows, he attained a degree of notoriety as one of the small and unpopular minority group then dominating the university. The president of Corpus, Morwen, belonged to the conservative majority and in attempting quasi-conformity to the new order fell afoul of the Privy Council and was called before it to explain his use of services other than those of the English Prayer Book. During his absence Jewel was appointed to assume charge of the college.[14] The easy-going Morwen, released on July 17, 1552, apparently held no prejudice against Jewel, or perhaps considered it impolitic to show prejudice. In December of the same year Jewel was selected to deliver the commemorative address on the founder of the college, Richard Foxe.

As a promising younger member of the reform party at the university, Jewel was included in the list of scholars who received funds from Richard Chambers, the layman who was to play such a prominent role during the next reign in financing the English exiles.[15] Chambers gave Jewel an allowance of six pounds a year for the purchase of divinity books and "exhorted him to set his mind intensely upon that study."[16] Although such advice was probably

[12] John Strype, *Ecclesiastical Memorials,* etc., 3 vols. (Oxford, 1822), II, ii, 268.

[13] Humphrey omits to mention either the degree or the ordination although he must have known the dates. There is no record of ordinations for these years. The license to preach and the preferment are fair evidence that sometime in the period 1550–1551 Jewel had received the degree and had been ordained.

[14] Strype, *Memorials,* II, ii, 52.

[15] *J. Juelli,* p. 32. Humphrey's reference is the first to Chambers in point of time that C. H. Garrett was able to find in her exhaustive research into the origins and identity of this mysterious figure. Her suggestion that he was an agent of the Earls of Bedford seems the most likely solution to the puzzling question of his relation to the exiled reformers during Mary's reign. See *The Marian Exiles* (Cambridge, 1938), pp. 111–114.

[16] Strype, *Memorials,* III, i, 225; *J. Juelli,* p. 32: "et serio in id studium incumberet."

formal and without particular significance, it may indicate a greater interest in profane letters on Jewel's part than his patron thought proper. Chambers' association with Jewel extended beyond the allowance. On his journeys to dispense funds and seek out worthy new recipients Chambers was usually accompanied by a cleric so that he could be sure of the learning of the candidate.[17] Martyr frequently went with him and when Martyr was unable to go Jewel took his place. It is ironical that one of Jewel's and Martyr's close associates in these activities, was the then radically inclined Thomas Harding, fellow of New College and professor of Hebrew, later to become Jewel's most important antagonist and a defender of the Roman Church.[18]

Humphrey has printed the *Articuli verae Religionis* which Chambers asked that the young men who were the recipients of his bounty be willing to accept. These articles include a denial of papal power; the rejection of transubstantiation as impious and diabolical and of the propitiatory mass as horrid blasphemy; the statements that justification is not dependent upon good works and that the doctrine of purgatory is ridiculous and superstitious; and finally the affirmation of a belief in the use of the vernacular in the service and of communion in both kinds. All of the articles, with the exception of that on justification, were to make their appearance later in Jewel's career when he included them among the challenge points in his Paul's Cross sermon of November 1559, the sermon that set off the great controversy between him and Thomas Harding.

The death of the young King and the succession to the throne of Mary Tudor in July 1553, brought to a sudden end the activities of the reformers at Oxford. Their dominant position in the university had rested wholly on governmental support since they were greatly outnumbered even at the peak of their power by the conservatives. With the certainty of loss of favor at Westminster many of the leaders left the university and, spurred on by a government only too happy to see the last of them, soon crossed the channel.

[17] Miss Garrett notes that Chambers had no Latin and suggests that the function of the divine was to test the candidate rather than instruct him.

[18] John Strype, *Annals of the Reformation*, etc., 4 vols. (Oxford, 1824), I, ii, 175.

The early exodus, however, was confined to those men whose reputation extended beyond the university. Martyr was one of the first
to go and was followed soon thereafter by the other members of
the small group of foreign divines and students at Oxford, together
with the late vice-chancellor, Dean Cox of Christ Church. Jewel
appears to have had no thought of leaving the university, even when
he was deprived of his fellowship at Corpus several months after
Mary's accession.[19] Two letters to Parkhurst written in October
suggest the observer rather than the active participant and give no
indication that he had anything to fear.[20] His welcome at Broadgates Hall, the future Pembroke College, by his friend Thomas
Randolph, the principal, and his selection as public orator to write
the congratulatory letter from the university to the Queen, no doubt
contributed to his sense of security.

The loss of Jewel's fellowship suggests that Robert Morwen had
disguised his feelings concerning Jewel, or that he bent to the wind
and followed the wishes of the extremists among his own fellows.
Humphrey declares that Jewel's removal from Corpus was regarded
even by some of the conservative leaders in the university as a
greater loss for Corpus than for Jewel. Jewel doubtless found re-
assurance in the willingness of the new vice-chancellor, Tresham,
Martyr's old opponent, to confer with him on the congratulatory
letter to Mary and give it his official approval. In the letter, or address to the Queen, Jewel acquitted himself well, appropriately
flattering the new sovereign but making no allusion to religion
except to pray for a peaceful and bloodless reign.

Jewel's farewell speech to Corpus, a quite characteristic and moving Latin oration, was well received. That he was allowed to give
the speech lends credence to the assumption that Morwen was
coerced into the dismissal and was not himself unfavorably inclined
toward his colleague.[21] Had Jewel been the victim of a real persecution he would hardly have been allowed to write the address

---

[19] Humphrey, the sole source for Jewel's activities during these months, shows his
usual disregard for chronology and gives no indication of the order of these events.

[20] Jewel, *Works*, IV, 1190–1191.

[21] This is Fowler's conclusion, *History of Corpus*, p. 96.

to the Queen or to find refuge in another college. Possibly he was a victim of a cabal among the fellows of Corpus, some of whom would naturally have resented his intimacy with such controversial and powerful figures as Peter Martyr and Richard Cox.

Despite the picture that Humphrey draws of the angry Romanists eagerly watching for a chance to destroy Jewel, he remained unmolested though most unhappy. The growing tension during the winter caused him to journey across the Cotswolds in the snow to Cleeve, only to find Parkhurst gone. He wrote Parkhurst later that he dared not commit to writing the things that were going on. Even so, he felt that he and Randolph, however miserable, were better off than their enemies might wish them to be.[22] And in a lighter vein, he noted that Richard Smith, Martyr's old enemy and now his successor as Regius Professor, "is thumping the anvil vigorously: there is some danger of his breaking his arms." Jewel himself was actually free enough from the attentions of the conservatives to be able to act as one of Ridley's and Cranmer's notaries in April 1554.[23]

The policy of Mary's government during the early months of the reign had been reasonably moderate, certainly no more extreme in its own way than that of its predecessor. In the spring and summer of 1554, however, under the pressure of rebellion, religious controversy, and the conscience of the Queen, harsher counsels prevailed and any hope which may have been held for a moderate policy soon disappeared. Mary married her Spanish Philip in July and the restoration of the Roman jurisdiction, toward which obvious steps had already been taken, was completed in November.

Any doubts that had lingered in men's minds should have been removed by the end of the summer; yet Jewel remained at Oxford. And sometime in the early autumn, possibly in October when the universities were subjected to a visitation,[24] he signed articles in agreement with the main tenets of Roman doctrine. Miss Garrett's

---

[22] Jewel, *Works*, IV, 1192.

[23] John Foxe, *Actes and Monuments*, 8 vols. (London, 1877), VI, 471; Nicholas Ridley, *Works* (Cambridge, 1841), p. 194; John Strype, *Memorials of . . . Thomas Cranmer*, etc., 2 vols. (Oxford, 1840), p. 483.

[24] Jewel, *Works*, IV, xi, n. 4.

comment that "he not only recanted but signed articles of recantation" [25] is pointless because his act of signing was his recantation. Humphrey attributes Jewel's action to the machinations of his enemies who forced the articles upon him, but he gives no indication of the nature of the articles or of their sanction. He makes no attempt to justify or to condemn the recantation. Perhaps he realized that only the martyrs themselves had any right to pass judgment; those who had taken refuge in flight might be asked with equal justice to defend their actions.

Jewel was no martyr, either in intent or fact. In these matters, however, the kind of recantation and the actions which followed it should be taken into consideration before passing final judgment. As Strype pointed out, one should be most lenient toward those who are forced to recant but do not persist in living in accord with their recantation. Far worse are those who of a sudden change their profession of faith merely because the government has changed and their career will benefit if their faith is in agreement with the official faith. This in general was the typical Tudor recantation, although the change was usually made easily and without the necessity of a formal recantation, as in the case of William Cecil, of Elizabeth herself, and we might add, as Jewel later pointed out, his opponent, Thomas Harding. There is no evidence that Jewel had anything to do with the new dispensation. Indeed early in the new year he fled precipitately from Oxford to London and the continent. Cranmer's editor argues convincingly that as a result of his recantation, Jewel, no longer under suspicion of the authorities, had been able to visit Cranmer in prison. At the same time, however, he had already determined to repudiate his recantation and thus knew he must leave the country.[26] As a result he became the obvious means for Cranmer to communicate with the reformers and thus the bearer of the Archbishop's very moving last letter to Peter Martyr.[27] Such a reconstruction does not explain or justify Jewel's recantation. But it does provide a reasonable explanation for his sudden departure

[25] Garrett, *Exiles*, p. 198.

[26] Thomas Cranmer, *Works*, 2 vols. (Cambridge, 1844–1846), II, xiv; II, 457, addenda to n. 6.

[27] *Ibid.*, II, 457; *Original Letters Relative to the English Reformation, 1531–58, chiefly from the Archives of Zurich*, 2 vols. (Cambridge, 1846–1847), I, 29–31.

for the continent after he had apparently made his peace with the authorities.

Years of Exile

During the years that followed the accession of Mary Tudor a steady stream of Englishmen, both lay and clerical, crossed the channel into exile. While some went their individual ways, the majority congregated in the cities of the Rhineland and Switzerland, the homes of the theologians and students who had visited England during the reign of Edward, and the recognized capitals of Protestantism.[28] In Strasbourg, Frankfort, Zurich, and Geneva, the English organized separate congregations which developed characters markedly different from one another, surprisingly so when we consider the brevity of their corporate existence. The congregation at Strasbourg, at least during the earlier part of Mary's reign, was not only the largest but included in its membership the most prominent of the exiles, churchmen and laymen alike. As a result it tended to assume general responsibility for the exiles as a whole and in the case of their fellow countrymen at Frankfort actively intervened in the affairs of another group. The Strasbourg congregation itself was generally moderate in outlook and its leaders consistently and vigorously sought to maintain the Anglicanism of Cranmer's Second Prayer Book. The Zurich group, though similar in point of view, took little administrative responsibility and became known primarily for its scholarly activity.[29] The Englishmen at Geneva constituted the most closely knit group of all, with their own separate church and English service book, but in complete and willing conformity to the Geneva Church.[30]

[28] For a more extensive treatment of the years of exile, see W. M. Southgate, "The Marian Exiles and the Influence of John Calvin," *History* 27 (1942).

[29] See R. W. Dixon, *History of the Church of England from the Abolition of the Roman Jurisdiction,* 6 vols. (Oxford, 1895–1902), IV, 690. Dixon calls attention to their expressed reluctance to become involved in the affairs of the Frankfort group to the extent of hurting their studies and dissolving "their exercises."

[30] Horton Davies characterizes the Geneva congregation as "the cradle of English Puritanism." Its order of service (developed from the form drawn up by the Calvinist party of Knox in Frankfort) remained the order of worship of the Puritans in England until superseded in 1644. *The Worship of the English Puritans* (Westminster, 1948), p. 118.

The Frankfort group, in contrast to the others, was characterized from the start by disunity and violent dissension.[31] Ironically, its quite atypical character has come to be regarded as representative of the Marian exiles in general. The reason is not far to seek. The most vigorous record of any of the exile groups is the contemporary *Brieff discours off the troubles begonne at Franckford* by one of the major actors in "the troubles," probably William Whittingham.[32] The conflict at Frankfort concerned the proper form of church service. One party, headed by Whittingham and John Knox, wished to introduce the Geneva service of Calvin. Another party, headed by Thomas Lever, vigorously defended a slightly modified form of the service of the English Prayer Book. The struggle became so violent that the very existence of the congregation was threatened, with the good burghers of Frankfort seriously considering the expulsion of the English. As early as August 1554 the Strasbourg group, disturbed by a letter from Frankfort to the other English congregations, discussed the possibility of sending one of the exiled bishops or Dean Cox to take charge. During the autumn Edmund Grindal and Richard Chambers, the former patron of the Oxford scholars, now serving as a kind of treasurer to the exiles, made several futile trips from Strasbourg to Frankfort to effect a settlement. Finally, in January 1555, a tentative agreement was reached upon the form of service. Complete acceptance by both groups, however, was to depend upon the verdict of several eminent divines, including Peter Martyr, Heinrich Bullinger, Zwingli's successor at Zurich, and Calvin himself. In the meantime it was understood that until the verdict had been received no steps were to be taken by either side.

A virtual armed truce seems to have existed for several months, although many letters passed back and forth and debate continued, though not in public. On March 13, the truce was suddenly broken by the appearance in Frankfort of Richard Cox, the dispossessed

---

[31] A detailed analysis of the "troubles" is given in Dixon, *History,* IV, 688–699; see also C. W. Dugmore, *The Mass and the English Reformers* (London, 1958), pp. 203–208.

[32] William Whittingham, *A brieff discours off the troubles begonne at Franckford A.D. 1554* (Zurich [?] 1575), pp. xiii, xxxvii–xxxviii.

dean of Christ Church and one of the most prominent of the Edwardian churchmen. Cox was accompanied by Jewel, who thus appears for the first time in the records of the exiles.[33] Cox was neither a peacemaker nor a compromiser. During the fortnight after his arrival much happened. The conservatives, bolstered by Cox's vigorous leadership, succeeded in bringing back the Second Prayer Book and at the same time convinced the magistrates that Knox must leave Frankfort, which he did on March 26; David Whitehead was elected pastor of the congregation two days later. During this same period Jewel made a public confession of his recent recantation and sometime thereafter he joined Martyr at Strasbourg.

Because of the casual statement of the writer of *The Troubles* that Cox had come to Frankfort from England it has been assumed that Jewel likewise had come directly from England. But Cox had actually left England much earlier.[34] It seems proper to assume with Miss Garrett that in the meanwhile he had been with another group of exiles, in all probability at Strasbourg. In view of the serious concern which the Strasbourg leaders felt over the situation at Frankfort and the doubts that they must have held in regard to the final agreement of the foreign theologians on the proper form of the service, it is altogether likely that they took the opportunity offered by the presence of the vigorous and pugnacious Cox and sent him to Frankfort to settle the quarrel by extreme means if necessary. If this assumption is correct then Jewel too must have been in Strasbourg prior to Cox's departure for Frankfort. He would naturally have gone first to Strasbourg and to Peter Martyr, especially if he were in fact the bearer of Cranmer's last letter to Martyr. And because of his Oxford associations with Richard Cox, Jewel was a logical choice to accompany the former dean of Christ Church on his mission to Frankfort.

In her census of the exiles Miss Garrett describes Jewel's visit to Frankfort as follows:

. . . Frankfort gave Jewell no welcome. He was referred to indignantly

[33] *Ibid.*, p. xxxxiii; Garrett, *Exiles*, p. 198.
[34] Garrett, *Exiles*, p. 134.

as "A stranger craftely brought in to preache, who had bothe byn at masse and also subscribed to blasphemous Articles." And although, on the advice of his friend Richard Chambers, he made a public apology for his recantation, John Knox, as publicly, preached against him, rousing the congregation's distrust to such a pitch that Jewell soon accepted Peter Martyr's invitation [to Strasbourg].[35]

There is no doubt that Jewel made a confession in the pulpit of having signed the articles of recantation. Both Humphrey and the author of *The Troubles* refer to it. But the latter carefully distinguishes Jewel from those whom he suspected of having been at Mass and Humphrey enlarges at length upon the sympathetic reception accorded his confession by the congregation and the favorable reaction of Richard Chambers. Miss Garrett apparently identified Jewel's confession sermon with the inflammatory sermon made by one of Knox's opponents, which was responsible for the final and irretrievable break in the congregation, and thus makes Jewel the central figure in the grand denouement of "the troubles." The sole authority noted for these conclusions is *The Troubles*. Yet on the page referred to, all that is said is that "many taunting bitter sermons were made (as they thought) to our defamings," so that Knox "was inforced to purge himself in sundry points." The points are given very briefly. There is no mention of Jewel, of people having been to Mass, even of anyone's having signed articles. Knox, in his own version of his remarks that Sunday afternoon, likewise made no reference to these matters.[36]

There is no record of the precise date of Jewel's return to Strasbourg. He did not sign the ministers' letter to Calvin written on April 5th,[37] so unless he was considered merely one of the congregation he had returned before this date. In view of Knox's departure on March 26th and the triumph of Cox it is hard to place any credence in the view that Jewel was driven from Frankfort. The signatories of the Calvin letter, including Cox, Whitehead, Edwin Sandys, Grindal, Robert Horne, and Thomas Sampson, were all

[35] *Ibid.*, pp. 198–199.

[36] John Knox, *Works*, 6 vols. (Edinburgh, 1846–1864), IV, 43–44.

[37] *Original Letters*, II, 755.

his friends and remained so. While he may have been uncomfortable in Frankfort—the Whittingham group did not leave until the end of September[38]—he probably chose to return to Strasbourg simply because Peter Martyr was there. Sandys and Grindal likewise left Frankfort for Strasbourg early in April.[39]

That Jewel parted from Whittingham and the remainder of the Knox group without friendly feelings, is attested by a letter he wrote to Whittingham and Christopher Goodman from Zurich a year or two later. It is clear, however, from this letter that if Jewel felt there was any apologizing to be done it was his to do, not theirs. Had their behavior been in any way obnoxious to him he would hardly have asked their forgiveness "if in that matter, which I cannot even now condemn, I have at all injured both or either of you, or, carried away with zeal and the heat of contention, have applied to you any unbecoming word." [40] It is not the letter of a man to those who have "preached against him" and forced him to seek a new place of residence.

Jewel's role in the events which took place during his early months abroad was not spectacular. He was one of a large conservative group concerned with the preservation of unity among the English exiles, the services of the Prayer Book being the common bond and symbol of unity. The tradition he represented was the tradition of unity and moderation for which Cranmer and Bucer and Martyr had labored. Throughout his exile and indeed throughout his subsequent career his belief in the necessity of unity and his ardent desire to promote it both within the English Church and among Protestants in general never wavered.

The effect of the troubles at Frankfort upon Jewel and his later colleagues in the Elizabethan Establishment was profound. Dixon, concluding his discussion of the troubles, observes that "where men are on a level and in narrow bounds, they fight implacably till one side departs for ever. This ineffaceable tendency is the justification

---

[38] Rudolph Jung, *Die englische Flüchtlingsgemeinde in Frankfurt am Main, 1554–9* (Frankfort, 1910), p. 25.

[39] "Die Standesliste" of the English in Frankfort, ca. November 15, 1555, printed by Jung, does not list Grindal, Sandys, or Chambers.

[40] Jewel, *Works,* IV, 1192–1193 and n. 3.

of empires, of kingdoms, of bishoprics, of all containing authority. Here were two secessions in one religious body in two or three years. The congregational system was not commended by this appearance." [41]

The troubles at Frankfort constituted Jewel's first experience in the practical problems of church administration. His immediate reaction was to retreat from the practical world of affairs to his studies. In the late spring of 1555 he accepted Peter Martyr's invitation to join him at Strasbourg. The value of the Frankfort experience to the development of his own ideas of church government could hardly have been apparent to him at the time. Although he had been on the winning side in the troubles, the ugly quarrels and the personal bitterness engendered gave to the city on the Main a character which could have little appeal to him. Richard Cox might thrive on conflict. For Jewel, especially after his tragic experience in Marian Oxford, the quiet atmosphere of scholarship which pervaded the study of Peter Martyr was infinitely preferable. Of Martyr's personal affection and of Martyr's very genuine respect for him as a scholar, he could have no doubt. And Martyr, of all the major Protestant leaders, came closest to his own ideal. After Bucer, Martyr was the most moderate of the reformers and among the reformers he yielded place to no one as a scholar.

In Strasbourg Jewel lived with Martyr. And there gathered the scholars among the exiles, laymen and clerics alike. Humphrey paints a pleasant picture of the group, "in hoc literatissimo Collegio," [42] occupying its time mainly with study. The major subject was the *Ethics* of Aristotle with Martyr directing them through lectures and Jewel acting as notary. Parallel to their work in the *Ethics,* Martyr conducted a detailed analysis of the Book of Judges which later provided the basis for his elaborate commentary. Again, he was assisted by Jewel. It was a happy combination of classical and biblical studies, characteristic of Jewel whatever his surroundings.

Until this year Jewel's friends and acquaintances had been drawn from a very narrow academic circle. His own connection with the

[41] Dixon, *History,* IV, 698.
[42] *J. Juelli,* p. 87.

world of politics and high policy had been secondhand, through such friends as Parkhurst, Cox, and Martyr. Now he was in the center of a group that included some of the major figures of the court circle of the late King, many of them Jewel's equals as scholars but worldly in a sense quite foreign to him. John Cheke, Richard Morison, Anthony Cooke, Peter Carey, Thomas Wroth, Bishop Ponet, and the remarkable Duchess of Suffolk with her husband, Richard Bertie, were all in Strasbourg, together with some of the ablest of the younger churchmen, mostly Cambridge men such as Edwin Sandys and Edmund Grindal. There were others, lay and clerical, and the friendships made were not only broadening for the Oxford clerk but significant for the future of the Church of England. Many from this circle were to play major roles in the government of Elizabeth; the central role that Jewel was called upon to take only two years later came in part because these men had come to know him and appreciate him during the exile.

In March 1555 John Calvin invited Martyr to become pastor of the Italian church in Geneva, but Martyr refused the offer on the ground that he could not obtain permission from the Senate to leave Strasbourg. Yet in 1556, when Bullinger invited him to Zurich to become Professor of Hebrew, "he quickly made it impossible for the Senate to permit him to remain." [43] Although Martyr respected Calvin highly, he apparently preferred the atmosphere of Zurich. He later refused another invitation from Geneva, this time because the Zurich Senate and ministers refused to give him leave.[44]

Jewel accompanied Martyr to Zurich as his assistant. Here he spent probably the happiest years of his life. The controversies of Oxford and Frankfort were far away. The very hopelessness of the news from England precluded any call to action and, from a personal point of view, the friends who had survived the Marian persecutions were safely out of the country. Indeed, his closest friend, his old tutor, John Parkhurst, was living quietly in Zurich together with young Laurence Humphrey of Magdalen and several Cambridge reformers. In contrast to Strasbourg where Jewel's circle

[43] Smyth, *Cranmer*, p. 124; *cf.* McLelland, *Visible Words*, pp. 45–53.
[44] McLelland, *Visible Words*, p. 54.

had been composed largely of English exiles, in Zurich he was particularly happy in the friendship of a group of congenial Swiss scholars and reformers, the printer Froschover, Josiah Simler, the younger Zwingli and many others, especially the great successor of the first Zwingli, Heinrich Bullinger. Jewel lived with Martyr in Zurich as he had in Strasbourg, "bettering him, and being bettered by him, and employing all the spare time from his more necessary studies in seeking to appease by word of mouth and epistle the contentions among his brethren, arising from difference of opinion, concerning ceremonies and Church-discipline." [45]

During his two years' stay in Zurich, Jewel is supposed to have made a trip to Padua. The authority for this journey is the *Epistle to Scipio*,[46] the short defense of the English view of the Council of Trent attributed to Jewel by Brent, the translator of Sarpi's history of the Council. Ayre, the Parker Society editor, makes an excellent case for Jewel's authorship of the *Epistle,* citing the intention expressed in a letter to Martyr to write such a defense, the similarity of the argument and expression with those found in the acknowledged works and even the same kind of mistakes which Jewel made elsewhere. But acceptance of this hypothesis does not necessarily imply that Jewel went to Padua, that he knew a certain Scipio, or that any such person even existed. The *Epistle* is introduced as an answer to one Signor Scipio concerning the latter's "expostulatory letter" on the failure of the English to participate in the Council. While Jewel may have been in Padua, while he may very easily have made the acquaintance of such a gentleman, "employed in the affairs" of his commonwealth when Jewel was employed in literary pursuits,[47] it is more probable that he was making use of a simple literary device in order to explain his writing and to justify a certain arbitrary setting out of points, each being, according to the device, an answer to specific queries of Scipio. The *Epistle,* so considered, is not sufficient evidence for the visit; Jewel's name is not

[45] Featley in *The Works of J. Jewell; and a briefe discourse of his life* (1609), par. 22.
[46] Jewel, *Works,* IV, 1094 ff.
[47] *Ibid.,* IV, 1094, n. 1.

listed among the foreign students at Padua for these years;[48] and Humphrey makes no mention of such a visit although he himself was in Zurich with Jewel.

During this same period the exiles were faced by the very serious problem of a shortage of funds. In the early years of Mary's reign they had been supplied with money through the agency of Richard Chambers and the generosity of certain London merchants. According to Humphrey, however, Bishop Gardiner had got wind of the source of supply and put a stop to it. The citizens of Zurich, having already provided the English exiles with a haven of refuge, came to their aid and together with Christopher, Prince of Wurtemberg, supplied funds sufficient for their support. Jewel never forgot the liberality of Zurich and in later years, when he became Bishop of Salisbury, rejoiced that he could repay, if only in part, the great debt he owed Bullinger and his friends.

[48] Garrett, *Exiles,* p. 199.

Chapter II

The New Reign

The Return of the Exiles and the Formation of the New Establishment

Queen Mary died on November 17, 1558. While the rumor of her death and the peaceful accession of Elizabeth reached the continent very early, the exiles were without definite and trustworthy news until nearly a month later. In the meantime the Strasbourg group made preparations to leave. Final confirmation of events in England was received in Strasbourg on December 19th. The next day Sir Anthony Cooke and a large party, which included the more prominent lay leaders, set out for England. On December 21st another group, including Sandys and Grindal, followed them.[1]

The English at Zurich moved more slowly. Although apparently the first to hear the rumors of Mary's death, they made no preparations to leave and did not finally set out from Zurich until several weeks after they had received Sandys' letter from Strasbourg verifying the news from England.

The contrast between the immediate departure of the Strasbourg leaders and the delay of Jewel and his friends at Zurich reflects the difference in character between the two groups of exiles. The Strasbourg congregation was dominated by men of action, laymen rather than clerics, who naturally wished to be in the center of activity in England as soon as possible. The Zurich scholars, though anxious to return to England, did not feel the same sense of pressure. Less

---

[1] *The Zurich Letters,* 2 vols. (Cambridge, 1842–1845), II, 1; I, 3–9; Edmund Grindal, *Remains* (Cambridge, 1843), p. 237.

politically minded than their Strasbourg friends, they tended to think far less in terms of possible opportunities in England, and parted from their friends and the congenial atmosphere of study in Zurich reluctantly. Their journey, once undertaken, proved extremely arduous, 57 days elapsing between their departure from Zurich and their arrival in London. The winter of 1558–1559 was unusually severe, the Rhine was frozen over and travel conditions were at their very worst. The travellers lingered awhile with friends at Basel and at Strasbourg and were held up for a time in Antwerp. Jewel did not reach London until March 18th.

By that date most of the exiles had returned. The significant exception was a group at Geneva. Whittingham and some others remained there to complete their translation of the Bible.[2] Poor Goodman, having sinned along with Knox in expressing views against female sovereigns, dared not "show his face." [3] Thus the Frankfort extremists and the exiles closest to Calvin played no part in the events of the early months of the reign.

Upon his arrival in England Jewel found conditions far less sanguine than he had anticipated. The news of English developments had been "far more pleasant in the hearing than . . . in reality," he wrote Martyr.[4] He had doubtless pictured an immediate and revolutionary change from Marian policies; his ignorance reflects the natural optimism of a returning exile, out of touch with reality and, like exiles in all ages, prone to an oversimplified view of circumstances infinitely complicated. The weeks and indeed the months that followed, represent for Jewel, as for his fellow exiles, a period of adjustment to the harsh realities of the world of affairs. The wonder is not that he became discouraged at times but rather that he did adjust, that he did come to accept the possible in place of the theoretically desirable, and to sympathize with his maddeningly deliberate Queen and the able but hardheaded ministers who shared her unexcelled grasp of the art of the possible.

The former exiles, both clerics and laymen, together with the

[2] Dixon, *History,* V, 34.
[3] *Zurich Letters,* I, 21.
[4] Jewel, *Works,* IV, 1200.

laymen who had remained in England during Mary's reign, constituted an unofficial party of reform, the laymen in Parliament, the clerics as their advisors and as a pressure group exerting influence upon the more moderate governmental leaders ʻand at times even upon the Queen herself. Professor Neale suggests that the direction of events during these crucial months owes much to their activities.[5] But they worked quietly and left no records. In his letters to Zurich Jewel refers only once to the parliamentary "alterations in religion."[6] His failure to mention the existence of an active group or party is puzzling only if we think in terms of a highly organized group such as Miss Garrett postulates in her analysis of the activities of the same men during the exile. Very probably the reformers constituted no such clearly defined party even in their own eyes. Their strength and therefore the importance of the group both within and without the Parliament was in all likelihood more obvious to the leaders of the government than to the reformers themselves, especially those, like Jewel, who had so little chance to assess the leanings of the House of Commons as a whole.

The parliamentary session was already half over when Jewel reached England. The decision to hold a disputation at Westminster between the reformers and the leaders of the Marian clergy, which he mentioned in his letter of March 20, may be regarded as the turn of the tide in favor of more vigorous action by the government in the direction of reform. He wrote Martyr that the disputation was to be held in order that "our bishops may have no ground of complaint that they are put down only by power and authority of law,"[7] a statement which has been quoted as evidence of bad faith on the part of the government, evidence that the result of the disputation was a foregone conclusion. The general tenor of Jewel's letter and his references to the Marian bishops in it and in later letters suggests that such was not the case. It was to be a bona fide disputation. The Marians would be given the floor to make their case if they could.

Jewel believed that his side had the stronger case. And, it is true, he felt reasonably confident that whatever the outcome of the disputation itself, it would not materially affect the nature of the eventual religious settlement, in view of Elizabeth's favor to "our cause." At the same time he was disturbed by the influence of Philip's ambassador, Count Feria, and "her own friends" whom he blamed for the Queen's having moved heretofore "somewhat more slowly than we could wish." Although these "friends" cannot be identified with any certainty, it is probable that Jewel had in mind the more conservative members of Elizabeth's Council and ascribed greater influence to them than they in fact possessed. The conservative policy followed by the government up until now was not theirs so much as it was the Queen's.

The disputation was held at Westminster on March 31st. Jewel, together with Cox, Scory, Grindal, Whitehead, Sandys, Horne, Aylmer, and "a Cambridge man of the name of Gheast," represented the reform side. All but Edmund Guest were former exiles and friends of Jewel and all except the elderly Whitehead were to become bishops.[8] In his detailed report to Martyr a few days later, Jewel wrote that it had been a useless conference that had proved nothing one way or the other.[9] Little can be added to Dixon's brilliant summary,[10] although further attention might be directed to the attitude of the participants, in view of the doubts expressed by Roman Catholic historians of the sincerity of both government and reformers. Pollen, for instance, characterized the disputation as a complete fiasco because its sequel, the imprisonment of several of the Romanists, was only too clear to their party from the start and they were therefore greatly handicapped.[11] One is tempted to compare the disputation with the Oxford disputation of 1554 when Cranmer and Ridley were made sport of by a large and unruly

---

[8] Professor Neale regards the constitution of the group as "striking proof of the government's dependence upon them [the exiles], and therefore of their latent power," *Elizabeth I*, p. 71.

[9] Jewel, *Works*, IV, 1204.

[10] Dixon, *History*, V, 74–86.

[11] J. H. Pollen, *The English Catholics in the Reign of Queen Elizabeth* (London, 1920), pp. 32 ff.

group of Romanist clergy. They had been brought out of prison for this purpose and were certain that they were to be thrust back to await a worse fate, since Cranmer was already adjudged guilty of treason and both were in fact on trial for heresy.[12] The Marian bishops were to die in comparative comfort and in their beds, most of them spending their later years with only nominal restrictions on their actions. In March 1559 it was still quite possible that they would continue as bishops. Jewel's remark that they were exulting as if "the victory was already achieved,"[13] suggests that they, at least, did not believe the disputation had been decided in advance against them nor that they had any presentiment of future imprisonment.

The disputation itself was a sorry show. The behavior of the Romanists "frustrated a great occasion, irretrievably damaged their cause, and exposed themselves to penalty."[14] Jewel was disgusted with the proceedings, including the first day's speech of Henry Cole, the dean of St. Paul's, which he described colorfully and with high good humor to Peter Martyr. He singled out for special comment Cole's point that ignorance "is the mother of true piety, which he called devotion."[15]

Although the reformers emerged victorious from the disputation, Jewel found little cause to rejoice. A letter written less than a week after his report on the disputation to Martyr is ironic, almost bitter, in its expression of impatience with the state of affairs.

O Mary and the Marian times! With how much greater tenderness and moderation is truth now contended for, than falsehood was defended some time since! Our adversaries acted always with precipitancy, without precedent, without authority, without law; while we manage everything with so much deliberation, and prudence, and wariness, and circumspection, as if God himself could scarce retain his authority without our ordinances and precautions; so that it is idly and scurrilously said, by way of joke, that, as heretofore Christ was *cast out* by his enemies, so he is now *kept out* by his friends.[16]

---

[12] Dixon, *History*, IV, 185–213.

[13] *Zurich Letters*, I, 11.

[14] Dixon, *History*, V, 76.

[15] *Zurich Letters*, I, 15; see below, p. 50.

[16] Jewel, *Works*, IV, 1205. Italics added by edition's editor, John Ayre.

The net result, he added, was to discourage "our brethren while it has wonderfully encouraged the rage and fury of our opponents." Yet there was another side to the picture. The very violence of the Marian churchmen might in the end prove their undoing. Jewel noted that their extreme stand already had driven many, heretofore favorably inclined toward them, especially among the nobility, to a greater sympathy with the cause of reform. In spite of governmental inaction, or because of it, Jewel was convinced that the Mass would most probably fall of itself—if only the Queen would banish it from her private chapel. In her defense he stated, probably quite unjustifiably, that she retained it "only from the circumstances of the times." Then in extenuation not merely for the Mass in the royal chapel but for the generally slow progress toward a religious settlement as well, he wrote:

this woman, excellent as she is, and earnest in the cause of true religion, notwithstanding she desires a thorough change as early as possible, cannot however be induced to effect such change without the sanction of law; lest the matter should seem to have been accomplished, not so much by the judgment of discreet men, as in compliance with the impulse of a furious multitude.[17]

Jewel and his friends simply could not admit, even to themselves, a fundamental difference between themselves and the Queen. "There was no rising sun to worship." [18] The obvious solution was to blame Elizabeth's advisors. Jewel himself was not above accepting this view at times and, good Tudor Englishman that he was, sought to explain away, even to justify actions on the part of the Queen which he would not have tolerated in any one else. His arguments to Martyr, insofar as he did seek to justify the political realism of the Queen, were fundamentally sound, though at times they might sound like mere rationalizing. In the long run, Jewel as an advocate was probably more successful in educating himself than in convincing the judge, increasingly so as his own experience with the problems of church organization and politics drove home to him the limits of the possible.

[17] *Ibid.*, IV, 1206.
[18] Neale, *Elizabeth I*, p. 84.

The Martyr letters are almost wholly silent concerning the passage of the all-important Acts of Supremacy and Uniformity. Jewel's sole reference to the Acts themselves or to activities directly concerned with them was a statement in his letter of April 14 that "many alterations in religion are effected in parliament, in spite of the opposition and gainsaying and disturbance of the bishops. These however I will not mention, as they are not yet publicly known, and are often brought on the anvil to be hammered over again." [19] It is a discreet, noncommittal statement, wisely so in view of the uncertainty concerning the results of the struggle then at its height over the Prayer Book, a struggle in which Jewel was deeply involved.[20] When he wrote Martyr again, two weeks later, the crisis over the revision of the Prayer Book had been resolved—not wholly to the satisfaction of either the Queen or the exiles but in a manner both were prepared to accept. Jewel could hardly defend the compromise in terms that would appeal to Martyr without suggesting an exegesis on the communion formulas which would have been indiscreet, even dangerous, in 1559. He sensibly therefore avoided all reference to the subject. He does, however, mention another problem closely related and of comparable importance. He wrote Martyr that "we have exhibited to the queen all our articles of religion and doctrine." [21] Although he does not describe her reaction, he refers in the same letter to her friendly attitude toward him and his friends in such a manner as to suggest not only that

[19] Jewel, *Works,* IV, 1206.

[20] Professor Neale in "The Elizabethan Acts of Supremacy and Uniformity," *English Historical Review* 65 (1950), 326, suggests that the Prayer Book revision was the work of the group of reformers who had participated in the Westminster disputation, not the "Prayer Book Committee" of Sir Thomas Smith mentioned in the "Device for the Alteration of Religion," usually accepted as a committee in fact—despite the total absence of any evidence that the "device" was followed or that the Smith committee ever existed at all. Professor Neale further suggests the possibility that Jewel may have been the writer of the letter to Cecil, generally ascribed to Guest, concerning the activities of the group, *Elizabeth I*, p. 77, n. 1.

[21] Jewel, *Works,* IV, 1208. Strype (*Annals,* I, 167 ff.) prints the introduction and conclusion. Dixon (*History,* V, 107–115) summarizes the articles in detail. From references in the introduction it is clear that the Westminster group were the authors. Dixon identifies them as the Paul's Cross preachers of the spring of 1559. The two groups were virtually the same.

her reception of the articles had been favorable but also that she had displayed no apparent resentment as a result of the compromise on the Prayer Book.

The articles themselves to a large degree were evidently a direct result of the bitter struggle over the Prayer Book. Sandys wrote Parker: "We are forced, through the vain bruits of the lying papists, to give up a profession of our own faith, to shew forth the sum of that doctrine which we profess, and to declare that we dissent not amongst ourselves. This labour we have now in hand and purpose to publish it so soon as the parliament is ended. I wish that we had your hand unto it." [22] If the struggle had in fact involved a fundamental disagreement between the former exiles and the more conservative of the non-Romanists whose real leader, as Professor Neale suggests, was the Queen herself, then Sandys' words made good sense indeed with their stress upon the necessity of a united front against the Romanists.

The articles do provide the firm common ground that was needed. As the Prayer Book itself is basically a moderate book in comparison with the Book of Geneva, so the articles, with their carefully worded introduction and conclusion, are moderate, even conservative in tone. Their thesis, strongly underlined in the introduction and carried out in the specific articles themselves, is that they represent a simple statement of Catholic doctrine; that the Church of England, whose teachings are thus set forth, is a true Catholic Church. Doctrinally the articles represent a modification of the Forty-two Articles in the direction of the Thirty-nine Articles and are in fact a link between the two. They are therefore at one and the same time a warranty of the exiles' determination to continue, at least doctrinally, the tradition of Cranmer, and a proof that the direction eventually taken by the Church under Elizabeth was the direction which they wished to take. Their tradition was an English tradition —despite their absence of many years, despite their relations with the continental churches and the influence of the continental reformers.[23] They were prepared to move forward in the direction

---

[22] Matthew Parker, *Correspondence, 1535–1575* (Cambridge, 1853), p. 66.

[23] Dugmore, *The Mass*, pp. 218–222.

which in retrospect can be described as the mainstream of Anglicanism, on their own volition, without prodding from the government, and independently of their own leader-to-be, Matthew Parker.

The *via media* is often presented as the reflection of Elizabeth's own position—a compromise between the non-Roman Catholicism of her conservative advisers and the Protestantism of the exiles. But from the beginning, for personal reasons as well as political, Elizabeth herself favored a more conservative settlement. The Prayer Book represented a compromise more satisfactory to the exile leaders than to the Queen. The articles from which the Thirty-nine Articles were developed were drawn up by the exiles, with the Queen's views in mind certainly, but without guidance from her. And as time was to prove, the Establishment itself took shape and character under their leadership. The clerics who had taken part in the Westminster disputation, together with Matthew Parker and the more moderate laymen like Cecil and Thomas Smith, these men rather than the Queen and the few churchmen she personally favored, were the true architects of the *via media*.[24]

Elizabeth's decision, given formal expression in the Supremacy Bill, to be styled *Governor* rather than *Head* of the Church in England, was accepted by Jewel as an indication of a fundamental change in fact rather than as a mere change of title.[25] The Queen may well have made the change to appease the Roman Catholic powers abroad and her own more conservative subjects at home, but she was also aware that the decision would be equally reassuring to the reformers. As a matter of fact, one of them, Thomas Lever, according to Sandys, was responsible for her decision.[26] Jewel praised

---

[24] *Cf.* G. R. Elton, *England under the Tudors* (London, 1955), pp. 273–274: "It is usual to call this settlement a compromise, and so it was—but not quite in the sense commonly supposed. . . . The compromise was between the queen and her protestant subjects represented in parliament, and it involved greater concessions from her than from them."

[25] Jewel, *Works*, IV, 1213. It is significant that Parkhurst, in a letter to Bullinger (*Zurich Letters*, I, 29) which probably accompanied Jewel's, expressed the view that the title of *Governor* "amounts to the same thing" as *Head*. The contrast between Jewel's reaction and the unbending rigidity of Parkhurst's is symptomatic of the difference in their thinking and an omen of the difference which the future was to reveal in their effectiveness as bishops.

[26] Parker, *Correspondence*, p. 66 (Sandys to Parker, 30 April 1559).

the decision and characterized it as the result of a sincere and basic conviction on the part of the Queen. For him it indicated a change in policy of vital significance to his own thinking. Later, in his *Defence of the Apology*,[27] he specifically condemned the all-inclusive Henrician term and welcomed its Elizabethan replacement. In appearing to limit the activities of the crown to the less debatable area of administration it reflected a point of view consonant with his own concept of doctrinal authority.

The Personnel of the New Establishment

With the closing of Parliament on May 8th, the government could now turn to the problem of selecting the personnel to man the new Establishment. Cecil had already given much thought to the matter, as memoranda in his papers attest.[28] These lists of bishoprics, of clerics without preferment, of clerics tentatively assigned to bishoprics, give little conception of the time that must have been spent by the Queen's advisors during the spring of 1559 on the vital question of personnel. Since the men whose influence counted most were in London, little written evidence has survived—only the meticulous jottings of Cecil's notes to himself. A record of the changes in prospective episcopal appointments, if it were available, would present an interesting and revealing story of the shifts in governmental policy during these months.

The events of the parliamentary session had made it clear that Elizabeth could expect little support from the Marian bishops. By May she had apparently given up hope for all but a handful—mostly old friends of her father's reign like Tunstal, from whom she continued to expect a measure of cooperation. Even these men in time made it clear that they would have nothing to do with the new settlement. One rarely thinks of 1559 as a revolutionary year. Yet developments through the year and the early months of 1560 follow very closely a pattern common to revolutions. The failure of conservatives to accept a measure of change forced the men in power to depend more on the left and so in turn to support policies which the conservatives found even more difficult to accept. Archbishop

[27] Jewel, *Works*, IV, 974 ff.
[28] Strype, *Annals*, I, i, 226–229.

Heath, for one, had shown moderation at the time of the Westminster disputation. But the actions of his more conservative colleagues drove the government further to the left, and as a result,
the final parliamentary settlement was as unacceptable to him as it
was to Bishops Watson and White. Likewise, the enforcement of the
oath upon the more conservative Marians, their deprivations and
the filling of the vacant sees with reformers, made it impossible later
in the year, even if it had been possible earlier, for men like Tunstal
to participate in the consecration of Parker, as the Queen had hoped
they would.

In the shifting picture, however, the most fundamental of personnel questions, the choice of an Archbishop of Canterbury, was
settled very early indeed, at least in the minds of the Queen's chief
advisors. Matthew Parker was to be the new Archbishop. Parker
appears to have been equally certain in his determination to avoid
the office. Since he was not in London except for a brief visit in
March, the story of his relations with the Queen's advisors is well
recorded in their correspondence.[29] During the crucial period from
March to mid-May, however, even the letters are silent concerning
the Canterbury appointment. Cecil was doubtless too occupied with
parliamentary affairs to give much thought during these months
to personnel. But on May 17th Bacon wrote Parker that at a meeting
on that day the decision had been made final and that shortly he
would receive orders to come to court.

In an undated letter written about the same time, Jewel lists five
appointments to bishoprics: Parker to Canterbury, Richard Cox
to Norwich, William Barlow, the Edwardian Bishop of Bath and
Wells, to Chichester, John Scory, the Edwardian Bishop of Chichester, to Hereford, and Edmund Grindal to London.[30] Very
likely the four additional appointees were selected at the meeting
with the Queen mentioned by Bacon. Oddly enough, only Parker
of the five had been listed as a possible appointee in Cecil's memo-

[29] The correspondence between Parker on the one hand and Cecil, Bacon, and the
Queen on the other, from December 1558 through June 1559, is printed in its entirety
in Parker, *Correspondence,* pp. 49–71.

[30] Jewel, *Works,* IV, 1210. This letter (to Martyr) duplicates much of the material
of a letter to Bullinger of May 22nd.

randum assigning clerics to specific sees. The group probably reflects therefore the adjustment of several points of view. Parker's appointment was the reaffirmation of the earlier decision from which apparently neither the Queen nor Cecil could be diverted. The Barlow and Scory appointments were the result of practical expediency, the necessity of using the two survivors of the Edwardian episcopate, regardless of their ability. Cox had played a more important role both at court and in the Church under Edward than either Barlow or Scory, he had the favor of the Queen, and he had fought for the maintenance of the *status quo* during his exile. Grindal, much the youngest of the group, was more representative of the exiles as a whole. If we may attach any significance to the absence of his name from any of Cecil's lists, despite Cecil's acquaintance with him during his Cambridge days, Grindal's appointment to London, the most important post in the Church after Canterbury, may represent an accommodation on Cecil's part with the more radical members of the Council and a reassuring gesture to the exiles. Jewel himself was unable, or at least unwilling, to draw any clear conclusions from a consideration of the list and closed with the cryptic statement to Martyr that "from this flowering I can easily guess beforehand, as you do of wine, what kind of a vintage it will be." In view of the generally depressed tone of the letter one is inclined to interpret such a remark as unfavorable. No doubt he was disappointed in the list—not so much that it indicated a positive direction of policy of which he disapproved, but rather because it actually indicated no real direction of policy at all, only a suggestion of the limitations within which the Establishment might be expected to operate and, in the case of Barlow and Scory, a willingness to place practical political necessity before any claims of distinction and ability.

Despite the many deprivations of the next two months, only two further appointments were made before the end of the summer, Edmund Allen and Jewel himself. Both Allen and Jewel, like Parker and in contrast to the other four, had been listed by Cecil for episcopal preferment, Jewel for Lincoln, Allen with no indication of see. Allen, a chaplain to Elizabeth in Edward's reign, had been abroad under Mary, although he had had no relations with the major groups of exiles. He had returned on Elizabeth's accession to his chaplainship and to diplomatic duties.[31] His early appointment to Rochester was the result, doubtless, of the Queens' favor and her desire to make use of him at court.

Jewel's inclusion in the first seven episcopal appointments raises a number of questions. Grindal, Sandys, and many others among the future bishops had been well known to Elizabeth's chief advisers as fellow Cantabrigians and in some cases as active participants in the Edwardian reformation outside the university. In contrast, Jewel had been a modest scholar known only to a restricted academic circle in Oxford. Only Cox, among the more prominent of the returned exiles, had known him at all well at the time. During the exile itself he had undoubtedly become better known to the leaders among the exiles, especially for his scholarly attainments and his association with Peter Martyr at Strasbourg, but he had spent most of the exile in Zurich away from the center of political activity. His sudden move to the front among the churchmen was the result, most likely, of his activities in England after his return. It was a period of numerous meetings and lengthy discussions. The month of April was largely taken up with the work on the Prayer Book and the articles. Here Jewel would have been at his best. He was one of the most learned of the extremely learned group of clerics in London. An informal committee concerned with theology and the liturgy would have provided a medium in which his own temperament and training would show to the best advantage. As a scholar, at Oxford during Edward's reign, and in Strasbourg and Zurich during the exile, he had not worked alone but with other men, academic in their interests it is true, but humanistic, as humanism in theory at least would always educate her sons. The humanity and reasonableness of Jewel is everywhere present in the long letters, vigorous, colorful and yet judicious, that he wrote through the years to Martyr. One has only to compare his letters with others in the Zurich collection, with those of Thomas Sampson, for instance, to realize the tremendous difference between the doctrinaire learning

[31] Garrett, *Exiles*, p. 70.

and narrow interests of the early Puritan and the humane learning and the wide ranging and human interests of Jewel. From the letters of his friends it is clear that the Jewel whom we meet in his letters is the Jewel whom they knew as a man, not unlike that earlier paragon of the Cambridge reformers, John Cheke, though without Cheke's worldly ambition. In the jungle of Tudor politics a gentle and lovable character like Jewel was rare indeed. As men came more and more to acknowledge his great learning, and as he himself made the successful adjustment, which so many scholars fail to make, to the world of political reality, he was an obvious man to watch. And it was no disadvantage that Jewel was unencumbered with a wife— in Elizabeth's eyes it may have been a decisive factor.

Unlike some of his friends, Jewel had no reservations concerning episcopal office.[32] He was convinced that the usage of the early Church, even as early as apostolic times, gave ample precedent for the office. Again and again in his controversial works he cited the powers and responsibilities of the early bishops as the effective and final answer to the claims of papal supremacy.[33] Logically therefore, since he believed episcopacy to have been an integral part of the structure and organization of the early Church, he accepted the institution as right and proper for the Church of England.

Congés d'élire were issued to Norwich on June 5th, to St. Paul's, Chichester, and Hereford on June 22nd, and to Canterbury, Ely, Salisbury, and Rochester on July 18th. Cox, who was originally to go to Norwich, received the richer appointment to Ely and no appointment was made to Norwich for another year. Except for the Canterbury appointment there seems little rhyme or reason in the apposition of persons and sees. The substitution of the rich see of Ely for Norwich and the appointment of Jewel to Salisbury, which, on Cecil's list, ranked fifth among the English sees in income, runs counter to the highly questionable Elizabethan policy that left the richest of the sees, Winchester, vacant for so long. The

[32] Jewel's references in his early letters to Zurich are in great contrast to Sampson's expression of distrust of the office and the consecration, "as we call it" (*Zurich Letters*, I, 63).

[33] Jewel, *Works, passim*, especially: *Reply*, I, 437; *Apology*, III, 100; *Defence*, III, 329 ff., 334, 337 ff.; IV, 906, 1069.

shift of Scory from his Edwardian see of Chichester to Hereford and the parallel shift of Barlow to Chichester from Bath and Wells, hardly reflects major policy though there may well have been personal reasons for not returning the bishops to their former sees.

The Visitorial Commission of 1559

Many months were to elapse between the issuance of the *congés d'élire*, the consecration of the bishops, and the restoration of the temporalities of their sees. In the meanwhile Jewel was occupied with work as strenuous as any he was to know as bishop. One of the first decisions reached by the government after the close of Parliament was the creation of visitorial commissions covering the whole of England.[34] There were seven commissions in all, if we include the rather extraordinary commission for the University of Cambridge. Excepting the latter, which included five prominent clerics and Mr. Secretary Cecil, and the Welsh commission with its three future bishops, the personnel follows a fairly regular pattern. Each commission included the lords-lieutenant of the counties to be covered and prominent gentry of these counties, together with several lawyers and one cleric.[35] The actual work of each commission, however, was normally carried out by a minority which always included a lawyer and the clerical member, the guiding spirit of the commission. All the clerics were former exiles, all had been singled out by Cecil for episcopal appointment, and all but Thomas Becon eventually became bishops.

From the existing records of the work of Jewel's visitation commission it is evident that the work was thoroughly done—in the most part by Jewel, Henry Parry, and one or two others. Parry, the lawyer of the commission, had been an associate of Jewel's at Frankfort and later was to become his chancellor at Salisbury. The painstaking work of visitation included the holding of a visitorial court in each parish, the review of the churchwardens' accounts, the reinstatement of clergy deprived during the previous reign, and the

[34] Jewel, *Works*, IV, 1210.
[35] C. G. Bayne, "The Visitation of the Province of Canterbury, 1559," *English Historical Review 28* (1913) 658–659.

furnishing of statutes to the cathedral chapters, in fact the full duties of a regular episcopal visitation extended over several dioceses and held after a change of government in both Church and State. The clerical commissioner, although provided with a preacher, usually delivered sermons at each sitting of the commissioners, in addition to his other work.[36]

The surviving records of Jewel's visitation give disappointingly little indication of his own personal views. Upon his return to London, however, he did write with considerable feeling to Peter Martyr of the state of affairs in the southwest.

We found everywhere the people sufficiently well disposed towards religion, and even in those quarters where we expected most difficulty. It is however hardly credible what a harvest, or rather what a wilderness of superstition, had sprung up in the darkness of the Marian times. We found in all places votive relics of saints, nails with which the infatuated people dreamed that Christ had been pierced, and I know not what small fragments of the sacred cross. . . . If inveterate obstinacy was found anywhere, it was altogether among the priests, those especially who had once been on our side. They are now throwing all things into confusion, in order, I suppose, that they may not seem to have changed their opinions without due consideration. But let them make what disturbance they please; we have in the mean time disturbed them from their rank and office.[37]

Among the articles issued by Jewel to the cathedral chapter at Exeter is a small but revealing item concerning the participation of the public in the service. Laymen, singing metrical psalms, had invaded the choir despite the opposition of the clergy. Jewel and two other commissioners advised the chapter not only to allow the singing but also to aid the singers, thus, as Frere pointed out, establishing an important precedent for the future. Jewel's action at Exeter reflected his own strong conviction that popular participation in the service constituted a vital means of strengthening the new Establishment in its fight against the old order and its tradi-

---

[36] W. H. Frere and W. M. Kennedy, *Visitation Articles and Injunctions of the Period of the Reformation*, 3 vols. (London, 1910), III, 42, n. 1.

[37] Jewel, *Works*, IV, 1217.

tions. He wrote Martyr later that the "practice of joining in church music" had contributed greatly to the improvement of conditions. For, as soon as the people

had once commenced singing in public, in only one little church in London, immediately not only the churches in the neighbourhood, but even the towns far distant, began to vie with each other in the same practice. You may now sometimes see at Paul's cross, after the sermon, six thousand persons, old and young, of both sexes, all singing together, and praising God. This sadly annoys the mass-priests, and the devil. For they perceive that by these means the sacred discourses sink more deeply into the minds of men, and that their kingdom is weakened and shaken at almost every note.[38]

Prior to the visitation Jewel had expressed to Martyr his intention to avoid the "burden" of a bishopric. During the course of the visitation he came to accept his appointment to episcopal office as a matter of fact, although he was by no means convinced of his qualifications for administrative responsibility. "As regards myself," he wrote, "you will know what an undertaking it is, especially for a man unskilled in business, and always brought up in inactivity and obscurity, to be raised at once to the government of the church; and, though scarcely able to manage his own affairs, to take upon himself the management of those of others." [39] Jewel's career until now had indeed been wholly free of administrative duties. During the visitation, for the first time, he had become aware of their extent and complexity. Furthermore, he had coped with them at least adequately. In these few months he had learned that he could do the job, his own protestations notwithstanding. But the visitation had meant more than this. It was a sobering introduction to the problems that faced the new Establishment. His knowledge of the paucity of capable workers and his recognition of the vast amount of work to be done simply overrode his feeling of inexperience and inadequacy.

Jewel was consecrated at Lambeth on January 21, 1560, by Archbishop Parker assisted by Bishops Grindal and Cox, and the Ed-

[38] *Ibid.*, IV, 1231.
[39] *Ibid.*, IV, 1219.

wardian Suffragan Bishop of Bedford, Hodgkins.[40] The temporalities of the see were formally restored to him on April 6th.[41]

The Crucifix in the Queen's Chapel

In spite of the long delay between his appointment and his consecration, and despite his anxiety to get to the multifold tasks which awaited him at Salisbury, it was several months before Jewel was able to leave London. Shortly after his consecration a debate over the use of the crucifix in the Queen's chapel reached its climax and if his remarks to Martyr concerning the controversy and its possible consequences are to be taken seriously, he had grave doubts of ever going to Salisbury as bishop.[42] The controversy appears at first glance to have been a veritable tempest in a teapot. In the eyes of the principal actors, however, it was far more—a struggle in which basic principles were involved and whose outcome would affect the very character of the Church of England.

In the course of the visitations under royal commission during the summer and early autumn the commissioners had addressed themselves quite thoroughly to the removal and destruction of the images in the churches, the rood-lofts, crucifixes, and other traditional symbols that they associated with Rome. Upon their return from the visitation in October and November they were faced with a disturbing state of affairs. The Queen was insisting upon the use of the crucifix and candles in the royal chapel, an example which could only be regarded as a precedent directly contradicting the visitorial work of the summer and which might even portend a fundamental change of policy on the part of the Queen. Among the bishops-elect there was complete unanimity against the Queen's action, Parker himself taking a leading part in the early protests.[43] When in January three of the bishops were selected to officiate in the chapel with the crucifix and candles, Cox made a plea to the

[40] W. H. Jones, *Fasti Ecclesiae Sarisberiensis*, 2 vols. (Salisbury, 1879–1881), I, 107.

[41] T. D. Hardy, *Syllabus of Documents in Rymer's Foedera*, 3 vols. (London, 1869–1885), II, 800.

[42] Jewel, *Works*, IV, 1229.

[43] Parker, *Correspondence*, p. 97.

Queen asking that he be excused.[44] At the same time an address stating their objections was presented by the bishops to the Queen.[45] This document, generally attributed to Parker, Frere believes to have been the work of Jewel.[46] As a direct result of the address of the bishops a disputation was held, the disputants being Parker and Cox for the crucifix, and Grindal and Jewel against it. It was this occasion which prompted Jewel's remark that he would probably not write to Martyr again as bishop. Sandys, too, wrote some time afterwards of having incurred Elizabeth's displeasure, but concluded that all was now well and the "stumbling-blocks" removed. Jewel, in his next letter to Martyr, makes no mention of the matter at all.[47] And Cox, writing a month afterwards, declared that there was no open quarrel among them now over the setting up of crucifixes in the churches.[48]

It is a confusing story. First Parker and Cox lead the opposition. Then the two of them apparently become the defenders of the very position they have previously attacked, against Grindal and Jewel. Finally, and in a very short time, all is peace. Several explanations have been offered. Frere for instance, suggests that the issue changed in the midst of the controversy from that of the cross in the Queen's chapel to that of the rood-images in the churches.[49] Dixon, on the other hand, suggests that the issue from the first was more fundamental, that the bishops were correct in suspecting the intention of the Queen to reverse the policy which the visitorial commission had so enthusiastically carried out.[50] If we accept Professor Neale's thesis that Elizabeth at the conclusion of the parliamentary struggle the preceding May had been forced against her own wishes to a com-

[44] Strype, *Annals*, I, ii, appendix xxii, 500–503.

[45] David Wilkins, *Concilia Magnae Britanniae*, etc., 4 vols. (London, 1737), IV, 196–197.

[46] W. H. Frere, *The English Church in the Reigns of Elizabeth and James I* (London, 1904), p. 54. J. Trésal in *Les Origines du schisme Anglican, 1509–71* (Paris, 1908) p. 393 attributes the work to Parker *and* Jewel.

[47] Jewel, *Works*, IV, 1231–1232.

[48] *Zurich Letters*, II, 42.

[49] Frere, *English Church*, p. 54.

[50] Dixon, *History*, V, 313, n.

promise with the exile leaders, then both suggestions must be regarded as contributions to the understanding of the problem rather than as explanations complete in themselves. The catalyst was the Queen herself and her position is the key to the problem throughout. Elizabeth, far from reconciled to what in fact had been a major defeat for her own policy,[51] was probing the defenses of the opposition, and her action, skillful as always, involved both the use of the chapel and the broader question of the use of the Church. It was a shrewd maneuver since she was free to dissociate the two issues one from the other, should strategy demand it, and retreat on the broader issue without endangering her position in regard to her own chapel.

The Queen's initial change of policy from that of the vigorous commissions issued to the visitors came while the visitations were still in progress. In October she authorized the celebration of a marriage in the royal chapel with crucifix and candles and the officiating priests in full eucharistic vestments. This step reflected, as did many of Elizabeth's actions in the ecclesiastical sphere, a particular venture in the field of foreign affairs, in this case the proposed marriage of the Queen to the Hapsburg Archduke Charles.[52]

Archbishop Parker took action almost immediately and, according to Elizabeth's Puritan councillor, Sir Francis Knollys, with complete success.[53] But both Parker and Knollys reckoned without their mistress. She simply bided her time and before the year was out the crucifix and candles appeared again in the royal chapel. From the beginning the bishops-elect had looked upon the use of the royal chapel as a precedent gravely undermining their own work in the visitations. Nor could they be at all sure that the Queen would not proceed further and reverse the fundamental policy which visitorial action represented. Jewel, as early as November, expressed dismay at the precedent created by the Queen's action.

[51] Neale, *Elizabeth I*, p. 83.
[52] Frere, *English Church*, pp. 52–53.
[53] Parker, *Correspondence*, p. 97.

He felt that the two issues, the use of the royal chapel and the general use of the Church were inseparable.[54] And now it appeared that the problem, supposedly resolved when the visitorial commissions were issued, was to be revived again.

Bishop Cox, presuming on his long friendship with Elizabeth, wrote a strong letter to her, protesting her actions and stating in unqualified terms that he dared not minister in the chapel, "the lights and cross remaining. . . . I cannot, without offence of God and conscience, yield to the setting up of images in the temple of my God and Creator."[55] Cox's protest is specifically against the use of the royal chapel. Unlike Jewel, in his letters to Martyr, Cox does not suggest the danger of the precedent and, more significantly, makes no allusion whatever to the possibility of a change of policy concerning the rood-lofts and images in the churches. Yet the broader issue came to the fore almost immediately and Cox capitulated to the Queen not only on the issue of the royal chapel but on the general issue as well.

Such a radical change on the part of the Bishop can only be explained by the hypothesis that Elizabeth herself at this point decided upon a complete reversal of policy in regard to the use of the Church as a whole. Why she should have done so at this precise moment is not clear, but it is quite possible that the letter of Cox itself provoked her to action. Despite its coating of humility, despite the grovelling tones with which the Bishop introduces his plea, it is an extremely positive letter. His assumption of fatherly authority may well have driven home to Elizabeth the extent of her own loss of control during the preceding months. She would therefore yield not an inch. And Cox, faced with an angry Queen and the charge of unwarranted interference in her own private affairs, doubtless crumpled. Elizabeth at this point then decided to proceed further. Her initial victory over Cox and the absence of other open opposition could easily have misled her. She would carry the battle far into the camp of the opposition and so let it be known that the use of the royal chapel was not only to stand but was indeed

[54] Jewel, *Works,* IV, 1225.
[55] Strype, *Annals,* I, ii, appendix xxii, 501–502.

to be considered a precedent for the Church as a whole. There need have been no time lag between what appear in the above reconstruction to be two separate actions. Elizabeth was quite capable of seizing the opportunity offered by Cox's surrender on the issue of the chapel and confronting him with the broader issue. Under the circumstances Cox would hardly have dared oppose her. Stronger men than Cox had wilted in the face of a frontal attack from an aroused Elizabeth. Thus his double capitulation and the embarrassingly defensive position in which he found himself later with his colleagues. His letter to the German Cassander written after all was over suggests that he was still seeking to justify his about face.[56]

Elizabeth, however, had only won the first round. The other bishops-elect, recognizing the seriousness of their position, closed ranks and drew up an impressive joint letter to the Queen. Their letter, unlike Cox's, was concerned primarily with the use of the Church, rather than with that of the royal chapel. The tone of the letter is neither grovelling nor authoritarian—Cox's letter had been an odd combining of both qualities. Instead of rendering a virtual ultimatum to the Queen, the bishops judicially and with great tact presented their case and concluded with the dignified request that the Queen "refer the discussion and deciding of them (all controversies of religion) to a synod of the bishops and other godly learned men, according to the example of Constantius Magnus and other Christian emperors: that the reasons of both parties being examined by them, the judgment may be given uprightly in all doubtful matters." [57]

The disputation of February 1560 followed, with Parker and Cox pitted against Jewel and Grindal. Since the letter of the bishops is concerned primarily with the broader issue it has been assumed that the subject of the disputation was the restoration of the rood-

[56] *Zurich Letters*, II, 41–42.

[57] Wilkins, *Concilia*, IV, 197. The tactful citation of "the example" of the Emperor Constantine may have suggested to Frere that Jewel was the author. The general argument of the letter does resemble very closely the Bishop's arguments in his controversial works.

lofts and images in the churches.[58] The only specific mention of the subject of the debate is Jewel's in a letter written the day before where he refers to the "little cross," *cruculam,* the same term he had used consistently in his earlier letters when describing the problem of the crucifix in the royal chapel. His use of the term at this point suggests that by the time of the disputation the issue had become narrowed again to the original question of the use of the Queen's chapel, although the disputants, concerned as they had been from the beginning with the importance of the chapel as a precedent, would hardly have ignored the broader issue. The result of the disputation was a compromise along lines decidedly favorable to the bishops. The reintroduction of the images in the churches simply disappeared as a problem; the policy carried out by the visitorial commission was to be continued. And finally, in the Queen's chapel, the crucifix was replaced by the simple cross. The candles apparently remained.

Such an interpretation makes good sense when we come to explain the role of Archbishop Parker. Perhaps even more important is the support offered it by the nature of the final solution itself. The compromise reached, that is, the use of the simple cross in the chapel, might logically have developed from a disputation over the chapel crucifix. It could not have emerged from a disputation in which the primate and one of his chief suffragans had defended the use of images throughout the Church, and that with the Queen's express support. I think it very likely that before the disputation proper the Queen was forced to retreat from her forward position. She was faced with the virtually unanimous opposition of the new bishops at a time when all hope of cooperation from the moderate Romanists had finally disappeared. So long as the bishops maintained a united front she had little choice.

There is no record of Parker's activities in this later stage of the controversy prior to Jewel's reference to him as one of the participants, unless we accept his authorship or joint authorship of the letter of the bishops. If he had a part in drawing up the letter, completely condemnatory as it was of the images in the churches, it is inconceivable that he could have executed an about face comparable

[58] Dixon, *History,* V, 311.

to that of Cox and supported the general use of images in the disputation. Even if he had had no part in drawing up the letter he would still stand convicted of an action impossible to reconcile with a reputation for integrity that few would question. I suggest that Parker, faced by the new policy consequent to the Cox letter and its repercussions, sought a compromise; that he made his own position so definite and interpreted the views of his colleagues so forcefully to Elizabeth that she felt compelled to give him assurances she had no intention of proceeding beyond the use of the royal chapel. He in turn, and Cox with him, would then defend the chapel crucifix in the disputation. True, his defense of the chapel crucifix involved a change from his stand the preceding October, but Parker was a realist, he was closer to the Queen than his colleagues and knew the danger of pressing her too far. It was better to give in on the lesser issue if by so doing he could save the broader one. And it would be within his jurisdiction as primate to see to it that the use of the royal chapel provided no effective precedent to the Church as a whole. It is also just possible that in his wisdom he saw his way even this early to the solution finally reached. Not only did he know his Queen; he was fully aware of the strength of the opposition she faced not only from the bishops but from many of her chief councillors. If he kept his counsel and used the disputation to demonstrate both the unanimity and the force of the opposition, he might very well bring Elizabeth to accept a compromise satisfactory to all. Whether or not he was in fact the architect of the compromise we do not know. Jewel, for one, is an unlikely candidate. He seems to have confused the crucifix and the cross in his own thinking so thoroughly that he was quite capable of condemning the cross as completely as he condemned the crucifix. If he did so in the actual disputation itself, he quite innocently played into the hands of the architect of the compromise. Had the opposition proposed the cross as an acceptable solution in place of the crucifix it would have ceased to be of any value as a compromise formula. On the other hand to insist categorically on the complete removal of all ornaments would be to leave the door open to the introduction of the simple cross as an acceptable compromise. Once the suggestion was made and the cross and its use clearly distinguished from the crucifix, it would be generally acceptable, as Cassander pointed out in his letter written afterwards to Cox.[59] There were doubtless individuals to whom the formula had no appeal. Parkhurst's puzzling references two years later indicate that to his forthright way of thinking the cross was still the crucifix. He first wrote Bullinger of his delight at the news of the destruction of the cross, then some months later quite dejectedly that the cross had been removed but was now restored.[60] For one who still identified cross and crucifix there was reason for confusion. He had been informed doubtless of the removal of the crucifix. The cross and the candles remained.[61]

For Elizabeth the compromise represented a very real defeat indeed. She had not moved forward at all to regain any of the ground lost in the last weeks of the 1559 Parliament. In fact, the confirmation of the policy which the visitorial commission represented meant that in this area at least there would be no further change, there could be no going back. While the character of the Establishment was not materially changed by the controversy, it had become more clearly defined and in terms satisfactory to the moderate men newly responsible for the administration of the Church. Here, however, it should be pointed out that Elizabeth was actually the gainer—to a degree that neither she nor the bishops could have recognized at the time. The bishops were committed to the compromise and, as with Parker and Cox in the case of the earlier compromise, they must perforce defend it against those of the extremists who continued to identify cross and crucifix and damn both equally. The alignment of the bishops with the primate within a month of their consecration provoked no comment at the time. But it can be regarded as a significant step toward the union of the leaders of the Establishment, a union of increasing importance as the division between the bishops on the one hand and the Puritans on the other moved toward the open rift of 1571.

[59] *Zurich Letters,* II, 42–47.

[60] *Ibid.,* I, 122, 129.

[61] Henry Machyn, *The Diary of Henry Machyn, Citizen and Merchant-Taylor of London, 1550–63* (London, 1848), p. 226.

Chapter III

The Defense of the Church

The Challenge Sermon

With the conclusion of the debate over the crucifix it seemed possible that Jewel could finally turn to the affairs of his diocese.[1] Already, however, a cause for further delay had arisen which would keep him in London until early summer. Some months before, he had preached a sermon at Paul's Cross which had attracted wide attention, according to the diarist Henry Machyn, being attended with as "grett audyense as (has ever) bene at Powlles crosse," including many prominent members of the court.[2] This was Jewel's original challenge sermon. Now, four months later, he was invited to repeat it at court on March 17th and then again at Paul's Cross the second Sunday before Easter. The Paul's Cross sermon of November 26, 1559, despite the size and prominence of the audience which heard it, might well have been regarded as no more than another tirade in the long series which the reformers had launched and would continue to launch against the Roman Church. Repeated before the court and then again from the most prominent pulpit in the city it assumed an altogether different character. The open and official approval of the government and the focussing of public attention upon the challenge made certain that the gage could be ignored by the supporters of Rome only at grave risk to their Church. The mere sermon of November 1559 thus became in the spring of 1560 the introductory chapter and thesis of what

[1] Jewel to Edward Nicolas, February 23, 1560 (British Museum, Add. MSS, Egerton 2533, fol. 1); Jewel to Martyr, March 5, 1560 (Jewel, *Works*, IV, 1231).

[2] Machyn, *Diary*, p. 218.

was to be a vast corpus of apologetic and controversial writing extending over the next decade.

In the last of the three sermons, shortly afterwards printed, Jewel described his original challenge: "If any learned man of all our adversaries, or if all the learned men that be alive, be able to bring any one sufficient sentence out of any old catholic doctor, or father, or out of any old general council, or out of the holy scriptures of God, or any one example of the primitive church, whereby it may be clearly and plainly proved" that certain current practices and teachings of the Roman Church were in use during the first six centuries of the Christian era, "I promised then that I would give over and subscribe unto him."[3] He was well aware that there had been many who believed he had said more in the November sermon than he "was able to justify and make good." Instead, he now felt more certain than ever of the position he had taken and to the original list of fifteen Roman practices and teachings added twelve more.

All but five of the twenty-seven points are concerned with the Mass, from the doctrine of transubstantiation itself to such matters as the plurality of masses, the preservation of the elements, the elevation of the Host, and other teachings which stem from the basic concept of the Mass held by Rome. The five points not directly related to the Mass are extremely varied, in Jewel's words:

that the people had their common prayers then in a strange tongue that they understood not;

Or that the bishop of Rome was then called an universal bishop, or head of the universal church;

Or that Images were then set up in the churches, to the intent the people might worship them;

Or that the lay people was then forbidden to read the word of God in their own tongue;

Or that ignorance is the mother and cause of true devotion and obedience.[4]

---

[3] Jewel, *Works,* I, 20–21.

[4] *Ibid.* The last point was apparently suggested by an argument made by Dean Cole in the Westminster disputation. In his report to Martyr on the disputation, Jewel had

Jewel had chosen his ground with great care. Later when he was criticized for having said nothing of justification, of the value of good works, of prayers for the dead, and many other doctrines around which so much of sixteenth-century religious controversy centered, he answered that since he knew that these might "have some colour or shadow of the doctors," he had thought it best to choose those points where you "should be able to find not so much as any colour at all." [5] Even so, he had been able to list twenty-seven teachings which were "the highest mysteries, and greatest keys of their religion" and without which Roman doctrine can never be "maintained and stand upright." [6]

The careful selection of points, the precision with which Jewel insisted upon terms, has little appeal to the modern reader. In the sixteenth century, an age still impressed by the intricacies of scholastic debate, and as deeply concerned with the problems of theology as the thirteenth century, men found the sermon convincing and even exciting. Had it been no more than a performance of technical virtuosity it would scarcely warrant our attention today. The reception accorded the challenge, however, by both the English leaders and the Romanists, is evidence that it was recognized as far more than merely another vigorous sermon skillfully argued.

Underlying the points and terms of the challenge is a premise basic to the most crucial problem which faced the English Church, the nature and character of the Church itself and the religion which it professed. Although the reign of Mary had greatly strengthened English opposition to Rome and to the papacy, the majority of Englishmen remained conservative in their thinking. Herein lay the advantage of the Roman apologists. Their claim that Roman Christianity alone was Catholic, that is, that it alone was apostolic and universal, repeated ad infinitum and present as a fundamental assumption in every statement made,[7] must inevitably find accept-

---

singled it out for acid comment. It is interesting that Cole should have been the first Romanist to accept the challenge.

[5] *Ibid.*, I, 28.

[6] *Ibid.*, I, 21.

[7] Philip Hughes, *The Reformation in England*, 3 vols. (London, 1950–1954), III, 48–100. In his very complete and detailed analysis of Jewel, Hughes accepts this

ance with a conservative people, unless it were vigorously and successfully challenged. Fundamental in the Roman claim to Catholicity was the further assumption that Catholic doctrine constituted an organic whole and that the denial or acceptance of any part of it necessarily involved the denial or acceptance of the entire organic structure.

Focusing his attention specifically upon this aspect of the Roman structure, Jewel stated categorically that the Church of Rome by professing doctrines which had no basis whatever in early apostolic and patristic Christianity, could no longer claim to be a Catholic Church. It mattered not that some, or even many Roman doctrines might be in this Catholic tradition. If only one central doctrine could be proven contrary to tradition, then the entire organic structure would crumble. But the terms upon which Jewel insisted implied even more than that. In declaring that the burden of proof rested upon Rome herself, Jewel reversed the roles which for so long Rome and her critics had played. Those who accepted his challenge must defend their teachings. This was no mere debater's trick. The demand is based upon the premise that Rome had no right to be considered the defender of Catholic tradition: that, in fact, the Church of England had the greater right.[8] Here Jewel had

---

basic assumption of the sixteenth-century defenders of the Roman position. Throughout his treatment of the English Reformation in the reign of Elizabeth, he refers to the Church of Rome as "the Church," to its members as "Catholics," and to its teachings as "Catholic." For instance: "The Catholic, learned or illiterate, found out what God had made known about all this by listening to the Church" (III, 65); "Whatever the general knowledge of the Catholic faith which this average Englishman possessed who was formed in the far-off time before 1529 . . ." (III, 52); or his paraphrase of Jewel's letter of May 1559 to Bullinger, "Many of the Reformed, they say, have been won back to Catholicism" (III, 54). Jewel, of course, used no such terms but wrote simply that "we . . . have . . . to combat . . . with those of our friends who, of late years, have . . . gone over to the opposite party" (*Works*, IV, 1212, as quoted by Hughes, III, 54, n. 1). Hughes, as a Roman Catholic apologist, should regard the Church of Rome as the Church and its teachings as Catholic. But as an historian he should at least point out that the English churchmen he is discussing would not for a moment have accepted his use of these terms and indeed that in this very fact lay the essence of the difference in points of view which the historian must analyze.

[8] Hughes, in his treatment of the controversy and Jewel's later writings (III, 96–114), ignores this fundamental premise of the challenge sermon. He grants that

simply developed the idea which the Romanists found so disturbing in the Westminster disputation. The parallel between the disputation and the challenge is immediately apparent. At Westminster, however, the Romanists had had to *disprove* positive teachings professed by the reformers. Now they must *prove* teachings which they themselves professed. Significantly, Henry Cole, the Marian Dean of St. Paul's and a prominent figure in the disputation, was the first to reply to Jewel's challenge and he adopted the same tactics against Jewel which he and his colleagues had pursued at the disputation.

The controversy with Cole took place during the weeks immediately following Jewel's sermon before the court on March 17th. It was on the whole a pleasant controversy, as sixteenth-century controversies go. Cole wrote Jewel a very short letter the day after the delivery of the sermon at court in which he took Jewel to task for limiting the challenge, and sought to enlarge the area under dispute to include points he considered more fundamental. In a brief answer written on March 20th, Jewel noted that Cole had obviously not heard the sermon since he listed only four of the articles and completely misconstrued the terms of the challenge. Jewel then repeated a number of the omitted articles and pointed out again that Cole had only to prove one point to make his case.[9] Having failed to tempt Jewel to shift his basic position, Cole now frankly recognized the issue which Jewel had raised and declared that it was up to those of the "new doctrine" to carry the burden of proof. It was, of course, the position maintained by his side at Westminster, the position of strength from which the Romanists up to this point had consistently, and wisely, refused to move. His complaint that Jewel had taken an authoritative tone merely because he held the office of bishop suggests that he was well aware of the danger of allowing Jewel to maintain his position. Until he could

---

Jewel and his contemporaries proved themselves astute controversialists in concentrating upon those practices which had only become an integral part of the Mass in comparatively recent centuries, but like Henry Cole, he condemns Jewel for avoiding fundamental issues. For Jewel, nothing was more fundamental than the issue of Catholicity. The doctrine and the practice of the Mass, the papal supremacy itself, were of importance primarily as evidence to that end.

[9] Jewel, *Works,* I, 26–28.

dislodge Jewel he apparently was unwilling to proceed further. Jewel replied in turn that in Cole's second letter he had found "many words to little purpose. It had been better for you to have alleged one sufficient authority, whereby I might have learned that I looked for." [10] Nevertheless, he analyzed Cole's arguments in detail, with the obvious purpose of drawing him into the debate—if that could be done without compromising the original conditions of the challenge.

Evidently Jewel's confident tone, his quiet assumption of authority, did provoke Cole, for the latter finally answered at some length. According to Jewel, the answer was not sent to him but circulated privately among some of Cole's friends. After making an effort to get a copy directly from Cole, Jewel replied, this time in the form he was to use in all subsequent controversies, printing a passage from his last letter, its answer by Cole, and a further rejoinder by himself.[11] The controversy remained a quibbling one since Cole never fully accepted the terms of the challenge. Whenever the debate did come close to the basic questions at issue, Cole was completely overwhelmed by the enormously superior learning of the Bishop. There can be no doubt of Jewel's complete victory in his first bout with the defenders of Rome.

To this verdict, to which historians from Strype to Dixon have subscribed, J. H. Pollen makes a strong demurrer. "The Catholics, remembering the violence to Jewel's opponents at the Westminster Conference, held their peace." Cole "wrote Jewel an adroit letter of inquiry which by insinuation effectively laid bare the weakness of Jewel's cause. 'Why not,' said the Catholic, 'prove the essentials of your creed?'" Jewel's failure to explain gave him in Catholic eyes "the appearance of shuffling." [12] In view of the fact that Jewel had initiated the challenge and had adhered scrupulously to its terms both in his sermons and in his letters, Pollen is merely accepting the position taken by Cole—the standard Romanist demand that Jewel, like the reformers at Westminster, defend a "new" position against

[10] *Ibid.*, I, 31.
[11] *Ibid.*, I, 40 ff.
[12] Pollen, *English Catholics*, pp. 107–108.

the "established and traditional" one.[13] Obviously the initial challenge itself did mark a radical departure from earlier attacks which the Roman Church had faced. But once the challenge was made there was no shifting.

Pollen concludes that Jewel answered "in the *de haut en bas* style so irritating to those who knew the answer, but were restrained by force from uttering it."[14] What disturbed Jewel's critics, in his own day and later, was not his tone *de haut en bas,* for Jewel was singularly free of pontifical airs. It was rather that Jewel refused altogether to accept the Romanist *de haut en bas.* For the first time a challenger had entered the lists which had heretofore been regarded by all as the peculiar domain of Rome and had denied the Roman claim to possession as of right.

The Apology of the Church of England

The publication of the correspondence with Cole brought to an end the first controversy over the challenge sermon. Jewel was to wait nearly four years for the appearance of a worthy reply, *An answere to maister Juelles chalenge,* of Thomas Harding, written abroad and published at Louvain in 1564. Long before Harding answered the challenge, however, Jewel had published a treatise which was destined to overshadow both the original challenge and its answer, his *Apologia Ecclesiae Anglicanae.* The Latin edition appeared early in 1562, and an English translation by Ann, Lady Bacon, later in the year.

The *Apology,* like the Cole and Harding controversies themselves, is closely related to the challenge sermons in point of view and in technique—hardly surprising in view of their nearness in time to one another. The composition and publication of the

---

[13] *Cf.* Hughes, *The Reformation,* III, 64: "The differences between the new version of the Christian religion (the English version) and the old (the Roman version) were well nigh infinite, said this leading apologist of the new." Thus Hughes paraphrases Jewel's basic argument of the *Apology*! By attributing Cole's terms to Jewel, Hughes has succeeded where both Cole and Thomas Harding failed. At one casual stroke of the pen he has caused Jewel to deny the premise upon which his entire life work rested.

[14] Pollen, *English Catholics,* p. 108.

Apology seems in fact to have been the direct result of the challenge sermons and the correspondence with Cole.

Jewel is of little help to us in reconstructing the story of the inception and composition of the *Apology*. His first specific reference to it occurs in a letter to Peter Martyr written in February 1562: "We have recently published an apology for the change of religion and the separation from the Roman church." [15] Except for a conventionally modest reference to its insignificance and a complaint concerning the errors of the printers, he is silent. His failure to refer to the *Apology* at any time prior to its appearance in print suggests that he attached little importance to it, that he looked upon it as a private and personal project in which no one else would be particularly interested. Actually the reverse is true. The writing and publication of the *Apology* was a matter of governmental policy— a major facet of the government's defense of the new Establishment. Such a view is strongly supported by the sequence of events preceding and subsequent to its composition.

On May 18, 1560, Jewel completed his final reply to Henry Cole. Three days later he dined at court with Cecil and on the following day departed for Salisbury. When he returned to London in mid-April 1561, he had completed the *Apology*. Within the next few weeks he attended an important series of conferences which the Queen held with Archbishop Parker, Thomas Young, the Archbishop-elect of York, Robert Horne, the newly appointed Bishop of Winchester, the Lord Keeper and Mr. Secretary Cecil.[16] On May 8 Cecil wrote to Throckmorton in Paris that

for the satisfaction of such doubts concerning the position of the English clergy I have caused the Bishop of Sarum to feign an epistle sent from hence thither, and have printed it secretly, and send you herewith several copies. If more be printed there the matter shall have more probability. I have caused an apology to be written, but not printed, in the name of the whole clergy, which is wisely, learnedly, eloquently, and gravely

[15] "Edidimus nuper Apologiam de mutata religione et discessione ab ecclesia Romana" (*Works*, IV, 1245).

[16] Quadra to Philip, May 5, 1561, *Calendar of State Papers Spanish, Elizabeth*, I, 201.

written, but I stay the publication of it until it be further pondered.[17]

It is a suggestive sequence of events. Jewel had remained in London during the spring of 1560 to complete his reply to Cole. Since the controversy had been initiated by sermons delivered at the invitation of the government it would have been most natural for him to have discussed the final version of his reply with Cecil before turning it over to the printer. I suggest that at the meeting with Cecil on May 21, 1560, possibly as a direct result of a review of the challenge controversy, a more ambitious project was broached— the writing of a formal defense of the Church of England. Such a project was an almost obvious corollary of the challenge sermons.

While Jewel's ostensible purpose in returning to London the following April was to preach at St. Paul's,[18] his actual purpose was more probably the discussion of the completed *Apology* with Cecil. In the meantime the Pope had issued his *Bulla Celebrationis* making definite at long last another session of the Council of Trent.[19] The convoking of the Council and the papal attempts to send a nuncio to England had forced the religious problem once more to the front in foreign affairs. Thus Elizabeth was present at a series of meetings predominant with ecclesiastics, and Cecil, whether by foresight or by fortunate coincidence, had the *Apology* ready when it would be most needed. It is not possible to know what consideration, if any, was given to it at the meetings with the Queen. But the steps concerning Jewel and the *Apology* which Cecil described to Throckmorton relate so closely to the subject of

[17] *Calendar of State Papers Foreign,* 1561–1562, p. 104. Of the various treatments of the period, only Pollen in his *English Catholics* refers to the letter, and he most inaccurately, declaring that in the attempt in 1560 by Throckmorton to convince the French of the Anglican *via media* "Jewel's pen was frequently employed by Cecil and at the end of the year his *Apologia* for Anglicanism began to be circulated abroad" (p. 108). The evidence submitted by Pollen for the first half of his statement is Cecil's remark quoted above. The "frequently" of Pollen's statement is not supported. Nor does he give any source for the statement that the *Apologia* was published abroad in 1560. The epistle to which Cecil refers has not been identified. *The Epistle to Scipio* appears at first glance to have been meant, but internal evidence makes it clear that it was written later. See Jewel, *Works,* IV, 1094, n. 1.

[18] Machyn, *Diary,* p. 225.

[19] The Bull was dated November 9, 1560.

the meetings that they most probably represent a direct outgrowth of the meetings. Such a conclusion is strongly supported by Jewel's devotion of the entire last chapter of the completed *Apology* to the problem of councils with specific and detailed reference to the Council of Trent. If this hypothesis be correct then the consideration of the *Apology* by the conferees named by Quadra may be regarded as the first step towards the official status which the work later attained. Certainly such status was in Cecil's mind as early as his letter to Throckmorton.

It is characteristic of Cecil that he should "stay the publication" of the *Apology* until it "be further pondered." This was a task for the Archbishop. Parker's study of the *Apology* confirmed Cecil's earlier appraisal. He only regretted, he wrote Cecil on August 11th, that the work had not been available earlier so that it could be "scattered in France" before the conference soon to take place at Poissy.[20] He apparently felt that the work needed no further pondering and proceeded at once to its printing, for it appeared before the end of the year. On January 1, 1562, Cecil wrote the Archbishop to thank him for the "heep of things wherewith you have gladded me," including "this last book, the Apology."[21] He regretted that the book had been so negligently printed and that the commonplaces had not been marked, evidence in both cases of the haste with which the first edition was put through the press.

Cecil's letter reveals an interesting aspect of the formulation of Elizabethan policy, one generally ignored. He wrote Parker that he especially welcomed the *Apology* in view of news he had only just received from Throckmorton in Paris, and forwarded the ambassador's letter to Parker so that the latter could consider at first hand Throckmorton's analysis and advice concerning the mingling of "policy and religion together." The Archbishop and the Church were not, as some would have it, the servant of the state, but rather a partner of it. Religious affairs might be influenced by political developments, but not necessarily prejudiced by them, and indeed, might themselves affect political policy. So intimately were they related one to another that neither could be considered separately.

[20] Parker, *Correspondence*, p. 148.
[21] *Ibid.*, p. 161.

In contrast to the vast controversial works of Jewel's later years the *Apologia Ecclesiae Anglicanae* is a little book, all the more effective because of its brevity. The longest of the controversial works, *The Defence of the Apology,* is simply an extension of the earlier work, an exegesis, as it were, on a text which is the *Apology*. The *Apology* is clear as well as brief and, despite the speed with which it was composed, despite the searching analyses to which it was subjected by its Roman critics, Jewel was never forced to change his stand in either essentials or particulars.

The work is divided rather arbitrarily into six chapters and a conclusion. Jewel takes as his point of departure the accusation of heresy leveled by the Romanists against the Church of England. His simple answer is that such accusations are untrue, the product either of malice or of ignorance. The teachings of the Church of England are Catholic. His first duty therefore is to set forth as clearly as possible beyond all chance of misunderstanding the main tenets of the Anglican faith.

The second chapter is a confession of faith, a positive statement of Catholic doctrine. It is therefore the core of the *Apology*. In it Jewel makes no effort to argue points, although he cites authorities from time to time by way of explanation. His technique is here strongly reminiscent of Melanchthon's stated purpose and technique in the Augsburg Confession, that is, to present, to demonstrate rather than to argue or attack. In making his case in the affirmative Jewel reverted from his own method in the challenge sermon to the method of the Westminster conference. While all the points of importance in the challenge sermon are appended, as it were, to their relevant affirmations to give further clarity to the affirmation and at the same time to make abundantly clear the distinction between the Catholic doctrines of the English Church and their Roman "perversions," the positive character of the confession is dominant. Jewel has stated the faith of his Church, saying in effect, if this be heresy make the most of it.

The remaining chapters constitute an extension of points of the confession and a development of Jewel's views concerning the fundamental issue of heresy versus Catholicity, together with a spirited defense of the major continental Churches and a frontal attack upon the claims of the Church of Rome. The *Apology* might well have been concluded with the fifth chapter. Instead, there is a sixth, somewhat longer than the preceding ones, devoted wholly to the current problem of conciliar authority, a vigorous defense of the unilateral action of the English in effecting their own reformation and their refusal to participate in or admit the authority of the Council of Trent. The topical nature of the chapter and its position in an otherwise tightly organic work lends credence to the view that it was inserted between the peroration of the fifth chapter and the brief recapitulation with which the *Apology* concludes, after Jewel's conferences with the Queen and her advisers in May 1561.

Although Throckmorton's correspondence with Cecil provides invaluable evidence concerning the *Apology,* the letters must be read with care. Considered without reference to the actual sequence of events they can be most misleading. In December 1561 Throckmorton wrote Cecil relaying the suggestion that a defense should be made of the English ceremonies and doctrines on the basis of the authority of the primitive Church. His adviser had pointed out that the English order was more highly regarded among "the adversaries than the novelties of Geneva." He had suggested furthermore that an apology be made for the English Church based upon its similarity to the early Church.[22] The adviser was a certain Baldwin, or Balduine, a doctor of civil laws and the representative of the King of Navarre at the Council of Trent.[23] Early in January Throckmorton again referred to the subject, writing the Queen that Baldwin "has written something in the form of an apology of the said order of religion in England." If the Queen were agreeable, Baldwin would "proceed in the whole as he had done in parts; or otherwise the same may serve (if it does not please her to employ him) as a pattern for some learned man in England to make a like apology for her formula which is thought necessary." [24]

On the evidence of these letters Dixon concluded that "it seems not unlikely that Jewel's work was suggested by the desire of foreign

[22] *Calendar of State Papers Foreign,* 1561–1562, p. 462. *Cf.* Dixon, *History,* V, 292.
[23] *Zurich Letters,* I, 118, n. 1.
[24] *Calendar of State Papers Foreign,* 1561–1562, p. 481.

theologians."[25] At the time of the "suggestion," however, the *Apology* was already off the press. The more likely explanation of the apparent coincidence is that Throckmorton, having heard nothing further from Cecil concerning a defense of the Church after the latter's casual mention of such a project in May 1561, forwarded the Baldwin proposal in the hope that should Cecil's original plans have bogged down, the new proposal would revive them or possibly provide an alternative. Shortly afterwards he received the most convincing of reassurances in the form of several copies of the Latin *Apology* itself. He wrote Cecil that he was greatly pleased with the work and only wished that Jewel had "as well answered the Calvinists and others who were grieved with retaining too many ceremonies in the Church of England."[26] Throckmorton, from the perspective of the Paris embassy, perhaps understood better than many in England the precarious and delicate middle path which the government was attempting to follow.

In a commendatory letter which prefaced Lady Bacon's English translation of the *Apology*, Parker referred to the careful examination of the translation by himself and "the chief author of the Latin work,"[27] a statement which at first sight suggests the collective authorship of the work. There is no further support for such a conclusion, however, and the statement itself can be otherwise interpreted. The *Apology* had received his careful attention before it was published. It may well have been corrected or amended during the summer of 1561. But such amendments or changes do not affect the question of authorship any more than the custom observed by scholars of submitting their manuscripts to fellow scholars before publication affects the question of authorship today. Parker's statement reflects rather his desire to give the *Apology* and the particular translation as much authority as was possible short of action by convocation. Such a conclusion is confirmed by the statement made some years later by Bishop Parkhurst. The author of the *Apology*, he wrote Wolfius, the translator of the German edi-

---

[25] Dixon, *History*, V, 319.
[26] *Calendar of State Papers Foreign*, 1561–1562, p. 504.
[27] Jewel, *Works*, III, 52.

tion, "was Jewel alone, although he published it in the name of us all."[28]

Some months before the appearance of Lady Bacon's translation, Parker and Bishop Grindal had effectively demonstrated their approval of the *Apology*. In preparation for the convocation of 1563, Grindal "drew up or at least annotated a paper" suggesting that articles of doctrine should be drawn out of the *Apology* by royal authority. Parker went even further and proposed that the *Apology* be appended to the Articles of Religion. If such a step was not taken he was prepared to accept Grindal's suggestion.[29] While neither suggestion was carried out by convocation, the proposals, coming as they did from the primate and the Bishop of London, brought the *Apology* to the attention of the leaders of the clergy and guaranteed its careful consideration as no mere archiepiscopal letter could ever have done. "And of what esteem and reputation it was in the church of England in these times," Strype wrote of the *Apology,* "appears by a state-book set forth the year after; 'I refer you to the Apology, which our church hath placed openly before the eyes of the whole Christian world, as the common and certain pledge of our religion.' "[30]

Not the least of the virtues of the *Apology* was that while it provided a defense of the English Church eminently satisfactory to the Anglican leaders, both lay and clerical, it could be enthusiastically received at the same time by the more moderate of the continental Protestants. Peter Martyr expressed his warm approval of his former student's work, a copy of which he had received from Bishop Grindal. He wrote that not only was he pleased with the *Apology,* as he was with all that Jewel wrote, but that Bullinger and the other leaders in Zurich consider it "so wise, admirable, and eloquent, that they can make no end of commending it, and think that nothing in these days hath been set forth more perfectly."[31] Then in a charming line, at its best in the formal Latin of the original, "I

[28] G. C. Gorham, *Gleanings of a Few Scattered Ears during the Period of the Reformation in England* (London, 1857), p. 460.

[29] Strype, *Annals,* I, i, 474; Dixon, *History,* V, 387, 397, n.

[30] Strype, *Annals,* I, i, 425–426, from Walter Haddon's *Epistle to Osorius.*

[31] *Zurich Letters,* I, 339.

exceedingly congratulate your talents upon this excellent fruit, the church upon this edifying of it, and England upon this honour: and beseech you to proceed in the same way you have entered."[32] To Martyr at least, if not to Jewel himself, it was clear that there would be much more to write, as events proved only too well. Martyr concluded his commendation with the declaration that "while you are alive, the truth of the gospel will not be attacked by its enemies with impunity. And I rejoice most exceedingly, that I have seen the day in which you are made the parent of so noble and elegant an offspring. May God our heavenly Father grant of his goodness, that you may often be honoured with the like fruit![33]

In their correspondence concerning the *Apology* neither Martyr nor Jewel referred to any debt which the work might owe to Martyr's teaching. The *Apology* was, in the last analysis, altogether too much the *Apologia Ecclesiae Anglicanae* to have been very much Martyr's. His influence was no longer a dominant factor in the thinking of the mature and English author of the *Apology*.

[32] Jewel, *Works*, III, 3: "Hanc ingenio tuo felicitatem, hanc aedificationem ecclesiae, hoc Angliae decus vehementer gratulor, teque obtestor, ut quam ingressus es viam pergas tuis vestigiis premere."

[33] *Zurich Letters*, I, 340.

Chapter IV

The Bishop of Salisbury

During the course of the controversy with Dr. Cole, Jewel had taken steps toward the ordering of his affairs in his cathedral city. He was fortunate in his connections there. Henry Parry, whom he had known as one of the leaders of the opposition to John Knox in Frankfort, had been chancellor of Salisbury during Edward's reign. When Jewel made his general visitation in 1559 Parry was his chief colleague on the commission and shortly afterwards was reinstated in his old post as chancellor. At the time of the visitation Jewel himself, as bishop-designate, took advantage of the visitation to become thoroughly conversant with the problems of the diocese. In Salisbury he became acquainted with a citizen of the town, one Edward Nicolas, and chose him as his agent against the day when the business of the diocese would become his own responsibility.[1]

While still in London, indeed, before his consecration, Jewel found himself subject to the pressure of patronage seekers. He refused to make any promises or commitments, however, until his affairs were in better order and he could gain a more detailed knowledge of the needs of the diocese and the quality of the individuals suing for office. The inexperienced scholar who had declared himself in November "scarcely able to manage his own affairs," [2] could write Nicolas in February that he well knew that the most part of these men "wolde serve themselves sooner than me." In the

[1] Edward Nicolas was the grandfather of Sir Edward Nicholas, secretary of state to Charles I. Six letters of Jewel to the earlier Nicolas are included at the beginning of Sir Edward's papers (British Museum, Add. MSS, Egerton 2533, fol. 1) each identified in Sir Edward's handwriting, "Bp. Jewel to my grandfather."
[2] Jewel, *Works*, IV, 1219.

preliminary planning of his new duties Jewel leaned heavily on Archbishop Parker "from whom I may obtain any reasonable things that I can demand.[3] Jewel's casual reference suggests a closeness and personal helpfulness on the part of Parker toward his inexperienced suffragans impressive indeed in view of the Archbishop's own overwhelming new responsibilities.

Until the restoration of his temporalities in April, Jewel could do little more than plan. Just how he and his friends subsisted during the long period after their return to England and before they could count on a regular income from their new preferments, has always been somewhat puzzling. Presumably they lived, as they had during the exile, on the bounty of their lay friends. But it is clear from Jewel's correspondence with Nicolas that he had gone heavily in debt—probably on the basis of his expectations. One of the first steps he took after the restoration of his temporalities was the transference of the collection of rents to Nicolas and the arrangement for Nicolas to pay his debts. The Nicolas correspondence, filled with details of business and ecclesiastical patronage, gives the lie to Jewel's own disclaimers of practicality. It is true that his experience in practical affairs before 1559 had been slight, but he had a hard core of common sense worthy of a Devon farmer and the ability to learn quickly and act effectively in areas far removed from the study.

Late in May 1560 Jewel was at last able to leave London for Salisbury. With the exception of brief visits to the capital he was to spend the remainder of his life in his diocese, devoting his time and energy to the vigorous administration of the see and to his literary labors, the writing of the *Apologia Ecclesiae Anglicanae* and his controversial works—*The Reply to Harding,* the final sequel to his challenge sermons, and the vast *Defence of the Apology.* Unlike Edmund Grindal, who was burdened with the provincial duties associated with the London bishopric and heavy diocesan labors under the immediate eye of the court; and unlike Bishops Cox of Ely and Horne of Winchester, who served with the Archbishop and Grindal for most of the period on the High Commission, Jewel could be thankful that he had no responsibility for the day-to-day administra-

[3] Jewel to Edward Nicolas, 23 February, 1560.

tive problems of the establishment as a whole. After a year of London and the complicated politics of the court his diocese was a welcome haven from which he departed only upon summons from Lambeth or the Queen.

One of Jewel's first tasks after his arrival in Salisbury was a review of the properties of the see. Writing to Zurich some weeks later he declared that everything was in wretched condition, his houses "decayed and lands all leased out."[4] He attributed the state of affairs to the rapacity of his Marian predecessor, Capon. While it is true that toward the end of Mary's reign some of her bishops, including Bourne of the neighboring diocese of Bath and Wells,[5] had done a thorough job of tying up the leases under their jurisdiction with the hope that the property would thus be preserved until another turn of the wheel brought them back to power, the see of Salisbury had actually suffered its greatest impoverishment during Capon's Edwardian and reformist days rather than during his later career under Mary. He had died in 1557 in his eighties.[6] The decay of physical properties which so distressed Jewel was more probably the result of the long vacancy of three years and the milking of the see during that time by both the Marian and Elizabethan governments.

Whatever had happened to Salisbury during the preceding years, it remained a rich see at the time of Elizabeth's accession. Cecil estimated its worth at a thousand pounds a year.[7] Although Jewel might not be able "to maintain the port his predecessors did"[8] he was never in want. Jewel himself did not object to the reduction in episcopal income for which the new government was responsible. On the contrary, he expressed his approval that the wealth of the bishops being "diminished and reduced to a reasonable amount,"

[4] John Harington, *Nugae Antiquae; being a miscellaneous collection of original papers*, etc., 2 vols. (London, 1769), I, 101.

[5] Phyllis M. Hembry, in her unpublished University of London thesis on Gilbert Berkeley, Jewel's friend and diocesan neighbor, has thoroughly documented Strype's harsh criticism of the policies of the Marian bishops (*Annals*, I, i, 232) in the specific instance of the diocese of Bath and Wells.

[6] L. B. Smith, *Tudor Prelates and Politics* (Princeton, 1953), p. 283.

[7] Strype, *Annals*, I, i, 227.

[8] Harington, *Nugae Antiquae*, I, 101.

they are "relieved from that royal pomp and courtly bustle," and thus "may with greater ease and diligence employ their leisure in attending to the flock of Christ." [9] Not that Jewel looked forward to a life of dour asceticism. Though he might disapprove of the royal pomp and courtly bustle associated with the great statesman prelates of an age gone by, he still held a thoroughly conventional view of the office. As he signed his own name, "John Sarum," as he addressed Parker as his "most revered father in God my very good lord, my lord archbishop of Canterbury's grace," so he accepted episcopal office as the great majority of contemporary Englishmen knew it. The office of bishop was an exalted position of great responsibility and its occupant must live accordingly. As a practical matter this meant a palatial mansion with a large staff of servants and retainers. For Jewel it could not have been an easy task. Unlike most appointees to high ecclesiastical office in the century, he had had no association whatever with episcopal establishments. Nor had he ever served as a chaplain in a noble or royal household. The Devonshire farm, the Oxford college, the simple life at Zurich provided little precedent.

The old episcopal palace at Salisbury is a huge pile, so extensive in fact that the bishops today, finding it too costly to keep as a residence, have converted it into a school and established their residence in one of the canons' houses. In 1563 Jewel's young friend from Zurich, Herman Folkerzheimer, wrote to Simler that the palace was so spacious and magnificent

that even sovereigns may, and are wont to be suitably entertained there, whenever they come into these parts. Next, there is a most extensive garden, kept up with especial care, so that in the levelling, laying out, and variety, nothing seems to have been overlooked. A most limpid stream runs through the midst of it, which, though agreeable in itself, is rendered much more pleasant and delightful by the swans swimming upon it. . . . [10]

Jewel's household was large. In addition to the many servants necessary to the maintenance of the palace and its grounds his

[9] Jewel to Josiah Simler, November 2, 1559 (*Works*, IV, 1221).
[10] *Zurich Letters*, II, 86.

family included a staff of clerics who assisted him in his diocesan
and scholarly work and several young gentlemen evidently attached
to the household in the manner of squires, as was customary in the
great houses of the day. The latter provided congenial company for
young Folkerzheimer. They shared his knowledge of the French
language and so could converse at ease. Together the young men
explored Salisbury and the surrounding countryside. On one occasion the Bishop himself took part in a lengthy outing to Old Sarum
and Stonehenge. Folkerzheimer was no less impressed than the
modern tourist by the strange monuments on Salisbury plain, and
the Bishop, like a modern guide, indulged in some interesting con-
jectures concerning the stones. He thought that they were probably
the work of the Romans who had built them symbolically in the
form of yokes!

On hunting expeditions the Bishop stayed at home. Folkerzheimer
noted that he took no pleasure in the sport, characterizing it, in fact,
as no sport at all. "What pleasure, says he, I pray you, can possibly
be derived from pursuing with fierce dogs a timid animal, that
attacks no one, and that is put to flight even by a noise?" Folkerzheimer had to admit that in this he disagreed with his host but
admitted that "were I frequently to repeat the same thing, I think
it would not afford me so much amusement. But although the
bishop never goes out a hunting, and I very seldom, the dogs are
by no means idle. The young men are required to provide a supply
of venison, that the table may always give proof of the activity of
the dogs and the labours of the huntsmen." [11]

According to Folkerzheimer Jewel set a very good table—and
an impressive one. He particularly noted the abundance and mag-
nificence of the silver plate. The young Frieslander, in fact, seems
to have been torn between a desire to report the great good fortune
of his erstwhile fellow exile and the fear lest he portray Jewel's new
life at Salisbury in such glowing terms that his Swiss friends would
feel Jewel had betrayed his reformist principles. Folkerzheimer
explained most carefully that luxury seemed to afford no great
pleasure to the Bishop, who regarded it all rather as a means to

[11] *Ibid.*

provide for the pleasure of others. His richest possession was his library, a form of riches to which the Zurichers would certainly not take exception. Jewel's library was in fact Folkerzheimer's primary justification for the extension of his stay in Salisbury, since it was especially rich in the field of his immediate interest, history.

The effort of Folkerzheimer to do justice to life at Salisbury without implying the scale of living of an earlier day suggests that the more puritan-minded among the reformers would hardly have approved of Jewel's establishment. A Martin Marprelate would surely have found in it considerable material for vigorous satire. Jewel consciously maintained a state in keeping with the dignity of the office and its traditions, to most Elizabethans altogether proper and fitting in the Lord Bishop of Salisbury.

So pleasant did Folkerzheimer find his stay with the Bishop that he requested a longer leave of absence and remained in Salisbury until the spring when he accompanied Jewel to London for the meeting of Parliament. From London he wrote his friends in Zurich that Edwin Sandys, the Bishop of Worcester, had entered into a friendly rivalry with Jewel as his patron and had even presented him with a beautiful and valuable horse. It is a pleasant picture, the former exiles, now bishops, endeavoring to repay, at least in part, the debt they owed their continental friends. Jewel regularly sent sums of money abroad and indeed made himself responsible for a pension for Peter Martyr's companion, Julius Santerentianus.[12]

Jewel's liberality was not confined to foreign friends and students. He took under his protection promising young Englishmen who were preparing for the ministry, the most notable of whom was Richard Hooker. Isaac Walton tells the story of the introduction of the young scholar to his future patron. John Hooker of Exeter, Richard's uncle, had made Jewel's acquaintance during the latter's visitation of the southern counties in 1559. Several years later, concerned over the poverty of Richard's family and the probability that they would not be able to continue his education, he arranged for Richard and his schoolmaster to be presented to the Bishop in Salisbury. According to Walton, Jewel was so impressed by the

[12] *Ibid.*, II, 55, n. 3; Jewel, *Works*, IV, 1256, 1269.

"boy's learning, and gravity, and behaviour" that he gave the school-master a reward and "took order for an annual pension for the boy's parents." [13] In 1567 Jewel procured an appointment for Richard to Corpus Christi, his own Oxford college. For the remainder of his life he continued his active patronage and interest in the young scholar. Indeed, his patronage extended beyond his own death in 1571. He had introduced Hooker to Bishop Sandys and had recommended him so highly as a promising scholar that Sandys, shortly after Jewel's death, chose Corpus for his son's education rather than his own Cambridge college, St. John's. His sole purpose, according to Walton, was that the boy might study under Hooker. It was in this fashion that young Edwin Sandys, together with George Cranmer, became Hooker's pupils and lifelong friends. The Sandys family and William Cole, the President of Corpus, to whom Jewel had also recommended Hooker, saw to it that the young scholar was not in want. Hooker never ceased to be grateful to the memory of his first patron, characterizing him in the *Laws* as the "worthiest divine that Christendom hath bred for the space of some hundreds of years." [14]

Although the cathedral of Salisbury was by definition the seat of the bishop of Salisbury and although the bishop's palace was the most impressive structure in the close after the cathedral itself, the bishop's authority and his duties, in so far as they had to do with cathedral and close, were relatively light. Theoretically the center of the local picture, he existed, as it were, by grace of the dean and chapter whose jealousy of episcopal power and determination to preserve their own rights was proverbial. The duties of the bishop were primarily diocesan rather than cathedral. Yet he too had his rights, in both close and cathedral. And Jewel had no intention of foregoing those rights, especially when they were accompanied by definite responsibilities. The great church, after all, was the center of the religious life of the diocese, or should be. And thus the broad responsibilities of the bishop for his diocese demanded that he exercise a modicum of control over his cathedral church. It is greatly

[13] Richard Hooker, *Works,* 7th ed., 3 vols. (Oxford, 1888), I, 10.
[14] *Ibid.,* I, 314.

to Jewel's credit that he was able to take part in cathedral affairs without provoking a conflict with the dean and chapter.

Shortly after he arrived in Salisbury as bishop he took the unusual step of "recognizing" an old statute of 1490 concerning cope money.[15] This statute provided that the bishop should give twenty pounds or a cope of the same value to be employed in the church. Similarly, the dean, the other officers and the archdeacons, certain prebends and canons of the cathedral, were to give in varying amounts. The money, it was specified, was not to be used for any other purpose than the purchase of copes. Jewel's was the first ratification of the statute since its original inception and the only one until it was again ratified by Seth Ward in 1672. The use of the cathedral church thus provided an example for the diocese, all the more effective in that many of the officers affected by the statute had administrative responsibilities beyond the cathedral, in the diocese as a whole.

Soon afterward Jewel did become involved in the old rivalry between bishop and chapter. A commission was issued to him on September 8, 1560, to visit the cathedral church and city and diocese of Salisbury and of Bristol, *jure metropolitico*.[16] The chapter at Salisbury objected strongly to that portion of the commission giving the bishop visitorial authority over the cathedral, as an infringement of its rights. The protest was not directed against Jewel personally but represented rather the concern of the chapter to protect the "rites, liberties, privileges, and immunities of the said church."[17] Therefore, though the Bishop of Salisbury was acting in the name of the metropolitan, another commission was issued to John Cottrel to visit the cathedral chapter of Salisbury. In explaining Cottrel's commission as an example of the jealousy of chapters for their rights, Strype failed to note, however, that the injunctions finally issued to the dean and chapter were issued by Jewel as metropolitical

[15] Christopher Wordsworth, *Statutes and Customs of the Cathedral Church . . . of Salisbury* (London, 1915), p. 355.
[16] *Diocesis Cantuariensis: Registrum Matthei Parker, 1559–75* (Oxford, 1907–1935), p. 675.
[17] John Strype, *The Life and Acts of Matthew Parker,* etc., 3 vols. (Oxford, 1821), I, 152.

visitor and not by Cottrel.[18] Since Jewel could hardly have over-powered his cathedral chapter in the face of an archiepiscopal commission, we can only assume that the dean and chapter permitted the Bishop to visit, the commission to Cottrel being considered sufficient legal precedent to protect their privileges for the future.

The record of relations between bishop and chapter, other than the merely routine, is scant, evidence in itself, perhaps, of amiable relations. Jewel did insist that the prebends of the cathedral live up to their responsibilities, especially in the matter of preaching, and to this effect renewed the order that the table of their preaching terms be placed in the choir.[19] But he did not rest with the mere renewal of an order. Leadenhall, a house in the cathedral close, was procured in 1560 for a term of seven years as an abode which the bishop might dispose of in order to encourage some of the nonresident prebendaries to live in Salisbury, especially during those periods when their residence was not required.[20]

A year and a half later, in April 1562, Jewel made his third visitation of the diocese. From a personal point of view the visitation is more significant than the earlier ones. That of 1559 was a general visitation by royal commission; that of 1560 a visitation rather as representative of the metropolitan than as bishop in his own diocese. The articles and injunctions of the two earlier visitations are therefore very similar to, if not identical with, those of other visitations undertaken at the same time by other commissioners with similar authority. The visitation of 1562 rested on no other authority than that of the bishop and the consequent articles and injunctions therefore represent his policies alone.

Visitation of the cathedral and chapter of Salisbury by the bishop was limited by ancient statute to five days.[21] Jewel's visitation in 1562 extended well beyond the period, evidence not only of his own thoroughness, but more important, of the degree to which he had

[18] Frere and Kennedy, *Visitation Articles,* I, 156, n. 1.

[19] Wordsworth, *Statutes,* 514–515.

[20] Christopher Wordsworth, "Elias de Durham's Leadenhall in Salisbury Close," *Wiltshire Archaeological and Natural History Magazine* 39 (1917) 434.

[21] Frere and Kennedy, *Visitation Articles,* III, 122.

won the confidence of the chapter during his residence in Salisbury, since the extension of the visitation period could be made only with the consent of the chapter. The set of statutes issued by Jewel on May 18 and accepted by the chapter eight days later represent a broad miscellany of problems, many of them on the petty side. But through them runs a constant theme, the basic concern of the Bishop for the proper functioning of his cathedral as the first church of the community and the diocese. It was not to become a private chapel for a group of canons, as so many cathedrals had tended to become in past years, nor merely an impressive ecclesiastical monument as some were to become in the years ahead. The statutes recur, for instance, to the problem of preaching by the prebends. The requirements for residence, especially for the principal officers, were strengthened, and in line with Jewel's earlier procurement of a house in the close for nonresident prebends, steps were taken to improve the living conditions of the resident members of the chapter, special attention being given to the repair of the houses in the close.

Several articles and statutes have to do with the restoration of the fabric of the cathedral itself. The great building had apparently fallen into a sad state of disrepair, for the chapter agreed that two thousand pounds would hardly be enough to cover the cost of the most pressing repairs. Jewel, or the chapter, had already taken steps toward meeting the problem and funds had been in process of collection toward the improvement of the cathedral since 1560. The state of the windows was a matter of special concern and during the next few years they were newly glazed.[22] Not only is Jewel to be credited with an active and effective interest in the care of the cathedral but, in the light of the evidence available, he is to be absolved from the charges of Puritan destructiveness which have been leveled so indiscriminately at the Elizabethan divines. The

[22] Captain Symonds, who visited the cathedral when the Cavaliers were in Salisbury in 1643, noted that "the windows in the body of the church are new glased at the bottome, north side. Written there in most of the Windowes: 'Joh's Jewell Ep'i. 1569.' " Richard Symonds, *Diary of the Marches of the Royal Army during the Great Civil War*, etc. (London, 1859), p. 140; Wordsworth, *Statutes*, p. 391, n.

visitation articles indicate that destruction at Salisbury antedated his episcopate.[23] A measure of the success of Jewel's visitation and the friendly reception which his statutes received was the chapter's request made shortly afterwards that he furnish additional statutes before the following Michaelmas.[24]

During his brief episcopate, and despite his tremendous literary labors, Jewel made a total of three visitations and was undertaking his fourth at the time of his death. Moreover, he had already visited the diocese as commissioner before he became a bishop. In comparison with the records of the other bishops, only Parker was more vigorous and painstaking in his work. Frere observes that such a record is a fair index to the nature and quality of a particular episcopal administration.[25] Cox, for instance, who was Bishop of Ely for twenty-one years, apparently made only one visitation of his compact little diocese in all that time. It is not an impressive record, even when allowance is made for the years Cox spent on the High Commission. Frere admits that the record of visitations is incomplete but suggests it is hardly by chance that articles and injunctions have survived in those particular dioceses whose bishops by common repute were the most conscientious administrators.

Jewel was a prolific letter writer. His letters to Zurich, in contrast to the other English letters in the vast Zurich collection,[26] are veritable newsletters reporting at length and in detail the state of

[23] E. F. Bosanquet, "The Destruction of Monuments at Salisbury Cathedral," *Wiltshire Archaeological and Natural History Magazine* 40 (1918) 147, implies that Jewel, in making inquiry for monuments of idolatry and superstition, destroyed the glass. J. M. J. Fletcher, in "Note on the Stained Glass in Salisbury Cathedral" in the same journal (45 [1930] 241) questions this. The inquiry of 1559, according to the royal injunctions (Frere and Kennedy, *Visitation Articles,* III, 16 ff.), is expressly concerned with repair.

[24] Wordsworth, *Statutes,* p. 397.

[25] Frere and Kennedy, *Visitation Articles,* I, 168.

[26] The four volumes of Zurich letters printed by the Parker Society (two as *Original Letters* and two as *The Zurich Letters*) represent only a small portion of the total Zurich collection. The Simler Collection at Zurich is in large folios, one to a six-month period, and includes correspondence between Zurich and Protestant leaders throughout Europe. It dwarfs in size many collections of state papers. The Parker Society editors printed only those letters written to or from the English or from correspondents visiting in England.

affairs in England—as if he felt it his personal responsibility to keep his Zurich friends informed of English developments, political as well as ecclesiastical. It was no mean undertaking in view of his isolation most of the time in Salisbury and involved a large supplementary correspondence within England. That his letters are to such a degree newsletters, however, is in a sense a drawback. As newsletters they are naturally less personal than one would wish and despite their number and length reveal his own views and reactions only incidentally.

As a result of their wide coverage, Jewel's letters have provided a mine of information for the historians of the reign. They are in fact a major source for the story of Anglo-Scottish relations during these early years. Jewel's surprising understanding of affairs in Scotland was the result of an old friendship. Thomas Randolph, the Edwardian principal of Broadgates Hall, who had given him shelter when he was cast adrift by Corpus in the early years of Mary's reign, had become a useful and trusted confidential representative of Elizabeth's government and was now very active in Scotland. From him Jewel received detailed information concerning the progress of events there and in turn relayed the story to Zurich.[27] Thus the Zurich leaders were kept abreast of the tangled events in the north through Salisbury rather than through London.

Of the thirty-six letters of Jewel in the Zurich collection, nineteen are to Peter Martyr. From references in other letters it is clear that Jewel intended the Martyr letters for the group of friends in Zurich as a whole. Thus the absence of more informative personal data. Not that the Martyr letters are cold and impersonal. Jewel's love and veneration for the older man is apparent at all times. His friends in Zurich, sharing his feeling and aware that he regarded Martyr as his adopted father, would have expected no less. But the letters lack the quality we would expect had they been altogether private. The few letters to Josiah Simler, for instance, with hardly a shred of news to their credit, are written on a personal note altogether delightful and far more revealing of their author, his humor, and his qualities as a charming friend.

[27] Of Jewel's thirty-six letters in the *Zurich Letters,* eighteen refer to Scottish affairs.

One theme, a puzzling theme, runs through the letters to Martyr, that of the prospect of Martyr's return to England. While the uncertainty of affairs in England was far greater than we with our wisdom of hindsight can possibly realize, it is another matter to find Jewel in 1560, after the settlement of the controversy over the crucifix and in view of his own growing prominence, as dubious as he had been in the early months of 1559 of the advisability of Martyr's return. One suspects that with the increase of Jewel's comprehension of the problems facing the Establishment and his understanding of the infinitely delicate and complicated nature of the pressures at work, he also had come to question the wisdom of having a major continental reformer present in England. It was one thing to advise with Martyr and his colleagues at a distance and subject to the vagaries of the sixteenth-century post. It would have been quite otherwise to have him in England, the natural focus for the hopes of the less compromising among the former exiles. Though the most moderate and conciliating of the major continental reformers, Martyr stood many degrees to the left of the Queen, and even of Archbishop Parker, on many questions. Nor was there any reason why a foreigner, however well acquainted with the English, should understand the necessity for compromise, much less share the unique ability of the English leaders, lay and clerical alike, in making compromise effective. With every year of the reign Jewel was drawn closer to the point of view of the Archbishop. Such a change in no way affected his feeling for Peter Martyr. But there was far less likelihood of embarrassment for either party were Martyr to remain in Zurich.[28]

As with many letter writers, Jewel wrote most frequently in the months which followed immediately upon separation from his correspondent. With the passage of time the gaps between letters

[28] *Cf.* McLelland, *Visible Words,* pp. 55–58. McLelland accepts the expressions of hope for Martyr's return to England at face value and interprets Martyr's own letter of July 1561 as a refusal of a formal invitation. A more likely explanation of the letter is that it was an answer to an inquiry of the possibility of his coming, not an invitation. We should also note that the addressee of Martyr's letter was the Earl of Bedford, one of the Puritan extremists on Elizabeth's Council, rather than the Archbishop or Bishop Jewel.

grew longer. Occasional visits of Zurichers to England and their expected return to Switzerland at times provided an excuse for not writing. Jewel's own health at other times confined him to those tasks which were unavoidable. But above all there was a natural and inevitable drifting apart in interests and common problems. During Herman Folkerzheimer's visit to Jewel came the news of Martyr's death.[29] It was as if *finis* had been written to a chapter which for some time had been ready to close.

Martyr's death left vacant a place that for Jewel at least was never filled. Henceforth it was to Heinrich Bullinger that Jewel wrote and henceforth it was to Bullinger that most of the former exiles looked for advice and approbation. But Jewel's letters to Bullinger have quite a different tone from those to Martyr. While he always showed profound respect for Bullinger, his letters suggest a more formal relation. Although Bullinger was five years younger than Martyr, his position as Zwingli's successor at Zurich, his extremely forceful nature in contrast to the milder Martyr, naturally created a gulf between him and the younger Jewel. Quite possibly Jewel did not regret this. In the absence of the very deep regard and the boundless debt he had owed Martyr he was freer to pursue the course he had determined upon, that of the English Church.

On January 12, 1563, Jewel took his seat in the House of Lords. The only record of his activities in this, the second Parliament of Elizabeth, is the presence of his name on the list of triers of petitions.[30] The list includes his fellow bishops, Parker, Grindal, and Pilkington, together wtih certain lay lords. In the convocation of the same year Jewel signed the Articles of Religion along with the other bishops.[31] It was at this time that serious consideration was given to the possible addition of his *Apology* to the Articles. His most important duty was the examination of the "book called the catechism," as a member of a committee which included Bishops Bentham, Alley, and Davies.[32] This was the catechism of Alexander

[29] *Zurich Letters,* II, 94, Folkerzheimer to Simler, March 15, 1563.

[30] Simonds D'Ewes, *The journals of all the Parliaments during the reign of Queen Elizabeth* (London, 1682), p. 61.

[31] Strype, *Annals,* I, i, 487.

[32] Ralph Churton, *Life of Alexander Nowell* (Oxford, 1809), p. 95.

Nowell which held a place of great importance in the Church "until the sacramental part was added to the prayer book," [33] and contributed materially toward the promotion of uniformity in the early years of the Establishment.

Jewel's activities in Parliament were not confined to ecclesiastical duties. Folkerzheimer wrote in March that he was deriving great advantage from his stay in London: "seeing our house is frequented by men of the first rank, I am daily hearing their grave conversation, . . . about fortifications, tolls, safe conduct, the importation or exportation of merchandise, and other things of the like kind." [34]

For the year 1564 there are no letters of Jewel's in the Zurich collection. He wrote Bullinger the following March that he had omitted writing since "all intercourse was everywhere prevented by the plague and pestilence." [35] He spent the year quietly in Salisbury attending to his diocesan duties. In November he wrote the Privy Council a report on the justices of the peace for Berkshire and Wiltshire concerning "their sundry inclinations towards the furtherance of God's truth." [36] The Elizabethan structure of local government was in process of review. The bishops who had of necessity to bear the brunt of any Romanist proclivities on the part of the local gentry, were able to provide in their reports a thoroughly trustworthy basis for the selection of loyal justices.

Jewel divided his list of possibilities into three groups: those who were "hinderers" of the gospel, those who were "no hinderers," and those who merited being called a "furtherer earnest." The Wiltshire list included no hinderers but the Berkshire list contained one whom he described "as it is supposed no hinderer, . . . one as it is supposed a hinderer," and one who was "no furtherer," very fine distinctions indeed. Compared with the reports of the other bishops which Miss Bateson has printed, Jewel's was extremely encouraging. The diocese in fact seems to have been singularly free of trouble

---

[33] Dixon, *History,* V, 409–410.

[34] *Zurich Letters,* II, 94; I, 126, Jewel to Simler, March 7, 1563: "Our mutual friend Herman is with me."

[35] *Ibid.,* I, 138.

[36] Mary Bateson, *Collection of Original Letters,* etc. Camden Society Miscellany IX (London, 1893), 37–38.

makers, Romanist and Puritan alike. Jewel could be grateful when he observed the endless tribulations which his friend Sandys had to face at the hands of the Romanists at Worcester or the discomfort of his old tutor Parkhurst as he failed repeatedly to deal effectively with the Puritan extremists at Norwich. Salisbury provided an unusually congenial atmosphere for scholarly work. At the same time the very absence of extremists and the problems arising from their activities may have made Jewel less aware than some of his colleagues of the pressing problems faced by the Church, especially from the challenge of Puritanism. In any case, the problems which beset the Church from within must occupy a secondary place in his thoughts. His task during these years was to meet the challenge from abroad, the attack of the English Roman Catholic exiles against the Church and against him as its chief apologist.

Chapter V

The Harding Controversies

In 1564 Jewel finally received an answer worthy of his original challenge sermon, Harding's *Answer to Jewel's Challenge,* published in Louvain. For the next six years he was to be mainly occupied with the one man and his writings.

Thomas Harding was no stranger. A Devon man, several years older than Jewel, he had been a fellow of New College when Jewel was at Corpus. His reputation as a scholar had been of sufficient distinction to justify his appointment as Professor of Hebrew toward the end of Henry's reign. He later blamed his scholarly efforts in Hebrew studies for his lapse from strict Roman orthodoxy, having been led into the reformist camp by his reading of the German commentaries on the Old Testament.[1] As one of the more promising of the younger reformers, he became chaplain to Henry Grey, Marquis of Dorset, and in the first year of the new reign was selected to give the official address of welcome to Richard Cox as the new vice-chancellor of the university.[2] Jewel knew him during the reign of Edward as an admirer of Peter Martyr and as "a most active preacher of the gospel."[3] Toward the end of the reign Harding was singled out by the government to become warden of his college when that office should become void.[4] The death of Edward VI, however, brought to a close his career as a reformer.

With Mary's accession and the restoration of the Roman juris-

---

[1] Nicholas Sanders, *Report to Cardinal Moroni on the Change of Religion in 1558-9,* ed. J. H. Pollen. Catholic Record Society, Miscellany I (London, 1905), p. 41.

[2] Strype, *Memorials,* I, i, 597; II, ii, 270; Wood, *Athenae,* I, 124, 402.

[3] Jewel, *Works,* IV, 1268.

[4] Strype, *Memorials,* II, ii, 270-271.

diction Harding returned to the Roman Communion. In view of the letter Lady Jane Grey wrote her father's former chaplain upon his apostasy,[5] Harding's conversion must have taken place some time in 1553. He was rewarded with a prebend at Winchester and became Gardiner's chaplain. The next year he was made treasurer of Salisbury. It is possible that he was in line for further preferment, for in May 1558 he was appointed to preach in the diocese of Salisbury during the vacancy of the see, with the provision that his work should in no way interfere with the income from his prebend.[6]

The parallel thus far between his career and Jewel's is close indeed. Not only were they both from Devon but they had been at Oxford together and in close association with Peter Martyr. Later, Harding's most important preferment was in the see which Jewel eventually filled. In fact, Jewel claimed that Harding as a member of the cathedral chapter, had voted for his future opponent's election to the bishopric. This, Harding denied.[7]

At Elizabeth's accession Harding refused to change his faith again, declaring "I will lose my head first." [8] No such fate threatened him. Indeed, he was not even imprisoned, as one of his biographers would have it. The ecclesiastical commission merely ordered him to remain in the town of Monkton Farleigh in Wiltshire or within sixteen miles of the same, or in Tollewilme in Dorset or within twenty miles of that town. In the margin of the order signed by the commissioners there is the following comment: "Learned. In King Edward's time preached the truth honestly and now stiff in papistry and thinketh very much good of himself." [9]

Shortly afterward Harding fled to the Continent where he joined

---

[5] This letter was published by John Aylmer and later incorporated by Foxe in his *Book of Martyrs* (John Strype, *Historical Collections of the Life and Acts of . . . John Aylmer,* etc. [Oxford, 1821], p. 7).

[6] *Calendar of State Papers Domestic, 1547–80,* pp. 102, 103.

[7] Jewel, *Defence, Works,* III, 334 and n. 7.

[8] Sanders, *Report,* p. 41.

[9] Hughes, *The Reformation,* III, 422–423. Hughes gives 1561 as the date of the order. No earlier date is possible. The list of signatures of commissioners transcribed by Strype (*Annals,* I, i, 411) includes "William Chester." William Downham did not become Bishop of Chester until May 1561, over a year after Jewel's election to Salisbury.

the group of English Romanist exiles at Louvain. With Nicholas Sanders, also of New College, he became an active leader in the early efforts to reconcile the relapsed English to Rome. Under the authority of Cardinal Ghislieri, the future Pius V, Harding and Sanders provided the principal liaison with the papacy, responsible for the execution of orders from Rome concerning the English and their problems. In 1567 they proposed and seriously urged that an orthodox translation of the Bible be made,[10] a suggestion of particular interest in view of Jewel's frequent recurrence throughout his controversy with Harding to a vigorous condemnation of the Roman attitude in the past toward the vernacular. Action was not taken on the proposal until after Harding's death in 1572. Harding is likewise to be credited, together with William Allen, for the establishment of the English college at Douai.[11] Evidence of the importance and the success of the work of the exiles is the citation of Harding and Sanders in a broadside of 1567 in which they are accused as "trumpettes of treason" of undermining the allegiance due the Queen and of being subservient to the orders of a foreign power.[12] The curia itself apparently accepted the English estimate of the effectiveness of Harding's activities for he was seriously considered in 1570 for a cardinalate. But the curia decided against naming an English cardinal until there should be greater possibility of a return to England.[13]

Harding's *Answer to Jewel's Challenge* appeared in England in the late spring of 1564, shortly after its publication at Louvain. The first public notice taken of it was a sermon by Alexander Nowell, the Dean of St. Paul's, who discussed it at some length from the pulpit four Sundays after Easter.[14] Jewel evidently began work on his reply immediately, for it was completed by the beginning of

[10] A. O. Meyer, *England and the Catholic Church under Elizabeth and the Stuarts* (London, 1916), pp. 475–478.

[11] H. DeVocht, "Thomas Harding," *English Historical Review* 35 (1920) 237.

[12] Meyer, *England and the Catholic Church*, pp. 125–126.

[13] Actually the step was postponed until 1587 when Harding's associate, William Allen, was named Cardinal of England as part of the grand design which included the Armada.

[14] Strype, *Annals*, I, ii, 113; Churton, *Life of Nowell*, p. 105.

1565. On January 30th he wrote Leicester that he knew his answer to Harding was "greedily looked for, both of many others and also of your honour,"[15] evidence of the seriousness with which the English leaders regarded Harding's work and their anxiety that Jewel demonstrate the soundness of the position he had taken in his original challenge to Rome. Jewel wrote Leicester that he was not at all surprised at the appearance of Harding's *Answer*. From the day he delivered his first challenge sermon a major effort on the part of the Romanists was virtually inevitable. He was aware, he noted wryly, that many of his friends were a bit fearful that he would be unable to live up to his challenge, that "I was overseen, to lay out the matter in such a generality, and to give the adversary so great a scope." However, "touching the possibility hereof, I need not greatly to stand in fear, as having well and particularly considered the whole case before I first began to speak." He added that his original confidence had been greatly strengthened when he finally received Harding's *Answer* and had the opportunity to examine it carefully.

Jewel's *A replie vnto M. Hardinges answeare* (London, 1565), is a tremendous work. In the Parker Society edition it occupies 731 pages. Not all of it, by any means however, is Jewel's own. Jewel adopted the mode of controversy common in the century, that of printing his opponent's work along with his own. The *Reply* is divided naturally into sections by the points of the original challenge. Jewel's method was first to print the particular point of the challenge, then to take Harding's answer to that point, divide it into subsections, and print each subsection with his specific reply to it. The method, in short, has less in common with a formal debate than with a dialogue composed of an endless procession of short speeches. This effect is of course greatly accentuated when, in later editions, Harding's rebuttal and Jewel's final reply were added to the various subsections. Jewel left no stone unturned, taking up one after another the authorities cited by Harding and either denying the validity of the citation or refuting the interpretation placed upon it. In the process the work was further enlarged by a tre-

[15] John Whitgift, *Works*, 3 vols. (Cambridge, 1851–1853), III, 624.

mendous wealth of quotations cited as positive proof of the soundness of his own position, first in their original Latin or Greek and
then in his own English translation. Unlike the first edition of the
Apology, the *Reply* was from the beginning intended for the English reader. In effect, it is a series of articles, only slightly dependent
upon one another, repetitious, and indeed quite complete in themselves.[16] As such it has little appeal for the reader of today. However, from the point of view of the sixteenth century the form of
the *Reply* was an advantage rather than a liability. The sixteenth-
century reader, deeply involved in the various issues at debate,
could pursue at length a particular point on which he had reservations or questions, and skim lightly over or even omit those points
on which he had attained a fair degree of certainty.

Jewel had hardly completed his labors on the *Reply* when Harding published *A confutation of a book intituled An apologie of
The Church of England.* Jewel did not have to face the attacks
from Louvain singlehandedly. Others took up the cudgels in his
defense, including Dean Nowell, and they in turn were answered
from abroad. The controversies stemming from the challenge sermons and the *Apology* were many and continued for decades.
From the beginning, however, the center of the conflict was the
battle between Jewel and Harding. Jewel recognized from the first
the quality of his opponent and ignoring all others confined himself
solely to Harding.

The sudden appearance of the *Confutation* so soon after the completion of his labors on the *Reply* was naturally disheartening. Yet
Jewel should have expected it just as surely as he expected an answer to the challenge sermons.[17] On the other hand, until the
nature of the attack was known he could hardly prepare a defense
of the *Apology* as he had made ready beforehand his support of his

---

[16] Jewel was well aware of this. He regarded the sixth article, for instance, as
virtually a separate treatise, in this case on the much debated subject of ubiquitarianism
(Jewel to Bullinger, Mar. 1, 1565, *Works,* IV, 1264).

[17] As early as January 1564 Cecil was informed that "one Alphanus Episcopus,
alias Noare, . . . writes against the *Apology* and that very shortly by the authority
of the King of Spain" (*Calendar of State Papers Foreign, 1563,* p. 70). There is no
evidence that this project was carried out.

challenge. The *Defence of the Apology* was therefore much longer in the writing than the *Reply*. It was likewise a much longer work, in the Parker Society edition nearly 1000 pages as against the *Reply's* mere 700. As with the *Apology* itself Jewel had the support and interest of the Archbishop and Cecil in his undertaking. He wrote Cecil in September 1567 that the *Defence* being "well-near past the printing," he thought it time to consider the dedication. Parker and "some others my friends here," had recommended he dedicate it to Elizabeth, particularly since Harding had had the effrontery to dedicate his *Confutation* to her.[18] His purpose in writing to Cecil, he explained, was to find out if she approved his doing so. Jewel apparently received the royal approval and the *Defence* was published with an elaborate epistle dedicatory to the Queen.[19]

In the *Defence of the Apology* Jewel followed very much the same procedure he had adopted in the *Reply* except that the natural chapter headings provided by the challenge points were lacking. In his *Confutation* Harding had dealt with the *Apology* almost sentence by sentence. Jewel accepted Harding's arbitrary divisions, printing the passage from the *Apology* together with Harding's critique of it,[20] and then appending his own reply. When Harding answered the *Defence* with *A Detection of sundry foul errors uttered by M. Jewel* (Louvain, 1568), Jewel simply inserted the new material in the relevant sections, added further comments of his own and included both in a new edition of the *Defence* in 1570. The only surviving example of Jewel's work in process is his own copy of the 1567 edition of the *Defence* now in the Magdalen Col-

[18] Jewel, *Works*, IV, 1273.

[19] *Ibid.*, III, 115–118.

[20] Jewel did not print the *Confutation* in its entirety. It was a much longer work than the earlier *Answer* and more repetitious. The omissions have been carefully indicated by Ayre in his edition of the *Defence* in the Parker Society edition of Jewel's *Works*. A comparison of the *Confutation* in the Antwerp edition of 1565 with the citations from it in the *Defence* indicates that while some portions omitted by Jewel are vigorous and well argued they are no more forceful than those quoted. No doubt Jewel weakened Harding's argument by depriving him of the effect of a more impressive accumulation of evidence, but the sense of Harding's argument is not affected by the omissions.

lege library. The copy is liberally underlined and the margins filled with corrections and notations in his own hand. The latter were included along with his answers to Harding's *Detection* in the 1570 edition.

The *Reply* and the *Defence* are actually enlargements of the original works, the challenge sermon and the *Apology*. Both are to the smaller works as objects seen through a microscope, magnified many times. Of the two, the *Defence,* unhampered as it is by the conditions of the challenge, is the more comprehensive. It remains, as Dixon declared, "one of the most complete pieces of controversy in the world."[21] Few works have been subjected to such a complete exegesis by their author as has the *Apology,* an exegesis in Jewel's case made in the full glare of the harshest and most adverse criticism. As a result, the points considered are enlarged and developed to such an extent that any doubt that may exist concerning his original meaning is clarified beyond question in the final edition of the *Defence.* In the process, incidentally, Jewel availed himself of the opportunity to make revisions from time to time in the English translation of the *Apology* thus bringing it finally into complete accord with the meaning of the original Latin as he had intended it.

In a letter to Bullinger written shortly after the publication of the *Reply,* Jewel complained that the fire of the Romanists seemed to be directed at him alone. It is difficult to accept his complaint as more than conventional, since by writing the *Apology,* no less than by delivering the challenge sermons, Jewel had invited the attack. No one knew better than he how fundamentally his own arguments struck at the foundations of the Roman position. From the point of view of the English Romanists Jewel was the most dangerous antagonist the Roman Church had to face and the exiles at Louvain, unlike Henry Cole and his fellow disputants at Westminster, met the challenge squarely. Hence the importance and the vitality of the resultant controversy. The essential requirement for any vigorous and productive debate is the acceptance by the two sides of common authorities. In the controversies between Harding and

[21] Dixon, *History,* V, 320.

Jewel at least a partial meeting ground of authorities had been found and agreed upon.

To convey an impression of the techniques of the two controversialists short of a detailed review of their works is extremely difficult. While both Jewel and Harding were skillful—judged solely in terms of their controversial technique—Jewel was the more skillful of the two. One example may serve to illustrate the point. Since his argument that the Church of England rather than the Church of Rome had remained faithful to tradition constituted the very heart of the controversy, Jewel took every opportunity to demonstrate that Rome had denied tradition in the person of the fathers of the Church. With consummate skill he succeeded time and again in placing his opponent in the position of having directly contravened patristic authority. In the heat of controversy Harding was not as level-headed as Jewel. His indiscriminate attacks resulted not infrequently in an unhappy attempt to rebut a point for which Jewel, with apparent ease, could cite a wealth of patristic evidence. Jewel made full use of his strategic advantage, insisting that the epithets which Harding had used against him or against a point he had made, were actually directed against a father of the Church and his teaching. These tactics were repeated again and again, at times with considerable justice and at times most unfairly, but always with telling effect. Jewel concluded one such passage by asking his reader to judge "what mystical catholic ears M. Harding hath, that cannot abide the phrases and speeches of the ancient fathers." [22]

In his writings Jewel was uniformly more even tempered and gentlemanly than Harding, indeed rarely so for sixteenth-century controversy.[23] He consciously sought to maintain a judicious approach, or at least the impression of judiciousness. Harding is more

[22] Jewel, *Defence, Works,* III, 484. Jewel differed from Calvin and Cranmer here only in that he used the device far more extensively, achieving in the process a cumulative effect not present in the work of his predecessors. See John Calvin, *Theological Treatises* (Philadelphia, 1954), pp. 284 and 338, and Thomas Cranmer, *Remains,* 4 vols. (Oxford, 1833), III, 17.

[23] *Cf.* H. M. Gwatkin, *Church and State in England to the Death of Queen Anne* (London, 1917), p. 162.

typical of the age, descending at times to ugly scurrility, Jewel in reply being content merely to reprimand him for his bad taste. Jewel's was a dryly humorous mind, capable of unusual detachment, and his raised eyebrow was far more effective than Harding's bludgeoning.

Jewel's private reaction to Harding and his arguments was another matter altogether. In a letter to Bullinger, describing the Harding controversies, he damned the man and his company in terms that leave no doubt concerning the depth of his commitment to his own position and his genuine aversion to that of the Romanists.

They are indeed our own countrymen, but enemies in heart, dwelling in a hostile land. For our fugitives at Louvaine began during the last year to be in violent commotion, and to write with the greatest asperity against us all. . . . Six years since, when I preached at court before the queen's majesty, and was speaking about the antiquity of ours and the popish religion, I remember that I said this among other things, that our enemies, when they accuse our cause of novelty, both wrong us and deceive the people; for that they approve new things as if they were old, and condemn as new, things of the greatest antiquity; that private masses, and mutilated communions, and natural and real presence, and transubstantiation, &c. (in which things the whole of their religion is contained), have no certain and express testimony either of holy scripture, or of ancient councils, or of fathers, or of anything that could be called antiquity.

At all this they were in great indignation: they began to bark in their holes and corners, and to call me an impudent, bold, insolent, and frantic boaster. Four years after, one Harding unexpectedly came forward; . . . This man would fain refute me out of the Amphilochiuses, Abdiases, . . . the decretal epistles, dreams, and fables. I replied to him last year, as well as I could. . . . I had scarce finished my work, when there suddenly flies abroad a Confutation of my Apology; an immense and elaborate work, and filled with abuse, contumely, falsehoods and backbitings. Here I am again pelted at. What would you have? He must be answered.[24]

On the score of scholarship, questions have been raised concerning the respective merits of the two antagonists only by the more

[24] Jewel, *Works*, IV, 1268.

extreme Roman Catholic historians who simply by the nature of the case cannot admit the superiority of Jewel's work. A moderately unbiased student reading Harding and Jewel, carefully checking the references, considering each argument and the evidence presented on each side, must admit that Jewel was the better scholar as well as the abler controversialist.[25] In Dixon's judgment "the superiority of Jewel in erudition and keenness is overwhelming." [26] There are many instances where Jewel was doubtless mistaken in his sources or wrong in his conclusions.[27] But without attempting to pass judgment upon the final rightness of the stand taken we must conclude that Harding did not cite the evidence necessary to prove him wrong. Whether that evidence exists or not is beside the point. Jewel, for his part, does cite the evidence and in such quantity that he literally overwhelms his opponent—and the reader. Much of the material cited, Harding simply ignored in the quibbling and ineffectual *Detection,* his final word in the controversy.

In the short space of three years between the appearance of Harding's *Answer* and the publication of the *Defence of the Apology* Jewel could hardly have assembled the vast body of authorities with which the *Reply to Harding* and the *Defence* are weighted down. Thus, specific preparation for the *Reply* must have antedated Harding's *Answer.* According to his literary executor, John Garbrand, "in times before" the writing of the *Reply,* Jewel "had gathered sundry books of common-places out of the Greek and Latin and later writers." [28] For how long a period Jewel had been accumulating these commonplaces, Garbrand does not say. Obviously they

[25] See especially *Reply, Works,* I, 341–360, an excellent example of Jewel's use of sound historical and textual methods in controversy and his superiority to his opponent in this respect.

[26] Dixon, *History,* V, 325.

[27] Hughes (*The Reformation,* III, 101), for instance, refers to Jewel's use of "bogus history" in his attack on the papacy but admits that while the "strange medley of medieval writers" may be "very dim figures to us perhaps . . . to Jewel and his generation" they were "not much further removed than are Burke and Chatham from our own time; and some of them are all but contemporaries." Among the "dim figures" cited (n. 2) are Marsiglio, Petrarch, and Valla.

[28] John Garbrand, "Epistle Dedicatory to Certaine Sermons" (1583), in Jewel, *Works,* II, 966.

antedate the first challenge sermon. Their existence suggests in fact that the challenge points had their roots in them, that the points in a sense represent conclusions based upon them, particular points being selected or rejected on the basis of the evidence accumulated. Jewel must have begun the collection as early as the Zurich period, if not before. Certainly the months in England between March and November 1559 were too crowded to allow any extensive research.

With these commonplace books in hand Jewel now returned to his sources and "did peruse afresh the authors themselves, and made every where in them special marks, for the difference of such places whereof he made choice. They were all drawn forth and laid to their themes by certain scholars, who wrote them out by such direction as he had given unto them."

Either the episcopal library which he inherited was very extensive or Jewel acquired a large collection in short order. Folkerzheimer was certainly impressed by it. Unfortunately it was scattered at the time of Jewel's death; however, Humphrey, then president of Magdalen, secured a number of volumes for his college library. There are not many of them, but the few volumes provide a remarkable cross section of the type of material which Jewel used—Jerome, Nicolaus of Cusa, Cardinal Pole. Throughout these volumes passages which appear as quotations in the controversial works are underlined and notated in the margin by a system of cipher notations together with occasional short notes in Jewel's hand. At the conclusion of each volume from five to eight signatures are affixed, followed by the significant "perfecit." Undoubtedly these are the names of the "certain scholars" mentioned by Garbrand.

Jewel made use of many of the passages specifically notated in these volumes both in his *Reply to Harding* and in his *Defence of the Apology*. So certain was he of having to support his challenge that he undoubtedly began the systematic review of his sources and the assembly of material around the challenge points soon after his arrival in Salisbury and not later than the spring of 1561 when he completed *The Apology*. Only in this way could he possibly have been able to answer Harding so quickly.

In his discussion of the controversies Strype raises the question of

Harding's originality, suggesting with Dean Nowell that Harding took most of his material from his predecessors and contemporaries among the Roman Catholic controversialists. Why this should reflect upon Harding is not clear. Certainly Jewel was well acquainted with the writers on both sides and never hesitated to make use of them. After all, the controversies with Harding represent a late chapter in a long series going back to Luther and his opponents. Since Luther's time the ground had been worked over quite thoroughly. Doubtless both Harding and Jewel had much of the material at hand. Jewel, and Harding too, for that matter, were often able to anticipate arguments and evidence to be met on a particular point simply by recalling previous controversies. Jewel in particular took perverse pleasure in being able on occasion to quote the writings of earlier Roman apologists against Harding's arguments— Eck and Bishop Fisher, for instance, and of course Stephen Gardiner in his Henrician period.[29]

Insofar as advice and help from his contemporaries is concerned, Jewel had probably far less than Harding, making use of his colleagues only when he needed their specialized knowledge. He corresponded with Parker, for instance, on the subject of the early English Church, having a profound respect for the Archbishop's knowledge of the Anglo-Saxon period. Nor was he averse to writing his friends in Zurich concerning special points. But the bulk of his work was his own. Since practically all of it was written at Salisbury where years went by without his seeing his colleagues, this is not surprising. Harding on the other hand was with his fellows at Louvain and could easily have received help if not actual collaboration. That he should have done so in no way detracts from his work, and indeed gives it additional authority in representing the point of view of the most important group of Roman Catholic exiles in the early years of Elizabeth's reign.

[29] Jewel, *Reply, Works*, I, 446; *Defence, Works*, III, 592; *Reply, Works*, I, 211.

Chapter VI

The Challenge of Puritanism

The Problem of Ecclesiastical Vestments

During the first decade of Elizabeth's reign the governmental structure of the Church remained remarkably free of criticism. And doctrine, as reflected in the Prayer Book and the Articles, stood unchanged without serious challenge throughout the reign. The controversies of the early years centered rather upon questions of ceremony, the ornaments of the churches, the vestments of the clergy—aspects of religion which many today would consider superficial. The debate over the crucifix in the royal chapel is a case in point. It was settled, however, soon after it came to a head early in 1560. In contrast, a controversy over the vestments of the clergy extended throughout the decade to merge finally with broader and more fundamental questions.

The religious revolution of the sixteenth century, like all movements affecting great numbers of people, had its popular symbols. In the medieval Church, ceremonies, the furnishings of the churches and shrines, the vestments of the clergy, had become an integral part of the total picture, indistinguishable in the popular view from the basic teachings of the Church and its organizational structure. When the reformers attacked Roman theological concepts and Roman authority they therefore attacked these symbols—images, crucifixes, symbolic gestures, apparel—as vigorously as if they too were essentials. The reformers recognized perhaps even more than had the medieval churchmen the central role that the symbols had come to play in the life of the ordinary layman. And the more extreme the reformer, the more vigorous his attack upon the symbols. The attitude of a particular reform group toward these seemingly superficial aspects of religion has thus come to provide a fair measure of the degree of radicalism in doctrine professed by the group. The modern observer suspects at times that with many of the reformers the symbols came to occupy a more prominent place in their thinking and a greater portion of their time and energy than did the fundamental doctrines themselves.

Since the English Church at the time of the initial break with Rome remained Catholic in doctrine, it retained the symbols associated with Catholic doctrine. Since the Church also maintained its episcopal form of government, the liturgy and vestments associated with episcopacy and the priesthood remained the same. Only the specifically Roman, as opposed to the merely episcopal, was done away with—the papacy, cardinals, the pallium—but the bishop and the priest, his ordination, his functions, his vestments, remained unchanged.

The contrast between the Church of England of the later years of the reign of Henry VIII and the continental Protestant Churches was extreme, but it remained unalterable until the death of Henry. In Edward's reign, however, as continental influence made itself felt in England, a major clash occurred, the focus of controversy being the question of ecclesiastical vestments. The controversy was not settled before the accession of Mary and the continental experience of the English churchmen during their exile under Mary guaranteed that the problem would rise again to face the new Establishment under Elizabeth.

Historians of the English Church under Elizabeth have tended to accept the view of the continental Protestant leaders that the symbols could not be divorced from the essentials of religion, finding confirmation perhaps for their view in the agreement on this point between the continental Protestants and Rome itself. They have therefore taken the simple approval or disapproval of the symbols by individual churchmen as a yardstick whereby these men could be categorized as Puritans or as conservatives.

Such an oversimplification unfortunately leads to the conclusion that the Anglican Church under Elizabeth survived only because the majority of its leaders sacrificed fundamental convictions for ulterior reasons, a conclusion manifestly wrong. The leaders of the Church under Elizabeth, not merely Parker and a handful of associates, but the majority of his colleagues, did not accept the view that the symbols, whether ceremonial or vestiarian, were inseparable from Roman doctrine and use. The English churchmen, including Parker, were fully aware of the public association of particular symbols with Rome and her teaching. As individuals therefore they frequently preferred to discard certain symbols either as a matter of practical expediency or because personally they found them distasteful. But however much they might distrust and dislike a symbol, it remained a symbol and no more, in itself not essential, and hence to be accepted or to be changed as the Church saw fit. Thus Cranmer had viewed the issue in Edward's reign and thus Jewel and his colleagues viewed it under Elizabeth.

For the first few years of the reign the question of ecclesiastical dress was not openly raised. Those clerics who preferred the simplest of vestments were apparently willing to bide their time in the hope that the tide would set in their direction, or at least until they had good evidence of a change in the other direction. The opinions of the Queen and the Archbishop might be suspect but the slight effort made to enforce conformity was encouraging. In retrospect it seems clear now that the tolerance of Parker and the government was likewise based on hope, in their case hope that differences would become less and the extremists conform. Both sides were wrong. Nonconformity in apparel increased; the Queen expressed strong disapproval; the Archbishop took action; the Puritans, faced with developments the opposite of those for which they had hoped, took the offensive; and the issue was joined. In the ensuing struggle the leading spokesmen for the Puritan point of view were Laurence Humphrey, the president of Magdalen, and Thomas Sampson, the dean of Christ Church. In 1564 Humphrey and Sampson formally protested to the Archbishop against the use of the vestments, on the grounds that they were inseparable from the use and teachings of Rome and thus not matters indifferent but of the nature of essentials. Should this premise be accepted their case would be won, for none would cavil at their primary premise that the essentials of religion themselves must be justified by scriptural warrant. The crux of the question therefore was the identification of *essentials* and its corollary, the definition of policy in regard to *non-essentials*. On these questions agreement was never reached.

As early as 1563 Humphrey and Sampson had appealed to the ministers at Zurich for advice and counsel.[1] Bishop Horne of Winchester wrote Bullinger at about the same time but in a different vein. While he expressed a dislike for the vestments, he insisted upon the necessity of conformity. Later Bullinger wrote to Horne noting approval of his views without in any way condoning the vestments. His concern was that the controversy over what he obviously considered non-essentials should weaken the English Church and give control to those who erred on fundamentals.[2] In 1566 Sampson sent a veritable questionnaire to Bullinger asking that the Zurich group carefully consider the matter and give full advice. Bullinger took action almost immediately and together with his colleague, Rudolf Gualter, sent a long and detailed reply to Sampson's questions, of pamphlet proportions. At the same time the Zurich ministers sent a copy of the document to Bishops Horne, Grindal, and Parkhurst with a request that it be communicated to Jewel, Sandys, and Pilkington.[3] The general tenor of the letter was so favorable to the stand of Horne and his fellow bishops that they proceeded to publish it, an action clearly not according to Bullinger's intentions, but extremely effective with many who tended to agree with Humphrey and Sampson. Sampson himself was not so easily satisfied and, disappointed in his old friends, turned from them to Geneva.[4]

While from the beginning the bishops, in varying degrees, had

---

[1] *Zurich Letters,* I, 134.

[2] *Ibid.,* I, 342–343.

[3] *Ibid.,* I, 345–356.

[4] Frere, *English Church,* p. 124; H. M. Baird in *Theodore Beza* (New York, 1899, p. 258), writing from a point of view highly critical of the bishops and the Queen and sympathetic to Sampson and the Puritan position, describes the Zurich pastors as being "less happy than Beza at Geneva in meeting these difficulties." In the following decade Beza was a supporter of Cartwright and the Puritans while Gualter in Zurich continued to support the bishops (*Zurich Letters,* I, 312–313; II, 249–254). See also Norman Sykes, *Old Priest and New Presbyter,* Cambridge, 1957, pp. 51–56.

sympathized with the objections of Humphrey and Sampson, they had never accepted the underlying premise of the arguments presented. As Sampson turned from authority to authority they became less sympathetic. In the end even Bullinger and Gualter lost patience.[5] The only authority which Thomas Sampson would accept was an authority in complete agreement with his own. Such a view was unacceptable to the Zurich pastors and they washed their hands of the whole matter. It was even more unacceptable to the English bishops, completely destructive as it was of all Church authority.

Jewel's position throughout the controversy has puzzled many. In his letters to Zurich he was outspoken in his opposition to the "papistical habits," providing, in fact, much of the evidence cited for the charge of Puritanism leveled at the entire group of Elizabethan bishops. At the same time he was as strict in his enforcement of the use of the vestments as Parker himself. As a result he has been characterized as hypocritical, or more generously, as inconsistent.

In a letter to Martyr in November 1559, he wrote scathingly of the "theatrical habits," of that "comical dress." These vestments, he declared, are indeed "the relics of the Amorites. . . . I wish that sometime or other they may be taken away, and extirpated even to the lowest roots: neither my voice nor my exertions shall be wanting to effect that object." [6] Early in 1562 he wrote that since now the "full light of the gospel has shone forth, the very vestiges of error must, as far as possible, be removed together with the rubbish, and as the saying is, with the very dust. And I wish we could effect this in respect to that linen surplice: for, as to matters of doctrine, we have pared every thing away to the very quick. . . ."[7] There are other references in the same vein. Nor is there any indication in the letters of a change in point of view as time passed. As late as 1566, having noted that the contest over the surplice was

<hr/>

[5] *Zurich Letters,* I, 360 (Bullinger and Gualter to Humphrey and Sampson, September 10, 1566); II, 152 (Bullinger to Beza, March 15, 1567).

[6] Jewel, *Works,* IV, 1223.

[7] *Ibid.,* IV, 1247.

not yet at rest, he added that the "matter still somewhat disturbs weak minds. I wish that all, even the slightest vestiges of popery, might be removed from our churches, and above all from our minds."[8]

Such statements are not to be taken lightly. Jewel's distaste for the vestments, even for the simple linen surplice, was unqualified; he stood for their reform in the direction of simplicity. We should note, however, that at no point in the letters does he characterize the vestments as essential or even suggest such a view. Furthermore, however strong his distaste for the vestments might be, he suggests no action against them other than that of personal suasion.

One of Jewel's first acts as bishop had been the renewal of the statute concerning cope money at Salisbury cathedral. It is difficult to visualize Sampson, or even Parkhurst for that matter, going out of his way thus to support a hated vestment. And it is a far cry from Martyr's advice to Sampson that he not give up his preaching because of the vestments but use the pulpit at all times to teach against their use[9]—virtual sabotage of the Establishment from within.

In 1565, at the height of the controversy, Bishop Horne, with Parker's consent, preferred Laurence Humphrey to a benefice at Salisbury.[10] Humphrey was a close personal friend of Jewel's, his companion in exile at Zurich, and later to be his official biographer. Yet Jewel in his capacity as Bishop of Salisbury refused him preferment in words that allow of no misinterpretation.

I would gladly admit (him) in respect of his learning, yet in respect of this vain contention about apparel I have thought it best to make a stay, until I might further understand your grace's pleasure. Unless your grace shall otherwise advise me by your letters, without good assurance of his conformity I mind not in any wise to receive him. Saving your grace's judgment, it were expedient that the matter were generally overruled. This long sufferance breedeth great offence.[11]

[8] *Ibid.*, IV, 1268.
[9] *Zurich Letters,* II, 27.
[10] Strype, *Parker,* I, 369.
[11] Jewel, *Works,* IV, 1265.

Parker naturally supported Jewel's decision and Humphrey did not receive his preferment. At a later date, unlike Sampson, he did conform.

Jewel's action was taken prior to his letter to Bullinger of February 1566 in which he expressed his own disapproval of the vestments. To what extent was he guilty of inconsistency? Bishop Burnet, on the basis of the general tenor of Jewel's remarks in the letters, concluded that while Jewel disliked the use of the vestments, "and treats the insisting so much on it with great contempt, yet, on the other hand, he blames those who laid too much weight upon that matter, and so looked on it as a thing of more importance than truly it was." [12] The vestments were symbols which well might be confused with Roman use and Roman teachings. But they remained symbols. Whether to wear the surplice in the pulpit or to celebrate Communion apparelled in a cope, these were not questions essential to religion. The Church had decided in their favor, and throughout the long controversy he consistently acted in accord with the Church's decision.

Jewel was an English churchman in the tradition which had included such diverse leaders as Gardiner and Cranmer. Although Gardiner had opposed the anticlerical and antipapal measures in Henry's Parliament, when they were enacted he supported them.[13] Likewise, Cranmer, against his deepest convictions, had to submit to the Six Articles. Jewel's acceptance of the vestments involved no such sacrifice as had his predecessors' acceptance of the fluctuations of the royal will. The vestments were matters indifferent and he could accept and enforce them with a clear conscience. His attitude toward the whole question is well summarized in a later letter to Bullinger. In it he noted that, while the affair of the habits still occasions much disturbance,

the queen is resolved not to be turned from her opinion; and some of our brethren are contending about this matter, as if the whole of our religion

[12] Gilbert Burnet, *History of the Reformation of the Church of England*, 4 vols. (London, 1839), III, 418.

[13] J. A. Muller, *Stephen Gardiner and the Tudor Reaction* (New York, 1926), p. 55.

were contained in this single point; so that they choose rather to lay down their functions, and leave their churches empty, than to depart one tittle from *their own views* of the subject: neither will they be persuaded either by the very learned writings of yourself and Gualter, or by the counsels of other pious men. However, we thank God that he does not suffer us at this time to be disquieted among ourselves by questions of more importance.[14]

In the conventional and generally accepted characterization of Jewel's position and that of his colleagues, is it possible that a fundamental error has been made in blurring the line between them and the active Puritans like Sampson while stressing the difference between their viewpoint and that of Parker? Should not the grouping be the other way round? The vital line of distinction ought rather to be drawn between Jewel and his colleagues on the one hand and Sampson and the Puritans on the other. The difference between the Archbishop, who may or may not have held the vestments in great affection but who certainly regarded them as non-essentials, and his bishops who did not love the vestments yet nonetheless regarded them as non-essentials, was far less than that between the bishops and the Puritans—perhaps not superficially, but surely so when the controversy was reduced to its fundamental issue.

The Year 1571

The difference in point of view between the bishops and the Puritan extremists became an open break in the Parliament of 1571. The Puritan leaders were convinced that "now was the acceptable hour to stop appeasement, suppress all compromise with the enemy, and stand in the strength of a purified church against 'the remnants of Antichrist.'"[15] Professor Neale observes at the conclusion of his extensive analysis of the events of the parliamentary session that "though the Queen herself was directly responsible" for the failure of the Puritan campaign, "the bishops also emerged as its critics and opponents."[16] Jewel became involved almost from the begin-

[14] Jewel, *Works*, IV, 1272 (February 24, 1567). My italics.
[15] Neale, *Elizabeth I*, p. 191.
[16] *Ibid.*, p. 217.

ning. An important part of the legislative battle was fought out in special committees of the two houses and he was a member of three of these, the committees concerned with the bills on simony and corrupt presentation and the committee responsible for the crucial religious bill of the session, that for coming to church and receiving Communion.[17] As a result he had ample opportunity to assess the true quality and significance of the Puritan program, not only through the Commons demands as reflected in the bills, but in the joint sessions with the Commons committees whose personnel included the most vigorous of the Puritan leaders. For Jewel it was the beginning of a new chapter. With the second revision of the *Defence of the Apology* he had concluded his controversies against the Romanists. In Parker's opinion his labors were sufficient in that respect.[18] Now, in the face of the Puritan attack, he must turn from the defense of the Church against Rome to its defense against the assault from within.

John Whitgift, in his answer to the Puritan admonition to Parliament, included a short paper entitled *Certain Frivolous Objections against the Government of the Church of England,* "the judgment," according to Whitgift, of the "late bishop of Sarum, avouched by his own hand."[19] The Puritan *objections* which the paper answers were four in number, all directed in one way or another at episcopal office. The first two *objections,* in the tradition of strict biblical authority, claim that although God left a perfect pattern for his Church, there is no mention of pope or archbishop or archdeacon in the Bible and that the synagogue must be regarded as God intended it, a model of the Church of Christ from which he had omitted nothing. The third *objection* was an interesting application of scholastic terminology, the contention that where the substance of anything is perfect the accidents are likewise perfect and while the substance of true religion was perfect in the primitive Church yet there was no archbishop. The fourth *objection* was the statement *ex cathedra* that ecclesiastical and civil government are not to be

---

[17] D'Ewes, *Journals,* pp. 146, 147.
[18] Parker, *Correspondence,* p. 410.
[19] Jewel, *Works,* IV, 1299–1300.

confounded or to be together in one person and that since "to be a chief or a ruler is a civil power," such power cannot be exercised by any ecclesiastical person.

The answers to these objections probe deeply the questions underlying them. The author of the paper begins with an unequivocal denial that "a perfect pattern of ecclesiastical government" is to be found in the letter of St. Paul to the Ephesians which had been cited as authority. He notes on the one hand that Paul mentions prophets and nowhere names presbyters, thus hoisting the Puritan on his own petard. As for the synagogue, the author will no more accept it as a model than he will the many details of the old Jewish law which the Puritans themselves had never accepted.

To the peculiar point concerning substance and accidents the author returns a strictly commonsense argument, accepting the inviolability and permanence of things substantial but arguing with great force and conviction that it is precisely for matters which might be referred to as accidents that the element of change is provided. For the specific needs of the Church at particular times God had indeed raised up prophets or apostles and had endowed them with gifts which men no longer possess. In accord with the needs of men today there are, in the place of prophets and saints, universities and schools, bishops and archbishops. The creation of offices and functions according to needs, the author noted, has been the history of church offices from the beginning. Then, moving from theory to precedent, he reminded his opponents that according to Chrysostom and scholars whom all accept, such as Erasmus, Paul himself was acquainted with the office of bishop and archbishop.

The fourth objection was apparently not understood to be as radical as it first appears. It was interpreted not as a denial of the power of the civil government over the Church, but rather as a denial of the civil powers and functions of ecclesiastical officers. The answer is based on two grounds, that of the necessity of Church discipline so insistently demanded by the Puritans themselves, and that of precedent, the biblical precedent of the Hebrew prophets and the patristic precedent of St. Augustine.

From the initial statement that the Puritan demand for the abolition of archbishops and archdeacons is *novitiorum assertio* to the olympian "stultitia nata est in corde pueri, et virga disciplinae fugabit illam, . . . It is but wantonness; correction will help it," of the conclusion, the paper is as thorough a condemnation of the Puritan point of view as any part of Whitgift's own work. Indeed, so closely do its arguments coincide with Whitgift's that the reader is tempted to ascribe it to Whitgift himself.

Although Strype and the Parker Society editor of the works of Jewel and Whitgift[90] accept Whitgift's word for the paper's authorship without further inquiry and proof, they appear to have been on solid ground. The most compelling evidence is Thomas Cartwright's failure in his *Reply* to deny forthrightly Jewel's authorship. Although he describes the paper as "put forth in the name and under the credit of the bishop of Sarisbury" to suggest, as it were, a shadow of doubt, his answer is to Jewel and not to Whitgift, even to the extent of apologizing for disagreeing with Jewel because of his "learning and gravity" and the debt which the Church owes him for "defending the case thereof against the papists." Cartwright, in fact, was in no position to deny Jewel's authorship. It was common knowledge among the Puritan leaders that the point of view expressed in the paper had been publicly stated by the Bishop in a sermon at Paul's Cross only a few months before his death. It was one of a series delivered by the bishops in their counteroffensive against the Puritans. The content of Jewel's sermon is known to us, ironically, only because the Puritans considered it so significant that they prepared and circulated an answer.[21] In the process they preserved enough of the Bishop's argument to make his position quite clear.

Jewel's sermon was a plea to the Puritans not to destroy the Church merely because of the minor flaws which they believed they discerned in it. He reviewed the question of vestments at some length and evidently made a detailed and spirited defense of them.

---

[20] John Strype, *The Life and Acts of John Whitgift,* etc., 3 vols. (Oxford, 1822), I, 76; Whitgift, *Works,* II, 336.

[21] *The Seconde Parte of a Register,* ed. Albert Peel, 2 vols. (Cambridge, 1915), I, 79–80.

On the subject of episcopal authority and ordination, the basic question now emerging as the Puritans pressed their attack, his stand was equally firm. He defended the use of the phrase, "Receive ye the Holy Ghost" in the ordination service in terms which the Puritans declared worthy of the papists themselves. His fundamental plea, however, was for the unity of the Church. Disputes on unimportant matters should never be allowed to endanger that unity and he termed those who would damn the existing order on superficial grounds mere sectaries, a charge which the Puritans deeply resented.

Thus in 1571 Jewel took his stand in vigorous opposition to the Puritan critics of the Establishment. In view of his part in the vestments controversy his position in 1571 is not altogether surprising, although it too runs counter to the impression of the man and his views generally drawn from his private correspondence, both by his contemporaries among the Puritans and by later historians of the Church. Jewel's published writings had given no cause of alarm to the Puritans, who received them as enthusiastically as did Archbishop Parker himself. The Paul's Cross sermon of 1571 surprised them and continues to puzzle those who still share their picture of the Bishop and his views. For the Puritans in 1571 the objectivity necessary to an understanding of Jewel's position was naturally lacking. The sermon and the very brief *Frivolous Objections* are the only pieces in all of his works directly concerned with the Puritan attack on the Establishment. Of necessity the questions considered were approached from a direction altogether different from that of his previous works and therefore the point of view which they express appeared to be a new one.

In his controversial works Jewel had found it essential to disregard the possibility of division within the English Establishment. As the defender of Anglicanism against the Church of Rome he had presented to the world a picture of Anglican unity which ignored the strains and stresses within the Establishment, the great divergence of views which existed from the start between the more conservative and the more radical leaders. The unity of the English Church, whether a reflection of his own deepest convictions or merely a wishful ignoring of the true state of affairs, is a constant theme of his writings, a basic premise in his defense of the Church. It continued to be a basic premise when he turned to the Puritans. An attack on this basis, and from Jewel of all people, was not expected. They had no disagreement with him on the question of the need for unity. But all along they had assumed unity to be unity on their own terms. This, the moderate churchmen, especially Jewel, removed as he was from the centers of Puritan activity, had been slow to recognize. That the pattern of Puritan opposition was to be the pattern indicated by the uncompromising Thomas Sampson rather than by the conforming Laurence Humphrey only became clear with the passage of the years. When the realization was driven home to him by the nature of the attack on the Establishment in 1571, Jewel turned against the Puritans with the impatience of an old warrior betrayed by the petty dissensions of politicians at home.

In reviewing Jewel's activities in 1571 it is essential to remember that the problem is not one of a change in one man's viewpoint in relation to immutable positions and principles. An element of change is undoubtedly present in Jewel's thought. But it is equally present in the views of the Puritans themselves and in the character and position of the Establishment. As Professor Neale has pointed out, the first decade of Elizabeth's reign saw a marked shift in the position of the Puritans, not so much in terms of beliefs as in terms of ways and means. Such a shift was in part a reflection of change in the position of the leaders of the Establishment and at the same time a cause of the change. There were few indeed of the non-Roman group of churchmen in the early years of Elizabeth's reign, including Archbishop Parker himself, who held rigidly to a view of Anglicanism so narrow that it excluded altogether any movement of the English Church in the direction of continental Protestantism. As the years went by, however, as necessary decisions were made in the face of differences of opinion and the resultant criticism, it became increasingly clear to both sides that the English Church was not to move gradually towards the Swiss ideal, at least in the natural order of development. As a result a growing rift appeared between the moderate churchmen in the Establishment and the Puritans. It became very real indeed in the parliamentary session of 1571.

Jewel's stand in 1571 actually represents no revolution in his thinking. When we review his early years, his life in exile, and his work as a controversialist and administrator under Elizabeth, it appears rather the culmination of a logical development. It only seems revolutionary because a changing situation brought into the foreground an aspect of his character and opinions heretofore largely unnoticed. His attitude towards the Puritan extremists, like that of so many of his colleagues, had not formed overnight. It had developed slowly, the result of his own growing awareness of the direction of Puritan aims and Puritan intransigence, and the threat to the unity of the Church in their refusal to accept a middle way. In the beginning he had been one of those who hoped to find a common ground of agreement near the continental position. The middle way that the English Church had come to occupy was perhaps further to the right than he would have wished, but to maintain unity he was willing to accept it. Such an acceptance involved no extreme and difficult adjustment, since Jewel himself was by nature a moderate—his moderation strengthend by humanistic study and reinforced by the experience of his own controversial labors. His works are overwhelming in their stress upon precedent. And respect for precedent, as with the common lawyers, does not make for a revolutionary outlook.

Moreover, Jewel was neither theoretical nor doctrinaire. Again, like the lawyer, he always argued to the point and, like the historian he fancied himself to be, he had great respect for the fact and the quotation. It is this practical side of the man of letters and controversialist that made him an excellent episcopal administrator whose education in the problems of the Establishment continued to the end of his life.

The moderation of the man and his commonsense practicality account for the passages running through his letters generally ignored by those who quote him so freely as a Puritan. He is distressed that the Queen delays making ecclesiastical appointments and decisions that concern the Church but he sees the reasons for delay as clearly as if he were William Cecil himself. He desires the presence of Peter Martyr in England but he is aware also of the possible troubles that might ensue were a continental reformer of Martyr's stature present in England to provide a rallying point for the critics of the Establishment. One has only to compare his letters with those of Thomas Sampson, or even with those of his old tutor, Bishop Parkhurst, to realize that though sympathetic he might be to Puritans and to Puritanism, in temperament and in point of view he was far closer to Archbishop Parker—even in the early years of the reign. In 1559 the differences within the group of returned exiles had been clearly enough seen by the government for some of the exiles to have been made bishops and some to have been omitted from the lists of preferments altogether. But among those deemed acceptable there were likewise differences, not too obvious to the government, or even to the men themselves. So in a later age Pym and Edward Hyde were associated together in the work of the early months of the Long Parliament. Yet no one would claim that they were two of a kind. The differences which placed them so soon in opposite camps were surely there from the start— in their character, in their temperament, in the very essence of their natures. Thus it was with the churchmen of Elizabeth's early years.

The unity of the returned exiles during the early months of the new reign was in reality the unity of the moment, a unity forced upon the churchmen by an almost "now or never" feeling. The creation of a new episcopate and the gradual clarification of the government's policy accentuated the differences that had been temporarily submerged. Some critics of the Church under Elizabeth have deplored the loss of leaders like Lever, Sampson, and Whitehead and have implied, at least, that the Establishment took its character entirely from that small group of clerics headed by Parker who had remained in England during Mary's reign. Such is simply not the case. Always including Parker himself, without whose leadership it is difficult to believe that a successful Establishment would have evolved at all, the substantial core of the Establishment was provided by the more conservative among the returned exiles.

Jewel, though he continued to remain on terms of close personal friendship with "the opposition," and though he continued to sympathize with the Puritan-minded concerning ceremonies and vestments, identified himself with the policy of the new Establishment in the interest of unity. He believed, as did his Puritan friends, that the great danger lay in Rome, but he placed his faith not in the negation of all practices resembling those of Rome but in broadening the area of agreement within the English Church to provide the strongest possible defense against the common enemy.

In 1571, as the Establishment began to arm itself effectively against the Puritans, Archbishop Parker and the Queen turned increasingly to Jewel. While the Parliament was still in session he served on the High Commission, although he was not appointed to the court until some months later. Christopher Goodman, in his protestation of obedience to the Queen in April, named Jewel as one of the commissioners sitting at Lambeth,[22] and in June, Jewel acted with Parker, Cox, and Horne in the final settling of the difficult case of Bishop Cheyney of Gloucester.[23] Further responsibilities followed as he was commissioned to be the keeper of the spiritualities and Parker's commissary general for the vacant diocese of Bristol in place of Bishop Cheyney.[24] In August he and Bishop Sandys, only recently translated from Worcester to London, were formally named to replace Bishops Cox and Horne as Parker's assistants on the High Commission.[25]

But the new chapter, with Jewel acting as a chief adjutant to Parker in the administration of the Establishment and its defender against the Puritans, was a chapter destined to be left unfinished. As if to prove to the Puritan critics his own regard for episcopal duties and to justify the office which they had assailed, he started upon his fifth visitation of his diocese in September, though ill and weary with the heavy labors of the preceding months. It became increasingly clear to his friends that he was seriously ill. Although

[22] Strype, *Annals,* II, i, 140–141.
[23] Strype, *Parker,* II, 53.
[24] Strype, *Annals,* I, i, 420.
[25] Historical Manuscripts Commission, *Calendar of Salisbury MSS.,* I, 519.

they protested, he would not give in and insisted upon the continuance of the visitation. After a sermon at Lacock he finally collapsed; he was taken to the episcopal manor house of Monkton Farleigh and died there on September 23rd.[26]

It is tempting to consider what the new chapter might have contained. Very possibly the burden of the defense of the Establishment would have fallen upon Jewel rather than upon Whitgift. That at least is suggested by the events of his last year. Such a defense, I believe, would have been more compelling than Whitgift's. Jewel was the greater scholar and his experience as a controversialist was unequaled. Above all, he would have had far greater influence upon the Puritans, at least upon the more moderate of them. They could hardly forget that it was he who had been the great antagonist of Rome, the chief defender of the English Church they labored to save. But it would not have been a happy task for Jewel. Even less congenial would have been the responsibilities of the administrator, the carrying out of an active policy of repression against the Puritans for whom personally he had deep sympathy. Though too realistic and clear sighted perhaps to have stumbled into the pitfalls that destroyed Archbishop Grindal, he lacked the rugged inner hardness which enabled Whitgift to pursue so unflinchingly a course pleasing to the Queen. Even so, it was a great misfortune for the Church of England to lose at this critical stage such a wise, able, and above all, moderate, champion.

[26] Jewel, *Works,* IV, 1130 (Garband's preface to *A View of a Seditious Bull*); W. H. Jones, "Aldhelm," *Wiltshire Archaeological and Natural History Magazine 3* (1863) 81; Charles Hobhouse, "Some Accounts of the Parish of Monkton Farleigh," *Wiltshire Archaeological and Natural History Magazine 20* (1881) 89–90.

Part Two

THE PROBLEM OF AUTHORITY
FOR DOCTRINE

Chapter VII

The Reformation and Doctrinal Authority

The problem of authority for doctrine should not be stated in terms of a simple choice between the authority of the Church of Rome and the authority of the Bible, despite the reformers' own view that they had rejected the Church to replace it with the Bible. The Church itself made ample use of biblical authority. Even in its stress upon the validity of its accumulated tradition which in fact did tend to become a "second principle of authority," [1] it taught that the foundations of such traditions existed in the original scriptural revelation. Thus, in spite of the oft-repeated indictment of the Church by the reformers on this point, the ultimate authority of the Bible was not actually in question. It was rather that from this single ultimate authority each side derived very different and even contradictory doctrines. The basic questions at issue therefore had to do with the nature and definition of the Scriptures as the ultimate authority, and above all, with the authority for their interpretation. The problem of authority for doctrine comes in the end to be the problem of the authority for the interpretation of the Bible.

The Church had solved the problem of interpretation by citing the authority of Catholic tradition and the living embodiment of Catholic tradition, that is, the institution of the Church itself. Buttressed as it was by centuries of acceptance throughout Western Christendom, such authority was formidable indeed.

Luther appears to have felt no need to cite an authority for an interpretation of the Bible in the sense of an authority external

[1] Emil Kraeling, *The Old Testament since the Reformation* (New York, 1955), p. 9.

to it, such as tradition or an institution. The meaning of the Scriptures was clear to him beyond the possibility of dispute. He approached the Bible with an unquestioned faith in his own understanding of its central message, the Pauline doctrine of justification by faith, and through St. Paul, as through a lens, he felt that he could read the Scriptures clearly and with complete authority.[2] Zwingli applied no such a priori test and took the stand that the clarity of the meaning of the Scriptures was manifest. His only concession was to interpret the Scriptures by the Scriptures. Calvin's answer to the problem of the interpretation of the Scriptures is contained in his answer to the primary question of the authority of the Scriptures. Their divine origin is self-evident and they gain credit in the hearts of men through the "internal testimony of the Spirit." [3] And so as with their meaning, their interpretation.

The obvious criticism of these views, including Calvin's, is that someone else besides the particular reformer in question might come to wholly different conclusions, "an endless variety of interpretations." [4] Who was to pass judgment upon the validity of Luther's interpretation of St. Paul or indeed by what authority does one accept the premise that St. Paul's teaching, however interpreted, is the heart of the Christian religion? Again, how can judgment be made between Zwingli's reading of the "obvious meaning" of a scriptural passage and the reading of someone else, should the two readings differ? Even with Calvin's solution it is quite possible that in all good faith someone might cite the internal testimony of the Spirit against an interpretation held by another and supported by the same authority. From the early days of the Reformation the defenders of Rome raised these questions, certain in their own faith of the interpretative authority of the Church. Nor was the question

[2] See R. E. Davies, *The Problem of Authority in the Continental Reformers* (London, 1946), p. 27–29. In his discussion of Luther and the problem of authority in general (rather than interpretative authority) Davies concludes that Luther "never thought of the problem of authority as a problem, properly so-called, at all."

[3] John Calvin, *Institutes of the Christian Religion,* 2 vols. (Philadelphia, 1936), I, vii, IV.

[4] J. T. McNeill, *The History and Character of Calvinism* (New York, 1954), p. 39, referring to Zwingli.

confined to the Romanists or to the century of the Reformation. There was John Bunyan's Master Cobb and his simple "who shall judge between you, for you take the Scripture one way and they another?" [5]

But an endless variety of interpretations did not come to pass. Indeed, insofar as basic and fundamental doctrinal differences were concerned, there was only a two-fold division, the division between the Lutheran and the Reformed Churches. Within each of these major divisions of continental Protestantism the degree of uniformity was actually greater than it had been in the pre-Reformation Church.

While the initial impulse and the guiding force for all of the major continental reform movements was spiritual, in Strasbourg and Basel, as in Wittenberg and Zurich and Geneva, the survival of the movements and their eventual character owed much to other factors, to the political framework within which the reformers worked, and to the personal character and ability of the individual reformers, as well as to the theological systems they developed.

The character of Lutheranism reflects all of these forces. A religious movement based on the spiritual experience of a great mystic had survived in the political framework of German particularism, in part because of the greed of the princes, in part because Luther's theology concentrated upon the inner aspects of religion rather than upon its social and ethical aspects. Lutheranism served the particularist ambitions of the princes without interfering in any way with the political power they sought. As a result the doctrinal system constructed very early by Luther and Melanchthon remained fixed and unchanged, undisturbed by a civil power satisfied to control the outward aspects of the Church. From the point of view of doctrinal authority it was an excellent practical solution. Luther's interpretation, authoritative because it was the "right" interpretation, received its practical authority from the civil power. There was no question of the civil power seeking interpretative power itself or interfering in the area of doctrine since the interpretation and the resultant doctrinal structure now in existence was final.

[5] A. Dakin, *Calvinism* (Philadelphia, 1946), p. 187.

Zurich rather than Geneva provides the typical pattern of Reformed Protestantism as distinguished from Lutheranism. Like Lutheranism, Zwinglianism bears the imprint of a powerful and exceedingly attractive personality. Unlike Lutheranism, however, Zwinglianism, in common with the other Reformed faiths, was oriented strongly towards the social and ethical aspects of religion, towards the creation of a godly society on earth. Hence, in contrast to Lutheranism, the adjustment of the purely theological and religious to the political facts of life was not so simple. Fortunately for Zwingli, as for the leaders of the other Reformed Churches, the political framework within which he worked was the city-state rather than the princely territorial state of Luther. More important, the polity of these city-states, now freed altogether of their old episcopal and feudal control, was that of the commune, oligarchical but broadly based. Nor should the factor of size be overlooked. The political unit which conditioned the Reformed Churches was minute and remarkably homogeneous. Thus the translation of the ideal of a Christian commonweal into practice was eminently feasible. Zwingli's Zurich however, and the other cities of Switzerland and the Rhineland, continued to be ruled by a civil magistracy, a godly magistracy perhaps, but laymen, and no matter how great the prestige of Zwingli, or of Haller in Berne or Oecolampadius in Basel, the magistracy retained the final authority.[6]

The similarity here between the authority of the Reformed magistracy and that of the Lutheran prince is only superficial. In the Swiss city-states no line could be drawn between civil magistrate and spiritual leader in terms either of status or of influence. Furthermore, even had Zwingli wished to construct a doctrinal system as final as Luther's, his stress on the social and ethical aspects of doctrine would have made finality impossible. The emphasis of Reformed Protestantism on the importance of a godly discipline made inevitable the necessity for continuing interpretative authority and made equally inevitable an extremely close relation between reli-

---

[6] McNeill, *History of Calvinism*, p. 84; *cf.*, Davies, *Problem of Authority*, p. 86: "The Council (in Zurich in 1528) is headed by the prophet, Zwingli." Zwingli's power in fact, however, was personal rather than constitutional.

gious authority and civil authority. As a consequence of the prestige of Zwingli and his successors at Zurich, the magistrates and citizenry were willing to accept their leadership in spiritual affairs. But this was a practical solution that depended on the ability of the pastors to persuade—a personal authority at best. The final decision lay with the civil magistracy.

The pattern of Zurich was duplicated to a greater or less degree by most of the Reformed Churches. The great exception was Geneva. In theory it was no different from the other Swiss cities with its government nominally in the hands of councils of lay magistrates. Peculiar to Geneva, however, was the institution of the Consistory, a small group composed of ministers and lay elders with full power over the spiritual life of the city. Originally the lay elders outnumbered the ministers and were elected by the councils, but by 1560 there were only twelve elders as against eighteen ministers and the ministers soon gained effective veto power over the election of elders. Since Calvin interpreted the spiritual life, the godly life, comprehensively to include every aspect of the life of the citizen and since the Consistory had absolute control over the spiritual life, in the end this body dominated by Calvin and his fellow pastors, held absolute power in the city.

It was the duty of the State, Calvin thought, to use its power—if need be, its sword-bearing arm—to enforce moral living and sound doctrine. But it was to do this always according to the direction of the Word of God, and it was the prerogative of the Church to interpret the Word and will of God. The Genevan theocracy may more properly be called a *bibliocracy,* for it was upon the Scriptures (and by implication upon Calvin's interpretation of the Scriptures) that the whole structure rested.[7]

Geneva was indeed the godly city, the ideal of the Reformed faith. And though deeply admired and widespread in its influence, it was not duplicated in Calvin's lifetime even in Switzerland.

The success of Calvinism owes much to the peculiar and indeed unique political circumstances of Geneva, both within the city and

[7] Georgia Harkness, *John Calvin: The Man and His Ethics* (New York, 1931), pp. 21–22; see also Dakin, *Calvinism,* p. 212, and W. A. Mueller, *Church and State in Luther and Calvin* (Nashville, 1954), p. 128.

without, but it owes even more to the force of intellect and the character of the man Calvin. Having supplied the most effective answer to the problem of authority in its theoretical aspects, he was able to forge a practical authority in the Genevan Consistory that could fully implement his theory. Small wonder that for so many, Geneva provided the final and effective answer to the authority and doctrine of the Roman Church.

The English Reformation, in contrast to the Lutheran and the Swiss Reformations, is the classic example of a religious revolution carried out by the temporal power almost wholly according to the dictates of political exigency.[8]

Henry VIII intended the English Church to remain Catholic in tradition and doctrine. Only the constitutional ties with Rome were broken. The English Church remained part of the visible Church Catholic but it was in no sense subject to the authority of the visible Church as Western Christendom had generally understood the term. The constitutional change, however, necessarily involved a basic change both in doctrine and the source of doctrinal authority, for Rome, deprived of any constitutional control over the English Church, inevitably lost authority over doctrine. This was a fundamental break: it set in motion, though to a less degree, the very same disintegrating forces which Luther had set in motion when he cast off Roman authority. The story of the English Church from the abolition of the Roman jurisdiction is the story of efforts made to replace Roman authority in doctrinal matters and thus to check the forces set free by the constitutional break with the Roman Church.

To Henry's Erastian mind doctrinal authority presented no great problem. The authority he possessed was sufficient not only to effect constitutional reform but also to insure the continuance of Catholic doctrine in the English Church. To Sir Thomas More and John Fisher the assumption of an authority of such magnitude was unsupportable. While they accepted the constitutional change, they could not allow Henry the right of judgment in purely divine

[8] *Cf.* E. S. Abbott, et al., *Catholicity: A Study in the Conflict of Christian Traditions in the West* (Westminster, 1947), p. 49.

matters. Stephen Gardiner, on the other hand, followed the King, thinking thereby to preserve the Catholic tradition. But the force loosed by the King's action was difficult to keep within bounds. Archbishop Cranmer, like Gardiner, Erastian, yet firm in his devotion to his own concept of Catholic tradition, developed ideas very different from those of his conservative colleague. No open break came while the strong hand of the King kept the English Church in its conservative course. But with Edward VI the evolution attained mercurial swiftness and Cranmer in turn found himself holding back the extremists. He too felt the need of authority, when spiritual affairs were subject to the whims of a boy king dominated by worldly and selfish advisers. Royal headship, a satisfactory replacement for papal authority in problems merely administrative, proved weak indeed as a bulwark of doctrinal authority and altogether inadequate as a bulwark of doctrinal stability. To achieve stability Cranmer undertook a series of tremendous projects, the formularies of the Prayer Book, the articles of religion, and the completion of the *Reformatio Legum Ecclesiasticarum,* all of which, by crystallizing the teachings of the English Church would tend to slow down the speed of change. As a source of authority for his views he looked increasingly to tradition, not the late papal tradition, but the tradition of the early Church. Without the balancing influence of royal conservatism which Henry had provided and which Elizabeth was later to supply, however, Cranmer had little chance of success. It is quite probable that had Edward lived, the English Church would have been torn free of Cranmer's control, to find a destination completely Reformed. But Mary became Queen and Cranmer, torn between his Erastianism and his own personal concept of religious truth, suffered martyrdom.

The reign of Edward proved to Bishop Gardiner that the solution he had hoped for, the preservation of Catholic doctrine, as he conceived it, in an Erastian Church, was illusory: he welcomed the Marian reunion with Rome convinced that Roman authority alone could preserve Catholic tradition. When Elizabeth came to the throne the question remained whether the evolutionary process which had gone so far under Edward might be halted without the acceptance of Gardiner's solution of a return to Roman authority, or whether the English Church must become one with the Reformed Churches on the continent. The solution of this problem was the fateful task of the churchmen of the reign of Elizabeth.

The secular-minded Queen and her closest lay advisers did not consider the theoretical problem of doctrinal authority of paramount importance. As long as practical authority was in the hands of the crown, any theory of doctrinal authority compatible with the royal supremacy would be satisfactory. This in itself, however, limited the choice of solutions. The Roman solution of an institutional authority independent of the state would have challenged the royal supremacy directly. The Lutheran solution, so compatible with the Tudor concept of the state, was not feasible, for obvious and thoroughly practical reasons. It was as unacceptable to the party of reform in England as it was to the large body of conservatives. And it had no positive support whatever.

By 1558 Calvinism had become the dominant version of Reformed Protestantism. The alternative to Rome was Geneva, an alternative as repugnant to the Queen as Rome itself. However sincerely Calvin may have respected the civil magistracy in its proper sphere, however generously he paid his respects to the godly princes of England, in his own Genevan theocracy the magistrates were subordinate. So it appeared to Elizabeth and her advisers. Goodman and Knox are not to be held entirely responsible for the Elizabethan view of Geneva.[9]

Elizabeth accepted neither the Genevan nor the Roman solution of ecclesiastical polity. The civil power remained supreme, in no way subject to the control of the spiritual power. If there was any continental pattern that the Elizabethan solution resembled it was that of the city-states of German-speaking Switzerland, especially that of Zurich. The possibility of any similarity has been almost completely obscured by the manifest absurdity of comparing a tiny Swiss city and its communal government with the English nation-state and its strong Tudor monarchy. While the very real and obvious differences between the two, reflecting the contrast between

[9] See McNeill, *History of Calvinism*, pp. 311 ff.

the power of the Tudor prince and that of the burgher aristocracy and, even more important, the contrast between the heterogeneity of the island kingdom and the homogeneity of the Swiss city-state, should not be minimized, the fundamental similarity is there. In both instances the final authority rested with the civil magistrate, yet in neither did the magistrate dictate doctrine to the spirituality. Rather, the magistracy, without abdicating its final power, deferred to the spirituality in religious and doctrinal matters, in England to the bishops it had selected, as in Zurich to the pastors it had appointed.

The problem of interpretative authority itself was solved by the Elizabethan churchmen within the framework provided by the permissive authority of the civil power. Bishop Jewel, upon the foundations provided by Cranmer's earlier tentative efforts, constructed a theory of doctrinal authority the basis of which was the interpretation of the Scriptures with the aid of the early Church and the fathers. Archbishop Whitgift accepted Jewel's work but added little to Jewel's arguments and was forced by the heat of the Puritan attack towards Erastianism. Richard Hooker, basing his thought upon the foundation of patristic tradition developed by Jewel, expanded the latter's appeal to reason in patristic exegesis to an equality with and beyond tradition itself as a basis of authority.[10]

Jewel, like the reformers who preceded him, accepted the absolute finality of scriptural authority, although he did not share their unquestioning faith in the absolute clarity of the meaning of the Scriptures. His chief concern therefore was to provide an interpretative authority without accepting either the solution of an authoritative church or the opposite extreme of complete dependence upon special revelation. While he accepted the Roman premise that traditional interpretation was of inestimable value, he denied the Roman conclusion that Rome was the rightful judge of tradition. Similarly, while he accepted the Protestant view of the necessity of divine inspiration in interpretation, he insisted that such inspiration

[10] *Cf.* P. M. Dawley, *John Whitgift and the English Reformation* (New York, 1954), 193–194: "The line of spiritual continuity is clear—from Colet to Cranmer to Jewel to Hooker, and then to the Caroline divines."

must meet the test of general agreement and consensus. He endeavored to find an authority which was objective and whose meaning was demonstrable by reason. This authority for interpretation he found in the early Church, particularly in the writings of the fathers.

It is probably true that Jewel's faith in his authorities and the demonstrability of scriptural meaning by their aid was just as naïve as the faith of the earlier reformers in the unaided clarity of scriptural meaning. Nor may one claim for him great originality. Yet, while he used the means which the humanists had developed, which most of the reformers in England and on the continent had employed in a subsidiary way, he stands alone in the completeness of his authoritative method. His writings constitute the first thoroughgoing attempt to prove to the world the Catholicity of English Doctrine, to demonstrate that the teachings of the English Church at no point departed from the Church of the apostles and the fathers. Jewel's was a singularly English point of view, distrustful of novelty, stressing as did the common law the derivation of all things from past usage and custom. Although most reformers, it is true, denied that their teachings were new, that they were in any way in conflict with the apostolic Church, it is quite another matter to emphasize the objective precedent of the early Church and to stress the primary importance of demonstrating the identity of a particular modern Church with the early Church.

Chapter VIII

The Authority of Rome and
the General Councils

The Church of Rome

The Church of England in the first decade of the reign of Elizabeth faced an antagonist stronger and more ably equipped than the Church that Luther had attacked or the Church whose jurisdiction Henry VIII had abrogated. The Elizabethan Establishment had to fight again the battles which Luther and his successors had waged. Despite the success of the continental reformers, indeed, in part because of their success, the Church of Rome presented a threat to the formation and growth of the new Establishment as challenging now in the intellectual, moral, and spiritual realm as it had been previously in the material and political. Jewel, as a leader of the English Church and its official apologist, undertook to meet the challenge. Moderate and reasonable in so much else, he was absolute and uncompromising in his denial of the authority of the Roman Church. So indeed had been every reformer who broke with the Roman authority, even the most conservative among them, for compromise would inevitably mean, as indeed it often had meant, an eventual and complete surrender.

Very early in his career, in a Latin sermon preached at Oxford in 1550, Jewel stated a principle which provided the basis for his approach both to the general problem of authority and to the particular problem of the authority of the Church of Rome. "Let us not unadvisedly think that men are so luckily born, that, whatever they say, they cannot err."[1] Man, being human, cannot hope to achieve infallibility. The Church of Rome is a human institution to be measured and judged in terms of the individual men who are its officers, never transcending the very human and hence fallible elements of which it is composed. "If it be so that the church of Rome cannot err, it must needs follow that the good luck thereof is far greater than all these men's policy."[2] And it is obvious to all who care to study the history of the Church, he added, that it has been in error many times. The Church is a human institution; the infallibility which it claims can be attributed only to God.

Jewel claimed with considerable justice that underlying all tne complicated and varied controversial questions was the simple issue of the authority of the Roman Church. He noted that his opponent had turned repeatedly to the Roman supremacy to establish a point or as a final line of defense. "Ye apply one salve to every sore. Whatever be alleged against you, it is sufficient for you to answer, The church of Rome erreth not; the church of Rome hath not erred; the church of Rome cannot err."[3] The infallibility of the Roman Church, as Jewel pointed out, was in fact the first premise upon which the entire structure of his opponent's thought was reared and around which the argument tended more and more to center.

Fortunately, for the further development of religious thought, the controversy was not settled by a mere rejection or acceptance of the authority of Rome. The Roman controversialists were willing, indeed they found it quite necessary, to descend into the controversial arena and defend their stand point by point, even though at times they did retire to the shelter and protection of the institutional authority. They had no choice but to fight proof with proof, if they were to save their Church in a world which no longer regarded it as the sole repository of grace and authority. The realistic acceptance of this choice by Loyola and his followers explains in large part the assumption of leadership by the Society of Jesus in the offensive of the Counter-Reformation.

[1] Jewel, *Works*, II, 950, n. 1; 960.
[2] Jewel, *Apology*, *Works*, III, 90–91.
[3] Jewel, *Defence*, *Works*, IV, 720.

Similarly for those who were opposed to Rome a simple rejection of Roman authority was by no means enough. It was necessary first to disprove its validity and secondly to replace it with an authority capable of logical defense consonant with the grounds upon which it had been denied.

As a student of the early Church, Jewel knew that papal supremacy and authority within the Church was more vulnerable to attack than the authority of the Church in general. He was also well aware that the papacy, as distinct from the Church, was not universally revered. Many Englishmen who still considered themselves faithful to the Roman Communion were one with those Englishmen of uncertain persuasion and anti-Roman leanings in their distrust of the papal power. For this reason and because he felt sure of success in his attack on the papal position, Jewel endeavored at all times to identify the Roman Church with the papal supremacy, knowing that the identification once definitely made, the disproval of the authority of the pope would inevitably mean the disproval of the authority of the Roman Church .

In the epistle to Queen Elizabeth which prefaced the *Defence of the Apology,* Jewel declared:

The main ground of [Harding's] whole plea is this, that the bishop of Rome, whatsoever it shall like him to determine in judgment, can never err; that he is always undoubtedly possessed of God's holy Spirit; that at his only hand we must learn to know the will of God; that in his only holiness standeth the unity and safety of the church; that whosoever is divided from him must be judged an heretic; and that without the obedience of him there is no hope of salvation.[4]

The Romanists even when they admit the existence of errors and abuses in their Church, will grant no redress save from the pope, ignoring the obvious failure of the papacy, despite untold opportunities, to remedy these very abuses.[5] Instead of an honest move toward reform there has been an even further extension of the papal claims. It has become "the very heart and root of all" their divinity, that " 'Christ hath prayed for Peter;' *ergo*, 'the pope can never err.' "

[4] *Ibid.,* III, 116.
[5] Jewel, *Apology, Works,* III, 81; *Defence, Works,* IV, 738–739.

Question after question, he felt, when submitted to thorough analysis, resolved itself into an acceptance or rejection of the papal claims. The whole vexed question of the validity of Anglican orders was in essence this question alone, "'Whether through the whole Church of Christ no man may be allowed for a bishop without the confirmation of the pope.'"[6] And again, the debate which raged over the Council of Trent in the end was concerned not with the authority of councils but with the papal supremacy and its domination of the Council.[7]

The supremacy of the pope within the Church was indeed a matter of fact. The Church which survived the fires of the Reformation was a papal Church, dominated not as the Church in the thirteenth century by an Innocent III, towering over a formidable hierarchy by the force of his personality, but by the position and office of the pope, whether that position was held by a Paul IV or a Pius V. Jewel characterized the power wielded by the contemporary papacy as arbitrary and wholly irresponsible, in the last analysis basically a denial of government under law. The pope is "tied to no law, neither of God nor of man."[8]

The charge that the rule of the Church was arbitrary and contrary to the law of the Scriptures was debatable in theory if not in fact. Certainly no Roman Catholic would admit its justice either in theory or in fact. Roman action and Roman doctrine were always justified, at least to the satisfaction of the Romanists themselves, by scriptural precedents. But to those who were not of the Roman Communion these scriptural precedents depended on interpretations they rejected altogether. It is again the old and basic problem of the authority for interpretation. To its critics, the Church of Rome, as the sole interpreter of the scriptural law, as the living embodiment of the law, was in fact and in theory above the law. Such must inevitably be the conclusions of men who do not accept

---

[6] *Ibid.*, III, 330. Dixon argues convincingly that this was the fundamental issue in the controversy, indeed, that it remains the issue upon which there can be no agreement. He notes his agreement with Jewel, quoting the passage cited above from the *Defence* (Dixon, *History*, V, 208).

[7] See below, pp. 128–131.

[8] Jewel, *Exposition on Thessalonians, Works*, II, 919.

the Roman premise that the institution of the Roman Church is the only visible and divinely ordained Church.

It is not within the province of the historian to judge whether the pronouncements of Rome were arbitrary or not. But he can and should observe that these pronouncements were absolute. Jewel was attacking no mere chimaera. Of all the monarchies which emerged in the sixteenth century the papacy alone was completely and divinely absolute. The doctrine of papal infallibility was to wait three centuries before becoming a part of the irrefutable dogma of the Church. But the Church itself already claimed infallibility, and to Jewel the Church was the pope. The pope, Jewel wrote, is in the eyes of the Church the universal bishop, the head of the universal Church; one who

hath authority above all general councils, and fulness of power to expound the scriptures; to whose determinations the whole church of God must of necessity submit itself without contradiction; whom neither emperor, nor king, nor clergy, nor the whole universal people, in anywise may control whatsoever he do; unto whom all appeals ought to lie from all places of the world; and who, wheresoever he happen to be, hath the full jurisdiction of a bishop.[9]

Although Jewel was convinced that these unlimited claims could not be substantiated by the history of the bishop of Rome in the early centuries of the Church, he did not distort the history of the early Church in order to make his case. He readily admitted that "the bishop of Rome had an estimation, and a credit, and a prerogative before others." Specifically, he "had the first place" of the four patriarchs, "both in council and out of council, and therefore the greatest authority and direction of matters in all assemblies."[10] Small wonder that many of Jewel's contemporaries were afraid that he had overstepped himself. Yet his thesis was actually very simple and, from the point of view of the historian, altogether viable: the bishop of Rome, for obvious historical reasons had achieved in these early centuries a certain preeminence; he had become *primus*

[9] Jewel, *Reply, Works,* I, 338.
[10] *Ibid.,* I, 375.

inter pares among the patriarchs. But this simple preeminence had gradually been changed until by the seventh century it was converted into unqualified supremacy in fact and in theory. Jewel developed this thesis in vast detail, devoting over a hundred pages to it and examining in full all the evidence presented by Harding and much more that he himself was able to add. All of it he was able to fit into the pattern of preeminence become supremacy, "the usurpation of power by the bishop of Rome," as he particularly liked to characterize it.

Modern scholars may well cavil at some of the specific evidence which Jewel cited, but his sixteenth-century opponents, including the ablest of them, Thomas Harding, failed signally to contravene the evidence or counter his arguments at any point. And few historians today would quarrel with his general thesis of the natural emergence of the bishop of Rome to preeminence and then to supremacy through an understandable historical process, though most would date the development of papal supremacy somewhat earlier than the seventh century.

While full credit must be given Jewel for his sound historical sense and his mastery of the subject, we should note that in this instance good history was also good controversial technique. A clear picture of the see of Rome in its early years which stressed the virtue of its actions and the simplicity of its doctrine, contrasted with the see under its Renaissance popes and its modern doctrines, was extremely effective in controversy. That Jewel dared to treat favorably a subject which a majority of the reformers avoided, is evidence perhaps of his more perfect knowledge of history and its uses. And it is also in keeping with his essentially reasonable approach to the whole problem.

He was most careful, however, to point out that the early preeminence of the see of Rome was not "de jure divino."[11] The respect which men like St. Augustine accorded the see was not due to any divinity in the see or its holder but was derived from simple historical causes, the antiquity of the see, the glory of its martyrs, and the

[11] *Ibid.*, I, 340.

position of Rome as the imperial seat. Most important of all was "the purity of religion, . . . preserved there for a long time without spot."[12] Apparently a dangerous admission of the Roman claim, such a view in reality completely reversed it. Doctrine was not dependent upon the Church for its validity; rather the possession of sound doctrine lent authority to the Church. Because the teachings of the apostles "at the beginning" were "exactly observed in Rome without corruption" the Church was then held "in reverence and estimation above others."[13] But now, since the Church has lost its purity of doctrine it can no longer command men's repect. Far less can it justify its claims of universal supremacy. Indeed, Jewel asserted, even at the height of its prestige in the days of the fathers it had never made such claims. Gregory the Great himself had stated that " 'Whosoever calleth himself universal bishop, or desireth to be so called, is in his pride the forerunner of antichrist, because in his pride he setteth himself before others.' "[14] The acceptance of papal absolutism with its acknowledgement that the pope cannot be judged by men, Jewel wrote, can only mean that he has "received liberty to do ill."[15] His rule is arbitrary in the worse sense of the word; it is capricious and wilful and therefore probably evil.

Jewel later developed from this premise a forceful appeal to those who feared a break with the one Church for the anarchy which would result. Arbitrary rule destroys one of the most fundamental and essential qualities of religion. If the pope can overrule councils, if he can overrule the pronouncements of his predecessors, "We shall evermore build upon sand and uncertainty and never be assured where to stand."[16] The Church of Rome has furthermore increased uncertainty a hundredfold by extending its contradictions of its own interpretations of the Scriptures to an overruling of the scriptural law itself. "It is a dangerous doctrine to say," Jewel wrote, that "the church is omnipotent and may allow or disallow God's command-

[12] *Ibid.*, I, 370.
[13] *Ibid.*, I, 365.
[14] *Ibid.*, I, 344.
[15] Jewel, *Defence, Works*, III, 339.
[16] *Ibid.*, IV, 773.

ments without difference, at her pleasure."[17] The rule of the Roman Church therefore has actually meant the destruction of the very attributes which men have thought to find in it. The results of arbitrary tyranny are no better than anarchy.

The Ecumenical Councils

As a result of the prestige of the ancient councils and perhaps also because conciliar tradition was largely unhampered by the prejudices which come with experience, the churchmen of the late fourteenth century had turned hopefully to the ecumenical council for a solution to the catastrophic schism in the Western Church. At its peak the conciliar movement gave promise of a thorough reform and a veritable reconstitution of the Church. While its failure and the dismal record of the fifteenth-century councils made almost inevitable the religious revolution of the sixteenth century, failure did not destroy men's faith in the general council as a possible answer to the problems facing Western Christendom. Throughout the early decades of the sixteenth century, interest in councils, demands for a council, disputes over the constitution and authority of councils, played a major part in theological as well as in ecclesiastical and political controversy.

By the middle of the sixteenth century the problems posed by the question of a general council of the Church had become focused on the Council of Trent. For Jewel, both as an individual and as the chief apologist of the Church of England, the questions at issue were particularly immediate and pressing. The first session of Trent had coincided with his formative years at Oxford. The last and definitive session was in the planning stage and under vigorous discussion throughout Europe when he was writing his *Apology*. During the final session he began his first major controversial work, the *Reply to Harding,* and in the years immediately following the close of the Council he wrote his monumental *Defence of the Apology.* Any

---

[17] Jewel, *Reply, Works,* I, 229. In almost the same words, Calvin had protested this "most pernicious error, that the Scriptures have only so much weight as is conceded to them by the suffrages of the Church; as though the eternal and inviolable truth of God depended on the arbitrary will of men" (*Institutes,* I, vii, I).

conclusions he reached concerning conciliar authority in general were naturally colored by his reaction to Trent. Indeed, the Council accentuated the peculiar problem which conciliar authority presented, that of the time element. Jewel found it necessary to work backward, in a sense, to deal first with the council in its contemporary form, then with its more immediate predecessors, and finally, having cleared them out of the way, to place the stress he wished on the councils of the early Church. In the process he found the usefulness even of the early councils considerably lessened, since, at least for the purposes of popular apology and controversy, the prestige of councils in general had been impaired and their authority rendered less trustworthy by the activities of the later councils.

Jewel's treatment of the Council of Trent, spread as it is over the writings of a decade, is anything but systematic.[18] It constitutes, however, an extremely detailed and indeed complete Anglican reply to the challenge of the Council. His basic indictment of Trent rested on the grounds, first, that it was not a true general council since it was far from being representative of the whole of Christendom, and second, that it was in no sense a free council but was instead a mere instrument of papal power entirely subservient to the pope.[19] Since it is composed only of Romanists it cannot represent all Christians. These man have "reserved the determination and whole judgment" to themselves; and themselves "are sworn to submit" their "whole judgment to the pope, and without his judgment to judge nothing."[20] "It is a madness to think that the Holy Ghost taketh his flight from a general council to run to Rome, to the end, . . . he may take counsel of some other spirit, I wot not what, that is better learned than himself."[21] Jewel could find no historical justification

---

[18] *The Epistle to Scipio* (Jewel, *Works*, IV, 1093–1126), printed and attributed to Jewel by Brent in his translation of Sarpi's history of the Council of Trent, is wholly concerned with Trent. Since its authorship cannot be finally proven, it should be studied only in conjunction with Jewel's acknowledged works. See above, pp. 22–23.

[19] Jewel, *Epistle to Scipio, Works*, IV, 1113, 1116; Harnack interprets the result of Trent as the triumph of the papal curia in the Church, in fact, if not in stated theory (Adolph Harnack, *History of Dogma*, 7 vols. London, 1896–1899, VII, 72 ff.).

[20] Jewel, *Defence, Works*, IV, 955.

[21] Jewel, *Apology, Works*, III, 94.

whatever for the papal dominance of the Council. In the early years of the Church, he declared, the bishop of Rome "had authority neither to summon councils, nor to be president or chief in councils, nor to ratify and confirm the decrees of councils, more than any other of the four patriarchs."[22] In those times the decrees of the councils could stand in force, "although the pope mislike them and allow them not."

The Council of Trent, as Jewel saw it, was more interested in protecting the vested interests of the Roman Church, and in particular the interests of the papacy, than it was in reforming the evils within the Church and in bringing its doctrine into closer conformity to the practices of the early Church.[23] "Let it be indifferently considered by the wise," he observed, "whether it be convenient that the pope, being notoriously accused of manifest corruption in God's religion, should nevertheless be the whole and only judge of the same, and pronounce sentence of himself. . . ."[24] Finally, Jewel insisted, Trent in the last analysis is but a travesty of a council. It is being used as the instrument of a Church which itself has openly declared against the final authority of councils. "When Luther made his first appeal from the pope . . . to a general council, they made him answer, that it was against the decree of pope Julius and pope Pius, that any appeal should be made from the pope to any council."[25]

Though his denunciation of Trent was uncompromising, Jewel acknowledged that much good could still come from a council. A council composed of devout and learned men could go far towards settling the many problems at issue between declared Christians. Nor was the authority of such an assembly to be scorned. But men must take care to distinguish between such a holy synod and a body which, calling itself a council, sets forth decrees and pronouncements clearly contrary to God's Word, acting always at the behest of authority other than its own.

As for our parts, we do not fear and fly, but desire and wish for a

[22] Jewel, *Reply, Works,* I, 413.
[23] Jewel, *Apology, Works,* III, 106.
[24] Jewel, *Defence, Works,* IV, 956.
[25] Jewel, *Sermons, Works,* II, 996.

council, so that it be free, honest, and Christian; so that men meet as the apostles did; so that abbats and bishops be freed from the constraint of that oath by which they are now bound to the popes; so that the whole conspiracy be dissolved; so that the men of our part may be temperately and freely heard, and not condemned without being heard; so that one man may not have power to overthrow and repeal whatsoever is done.[26]

Jewel's appeal is virtually a summary of the appeals the earlier reformers had made, beginning with Luther and including Cranmer and Calvin.[27] But the conditions had not been met in the crucial years before 1544. With the issuance of the Bull *Laetare Hierusalem,* and the initial meetings of the first session of the Council, it had become clear that the acceptance of the jurisdiction of Trent could only mean the acceptance of the papal supremacy. The rock upon which all movements toward unity had foundered remained an insuperable obstacle to a true ecumenical council.

Jewel's indictment of the Council of Constance, though not as detailed, was in every respect as vigorous and uncompromising. He condemned it both for its doctrinal pronouncements and for its treatment of the fourteenth-century reformers. Of the decrees of Constance he felt that the decree concerning Communion in both kinds provided ample evidence of untrustworthiness. The Council, in declaring Communion in both kinds for the laity to be schismatical, "pronounced openly, against Christ himself and all the primitive church."[28] Concerning its action in regard to Huss and Wycliffe, he declared that although "John Wicliffe, John Huss, Valdo, and the rest, for ought we know, and . . . setting malice aside, for ought you know . . . were godly men,"[29] yet, this council burned John Huss, "contrary to the emperor's safe-conduct and their own special promise; and, contrary to all humanity and sense of nature," dug up and burned "the body of John Wicliffe forty years after he had been buried."[30]

[26] Jewel, *Epistle to Scipio, Works,* IV, 1122.

[27] See John T. McNeill, *Unitive Protestantism* (New York, 1930), 101–102, 229–232, 111–112.

[28] Jewel, *Reply to Cole, Works,* I, 28; *cf.* Calvin, *Institutes,* IV, ix, XIV.

[29] Jewel, *Defence, Works,* III, 161.

[30] *Ibid.,* III, 163; *cf.* Melanchthon's appendix to the Schmalkaldic Articles (cited in McNeill, *Unitive Protestantism,* p. 109).

The earlier medieval councils, including the Lateran Council of 1215, are mentioned by Jewel only to receive the same cavalier treatment. Even as early as the eighth century, he declared, a council was capable of actions and pronouncements demonstrably false and contrary to the spirit of the Gospel. "Let no man beguile thee by the colour of councils," he adjured his reader; consider the second Council of Nicaea,[31] "read this second Nicene council throughout, if thou be able. Thou wilt say, there was never any assembly of Christian bishops so vain, so peevish, so wicked, so blasphemous, so unworthy in all respects to be called a council." The blasphemy of these "blessed bishops" was so great that they "there agreed together with one consent, that images in churches are not only to be allowed, but also devoutly and reverently to be honoured, and that with the same honour that is due to God himself."[32]

From the later councils Jewel turned back to the councils of the first six hundred years of the Church. Only these, and especially the ecumenical councils, were worthy in his eyes of consideration as valid authority. They alone of the councils represented the true tradition of the early Church. Since they were more nearly contemporaneous with the age of the apostles, with the great period of divine revelation, they were more likely to have understood the meaning of that revelation. "Whensoever contrariety in sentence is found in the acts of councils, let the sentence of that council be taken that hath the elder and better authority."[33] The conception is a corollary of Jewel's denial of the continuance of special revelation either to individuals or to institutions. If the Roman Church continued to receive special revelations through the centuries, then the Council of the Church in the year 1563 was of equal authority with the first Council of Nicaea. Jewel's denial that the grace which alone can insure a complete and absolute understanding of the original revelation had been given to any institution in perpetuity, destroyed

[31] The seventh ecumenical council was held at Nicaea in 787.

[32] Jewel, *Defence, Works*, IV, 792.

[33] Jewel, *Reply, Works*, I, 233.

the element of timelessness and forced him always to move closer to the apostolic age for authority.

In view of the favorable nature of his references to the early councils in his lengthy discussions of Trent and its immediate predecessors we would expect Jewel to make full use of the decrees of the early councils as authority for doctrine. As a matter of fact, however, his use of them is almost entirely negative. While he consistently emphasizes the agreement between the teachings of the Church of England and the early councils, the agreement stressed is usually of a general sort. For instance, he stated categorically that nothing could be alleged against the Church of England out of the first four councils while much could be cited from them expressedly against the teachings of Rome;[34] that the Church of England has "restored again, so much as in us lie, the decrees and canons of the ancient councils."[35] From this stand he never departed, but in proving points of doctrine he rarely relied upon conciliar authority. When we consider the great length of his works and his tendency at every turn to overwhelm the reader with patristic references and quotations ad infinitum, we cannot but be impressed by the small number of references made to specific conciliar decrees. With very few exceptions[36] his use of conciliar authority in positive proof is confined entirely to the problem of papal power in the early Church. Here he makes ample use of citations from the decrees of the first Council of Nicaea, the first Council of Constantinople, the Council of Chalcedon, and even from the decrees of the second Council of Constantinople, which was the fifth ecumenical council,[37] to show that the great metropolitan sees of Antioch, Alexandria, and Constantinople were equal

[34] Jewel, *Defence, Works,* III, 225.

[35] *Ibid.,* IV, 1054.

[36] The Council of Nicaea, quoted in proof of his interpretation of the nature of the sacramental bread and wine (*ibid.,* III, 592), and the second Council of Constantinople, quoted against a priest's putting away his wife (*ibid.,* III, 404).

[37] Since this council falls within the dates set by Jewel in his challenge, he tends to consider it in the same category with the first four councils to which he more frequently refers.

in authority to the see of Rome, and at the same time to stress the supremacy of the civil magistrate in the person of the emperor over both the councils and the patriarchs. While even these points are to a great extent negative, in that their primary purpose is to deny the papal supremacy, their positive side is of importance in the obvious implications they carry, first for the position of the metropolitan see of Canterbury, and secondly for the ecclesiastical jurisdiction of the king of England.

There were several reasons for Jewel's apparent slighting of conciliar authority. Although he hardly conforms to our concept of a popular publicist, Jewel always wrote with the layman in mind, and the layman could not be depended upon to keep clear the distinction between the authority of the early councils and the authority of councils in general. It was natural to expect confusion to arise. The Roman controversialists admitted no such distinction and endeavored to extend the authority of the councils that their opponents admitted to councils in general, and from there to the later councils which were so unquestionably on their side. It was because of this that Jewel always referred to the *early* councils, to the *first four* councils, with the care of the legalist for the qualifying phrase.

More important than the possibility of confusing authorities was a problem inherent in the very nature of the decrees and pronouncements of the councils themselves. Like the Scriptures, the first four councils were a heritage claimed by both the Church of Rome and the Church of England, of such a nature that depending upon the interpretation accorded them, they provided each with a solid basis for doctrine. Thus, while the decrees and pronouncements of the early councils were an essential part of the tradition and custom of the early Church, and, as such, possessed of complete validity as authority for scriptural interpretation, they simply did not go far enough. Like the Scriptures themselves, they at times needed implementing and interpreting. As they stood, they did not provide those who were not of the Roman Communion with sufficient authority for doctrine held in clear contradistinction to the doctrine of the Roman Church. It is primarily for this reason that Jewel appealed so rarely to conciliar authority.

Chapter IX

The Element of Rationalism
in Jewel's Thought

Before undertaking a systematic study of Jewel's solution to the problem of doctrinal authority we must consider a broader question, the extent and importance of the part that reason played in his thought. If Jewel is in truth the precursor of Hooker, we should expect to find at least elements of rationalism in his work. But a word of caution is necessary here. Jewel was faced with an extremely difficult problem. He was writing with two major groups in mind, those who were accustomed to the traditional and conservative authority of the institutional Church and those who in revolt against Rome had come to stress the complete sufficiency of biblical authority. To neither group would the authority of reason have been acceptable. Thus the appeal to reason is generally implicit rather than explicit in his writings. It is nonetheless there, an important element in his thought and of vital significance when viewed in the light of its subsequent development by Hooker.

The nineteenth-century historian of rationalism, H. T. Buckle, in emphasizing the rationalism of Hooker, contrasted him specifically with Jewel, making a distinction between the views of the two Anglican apologists which does grave injustice to Jewel and suggests an interpretation of Hooker equally fallacious. Buckle was highly critical of Jewel's innumerable citations from patristic writers "whose mere assertions, when they are uncontradicted by scriptures, he seems to regard as positive proof. . . . Jewel inculcates the importance of faith; Hooker insists upon the exercise of reason."[1]

Buckle ignored the reasonable element in Jewel's appeal to patristic authority and at the same time stressed the appeal to reason in Hooker to the exclusion of his appeal to tradition. There is, admittedly, a great difference in the points of view of Jewel and Hooker, but it is a difference in degree, not an absolute difference between one extreme of faith in authority and the other extreme of complete reliance upon reason. Because of his emphasis upon reason, historians have tended to think of Hooker in terms of seventeenth-century rationalism. Hooker, though, was very much of his own century, far closer to the climate of thought of the Reformation than he was to the age of Descartes. It is essential that this be recognized, that the rationalism of Hooker be understood in proper perspective before we can assess the significance and indeed the very nature of Jewel's contribution. To define rationalism in terms acceptable to the seventeenth-century philosophers would be to proscribe its use altogether in reference to Jewel. To define it in terms acceptable to Hooker, however, will allow it to be used with justice in an analysis of Jewel.

The rationalism of Hooker was a qualified rationalism. He did not dispense with revelation to replace it with reason. Like the reformers before him, he accepted Christian revelation as the primary basis of authority; but his chief interpretative authority was reason, and he insisted furthermore that it be regarded as a valid supplementary authority.

It was his intention to free the Church from the domination of the literal scriptural word. In order to do this he did not find it necessary to lower the authority of divine revelation. Revelation he declared to be perfect for the end for which God had intended it, that is, for salvation.[2] Concerning those things which relate to that end men must trust to revealed authority. The essentials necessary for salvation, those teachings requiring "the religious assent of

---

[1] H. T. Buckle, *History of Civilization in England,* 2 vols. (London, 1857–1861), I, 313.

[2] Hooker, *Works,* II, viii, 5; III, viii, 10.

Christian belief,"[3] must be shown from the Scriptures. Anything less fundamental than these bare essentials, however, he accepted upon an authority "grounded upon other assurances than Scripture,"[4] as long as it was not contrary to the manifest scriptural teachings. Thus the limitation which Hooker placed upon the authority of revelation was a limitation in extent and not in any sense a limitation in degree.

In such a conception there is great need for further authority, first to interpret revelation concerning those matters for which it was perfect authority, and secondly to make clear those matters that God had not seen fit to make final and absolute in the Scriptures. For Hooker interpretative authority and the supplementary authority for matters not dealt with by scriptural law were the same, the reason given to men by God. He accused Rome of having denied the sufficiency of scriptural authority for the ends for which God had created it. The Puritans also, he felt, had erred greatly in extending the meaning and the uses of revelation beyond God's intentions. And both had erred grievously in that each, in their own manner, had done away with the natural law and the reason that was the gift of God.[5]

Hooker thus denied the absolute authority of the institution of the Roman Church and at the same time refused to admit the absolute clarity and the limitless scope of scriptural authority. Nor did he accept the authority of special inspiration either in its extreme individualistic form or in the authoritative form of Calvinism. While he granted that man was helpless without the aid of the Holy Spirit,[6] he denied man's dependence upon visions. The proper channel for divine guidance was man's reason. At the same time Hooker insisted that the authority of reason was not to be regarded as an individual matter. The anarchy and chaos which he feared as the result of unchecked individual inspiration might just as easily result, as Professor Jordan has pointed out, from the full

---

[3] *Ibid.,* II, v, 3.
[4] *Ibid.,* II, v, 1.
[5] *Ibid.,* II, viii, 6–7.
[6] *Ibid.,* I, viii, 11; III, viii, 18.

liberty of personal interpretation based upon reason.[7] Reason had not been given merely to one or two in the manner of a special revelation. It was the common possession of mankind. Hence the reason to which Hooker turned for authority was a collective reason both in time and in place. "The general and perpetual voice of men," he wrote, "is as the sentence of God himself."[8]

By the "general and perpetual voice of men" Hooker meant the traditions of Christian teaching in the past and the agreement of reasonable men in the present. Concerning tradition, however, he was quick to point out that it was not to be considered authoritative as a "part of supernatural necessary truth."[9] Insofar as it represented the reasoned judgments of the wise men in the past it was of inestimable value toward the further understanding of God's Word. It was not authoritative in the sense of being infallible. Hooker asked that the teachings of the Church be capable of demonstration and that their acceptance be based not upon their infallibility but upon their demonstrability.

In the present "the universal consent of men"[10] could best be found in some collective body. Hooker "appears to have believed that the rational decision of Parliament and Convocation on a religious issue was considerably more likely to be in accord with the will of God than the inspiration of the most saintly individual,"[11] or indeed of the reasoned judgment of an individual. Such authority, however, was neither final, complete, nor continuing. The group or institution was right only insofar as its decisions were rationally sound. It had no intrinsic claim to authority. The underlying test of doctrinal teachings was their reasonable demonstrability and the recognition of their rightness by rational men.

In the end Hooker's solution is incomplete. And indeed, it must necessarily have been. Conceivably we might predicate finality upon the authority of reason when it is provided that none but the most

[7] W. K. Jordan, *The Development of Religious Toleration in England,* 4 vols. (Cambridge, 1932–1940), I, 231.

[8] Hooker, *Works,* I, viii, 3.

[9] *Ibid.,* I, xiv, 5.

[10] *Ibid.,* I, viii, 3.

[11] Jordan, *Toleration,* I, 226.

rational of men, indeed men wholly rational, may make the final pronouncements. But that can hardly be. Therefore we are forced to conclude that where reason is the test, finality and absolute completeness can never exist, men being men and capable of error. Hooker was well aware of this. He did not expect to find "proof infallible."[12] Thus he may be said to have returned to a position comparable to that of the early humanists. It was, as the humanists had found, a position difficult to support in a world where men demanded absolute certainty in divine matters. Yet Hooker was willing to rest upon such a position. His was a demand that truth be sought, not a claim that truth had been found; it was a faith in the method and a hope in the eventual attainment of success in the search, not a statement of the finality of results already attained. For Hooker, faith is no longer an easy acceptance of certainty. Faith is rather a belief in the capacity of the human reason to strive toward and eventually to attain an understanding of God's will.

When we examine the element of rationalism in Jewel's thought we are struck with the extent to which he anticipated the views of his protégé. Even less than Hooker was he the rationalist according to Cartesian standards. He was a man of religion primarily concerned with religious problems, with the Bible, with patristic literature, with the Church. He accepted the traditional Christian view that man was helpless without the aid of divine grace. He studied and did his thinking entirely within the framework of divine revelation. But the alternative to Cartesian rationalism, as in the case of Hooker, need not be the unquestioned and virtually anti-rational faith of Loyola or Luther. Rationalism as we find it in Jewel is Christian rationalism, but it is rationalism nonetheless. Jewel's work, like Hooker's, is based on the premise that reason is to be used in man's effort to comprehend the will of God.

That human beings are reasonable, that the human mind is capable of recognizing the truth when confronted with it, is a basic assumption of Jewel's. He believed that if all the evidence concerning a problem were clearly set forth, if all sides of a question were presented without color or prejudice, the normally intelligent man

[12] Hooker, *Works*, II, vii, 5.

would be able to judge and to choose the right. The advocate had but to present his case in full.[13] In his preface to the *Defence of the Apology* he declared:

> I cannot imagine that any my poor labours shall be able to end these quarrels;—Notwithstanding in this augmentation I have endeavoured, for my simple part, to say so much as to a reasonable man may seem sufficient. I have cleared such places as seemed dark: I have supplied such things as seemed to want: I have reformed so much as reason required: briefly, I have answered the substance of all M. Harding's long discourses. . . .
>
> May it please thee, good christian reader, to peruse both, and to judge uprightly. Endeavor thoroughly to know the cause. An ignorant judge was never indifferent.[14]

Such a view reflects Jewel's fundamental humanism. He himself was reasonable and gentle. If a cause were right he would prefer to persuade men to it rather than coerce them. " 'Forced faith is no faith,' " since " 'faith may not be compulsed by force or rigour, but gently brought in by persuasion.' "[15] Christ himself preached to the people and instructed them. It was not God's will that men should be harried and driven to faith, but rather that they should be led and persuaded to it.

In his early controversy with Dr. Cole, Jewel censured the Romanists for having chosen as the grounds of their "persuasion" during the six years of Mary's reign the force of law rather than " 'scriptures and reasoning.' "[16] In the *Apology* he condemned them bitterly in that "fire and sword they have had always ready at hand. . . . They did surely against all reason to begin first with these so bloody and extreme means, if they could have found other

---

[13] In his great controversial works, Jewel quoted a large portion of his opponent's work, confident that his own arguments and the weight of the evidence presented in their support would convince the reader. It is significant that Bishop Parkhurst, Jewel's old tutor, was so doubtful of the safety of the method, so lacking in Jewel's confidence in the judgment of his readers, that only after considerable protest was he persuaded to comply with Parker's ruling that the *Defence of the Apology* be placed in the parish churches (Parker, *Correspondence*, p. 416, n. 2).

[14] Jewel, *Defence, Works*, III, 136.

[15] Jewel, *Sermons, Works*, II, 1023.

[16] Jewel, *Reply to Cole, Works*, I, 45.

more easy and gentle ways."[17] With the Marian persecutions fresh in the minds of his readers, Jewel vigorously underlined the contrast between the policy of persecution which had become associated with the Rome of Paul IV, and the policy of Queen Elizabeth in the first decade of her reign. It is our policy, he wrote of the Church of England, to

allure the people to read and to hear God's word: they drive the people from it. We desire to have our cause known to all the world: they flee to come to any trial. We lean unto knowledge; they unto ignorance. We trust unto light; they unto darkness. We reverence, as it becometh us, the writings of the apostles and prophets; and they burn them. Finally, we in God's cause desire to stand to God's only judgment: they will stand only to their own. Wherefore, if they will weigh all these things with a quiet mind, and fully bent to hear and to learn, they will . . . join of their own accord to our side.[18]

It is a noble statement, an ideal which, when followed even in part, did much toward bringing into the Anglican fold the great army of waverers whom Jewel had always in mind. The Anglican Church under Elizabeth was in fact an essentially reasonable and moderate

---

[17] Jewel, *Apology, Works,* III, 86.

[18] *Ibid.,* III, 92–93. *Cf.* J. W. Allen, *A History of Political Thought in the Sixteenth Century* (London, 1928), 71 and n. 2: "To be convinced that you are right is one thing; to believe that no honest and reasonable person can disagree with you is quite another. . . . All the later Calvinists took the same view." The reference for the latter part of this statement is Jewel's preface to the *Defence of the Apology,* specifically the following passage: "God in these days," wrote Jewel, "hath so amazed the adversaries of His Gospel and hath caused them so openly and grossly to lay abroad their follies to the sight of all the world, that no man now, be he never so ignorant, can think he may justly be excused" for not seeing the truth.

Out of context the passage seems to indict Jewel for the intolerance which Allen decries. But in fact Jewel's "intolerance" is of an altogether different order. The "follies" for which he damns the Roman controversialists and which he believes invalidate their work, are their continual citations of evidence which Jewel declared had long since been buried and forsaken as valid by their own scholars. Harding, for instance, had in all seriousness cited the *Donation of Constantine* in proof of the papal supremacy. Surely it would be an odd kind of toleration which would demand the acceptance of such evidence. Jewel made no blanket claim that every one who disagreed with him was either dishonest or ignorant. He did feel that on the specific questions at issue he was on sound historical ground and he believed that on the strength of the evidence he presented he could demonstrate that his opponents were wrong.

establishment, less unyielding in its demand for ecclesiastical obedience than the Church of Rome, less committed to "the task of securing the conformity of men's thoughts and conduct"[19] than the Church of Geneva.

Jewel's insistence upon reasonable persuasion and a rational approach to authority extended to all of his interpretative authorities. He would not follow blindly even the fathers of the Church, whom he so deeply reverenced and to whom he consistently turned, but only as they were able to persuade their readers of the rightness of their teachings. To support this view he cited the fathers themselves, noting that they had never claimed unqualified and absolute authority, but reserved it for the scriptural writings alone. They expected to be accepted only insofar as they were able to convince their hearers of the reasonableness of their interpretations. As Augustine himself had written: " 'Other writers or fathers,' besides the holy scriptures, 'I read in this sort, that, be their learning or holiness never so great, I will not think it true because they have thought so, but because they are able to persuade me so, either by other canonical writers, or else by some likely reason.' " And these writings " 'must be read, not with the necessity to believe each thing, but with the liberty to judge each thing.' "[20]

Logically, if men are to be free to judge, they must have freedom to examine the evidence, to seek the truth where it is to be found. In words which foreshadow the eloquence of John Milton, Jewel argued for the absolute necessity of free inquiry:

> Unless thou know, thou canst not judge: unless thou hear both sides, thou canst not know. If thou like ought, know why thou likest it. A wise man in each thing will search the cause. . . .
>
> Say not thou art settled in thy belief, before thou know it. Vain faith is no faith. . . . 'Fond faith is hurtful, and doth no good.' . . . Let reason lead thee: let authority move thee: let truth enforce thee.[21]

Deprive men of knowledge, Jewel declared, and you inevitably lay the foundations for error and heresy, since ignorance rather than

---

[19] A. M. Hunter, *The Teaching of Calvin* (London, 1950), p. 223.

[20] Jewel, *Defence, Works,* III, 227.

[21] *Ibid.,* III, 122–123.

knowledge is to be found at the root of all heresy.[22] The heretic seeks to keep closed the doors of learning, knowing well that when the doors are opened the people will forsake him. He prefers darkness and concealment, aware that the better the error of idolatry be known and understood the easier it can be condemned and destroyed.[23] "As learning is dangerous and hurtful without religion, so is religion unable to defend itself, and to convince the gainsayers, without learning."[24] Because the enemies of religion recognize this truth they have always been the enemies of learning. In every age it has been the policy of evil and ungodly rulers to "practice cruelty upon learned men;" they have ever "utterly hated all manner of learning," for they know that "if learning decay, it is likely that religion cannot abide."[25]

Jewel was deeply concerned over the state of education and of educational institutions in the early years of the reign. Repeatedly in his sermons he returned to the charge that their decay in the previous reign and the failure of the present leaders to take steps to improve conditions constitued the gravest of threats to the new Establishment.[26] Although the end he hoped for and expected was a particular one, indeed thoroughly partisan, he had faith enough in the rightness of his position to trust the free inquiry which must result from the full development of the universities. In the best tradition of the humanism in which he had been trained he declared that only through the promotion of sound learning, in the training of men in good letters and study to increase knowledge can ignorance and its resulting heresies be destroyed.[27]

[22] *Ibid.*, IV, 1039.

[23] *Ibid.*, IV, 1075.

[24] Jewel, *Sermons, Works*, II, 980–981.

[25] *Ibid.*, II, 1011.

[26] Many of these sermons were delivered at Court before the very people whom he indicted. Of the first five sermons in Garbrand's edition of 1583 (*Works*, II, 968–1034), Sermons III, IV, and V, to judge from their references to the Queen, were preached in her presence. Of the first two in the edition, Sermon I was a Paul's Cross sermon (J. A. Froude, *History of England from the Fall of Wolsey to the Defeat of the Spanish Armada: The Reign of Elizabeth*, 5 vols., New York, 1912, II, 344, n. 1), and Sermon II was preached before the Court, although probably not in the presence of the Queen, judging again from the references to her.

[27] Jewel, *Sermons, Works*, II, 1011.

When we stress the element of rationalism in Jewel's thought it is essential to remember an important qualification made earlier. Reason, as he used the term, explictly was not the natural reason of the Enlightenment. It does not stand alone. Truth, the objective of reason, by definition Christian truth, cannot be reached independently of divine revelation. Here Jewel differed not at all from the main stream of Christian tradition, Roman and Protestant alike. The mysteries of God were beyond nature, they were beyond the powers of natural reason to realize. "God is omnipotent, and his power infinite: ye may not make him thrall and subject to your senses. That were natural reason: that were infidelity."[28] Reason, independent of all revelation, cannot be trusted. And, Jewel added, when reason is used to contradict the manifest word of God, when it is " 'alleged against the authority of the holy scriptures, be it never so subtle, it beguileth men by a likeness or colour of the truth; for truth it cannot be.' "[29]

Such a statement reads like a veritable manifesto against rationalism, proof surely of the wide gulf that separates the Bishop of Salisbury from Richard Hooker. Yet on this point, as a matter of fact, there would have been little or no disagreement between the two men. Neither could accept pure rationalism. They were Christian thinkers concerned above all with understanding the revealed will of God. Reason was of value as an independent authority only for those areas not included or made clear in revelation. In those areas "nature of herself is oftentimes able to discern between truth and falsehood."[30] Here, of course, Jewel placed greater dependence than did Hooker upon the tradition of the early Church. He differs at this point, however, only in degree. Hooker likewise appealed to the authority of tradition, but he stressed it less than did Jewel and made a much stronger appeal to reason.

All of this, of course, has to do with the very limited area which is not covered by scriptural authority. In regard to scriptural authority itself reason also played an important role. In the interpretation

[28] Jewel, *Defence, Works*, III, 260.
[29] Jewel, *Reply, Works*, I, 378.
[30] Jewel, *Defence, Works*, III, 198.

of the Scriptures, in the process by which men seek an understanding of God's will through their study and the study of the great interpretative authorities, reason is a primary instrument. "Natural reason, holden within her bands," which is revelation, "is not the enemy, but the daughter of God's truth."[31] It is the function of reason to recognize the revelation of God and to seek there the understanding of the truth. That is God's will. God "has given us reason to see what is good," and the "will to seek after that which is good."[32]

Careful as Jewel was to point out the limitations of reason, it nevertheless occupies a central position in his thought. Every aspect of his approach to the problem of authority, the presentation of his case, and the examination both of the original authority of revelation and of the various authorities for interpretation, presupposes the use of the human reason.

[31] Jewel, *Reply, Works*, I, 500.
[32] Jewel, *Exposition on Thessalonians, Works*, II, 885.

Chapter X

The Authority of the Bible

When the reformers took their stand upon the principle that the Bible was the sole source of authority, they were faced with a series of fundamental though derivative questions: How could they authenticate the Scriptures as the Word of God, that is, how could they prove the ultimate divinity of the Bible? They then had to decide what in fact constituted the Bible. This, of course, was the problem of the canon. Thirdly, there was the question of the extent and scope of scriptural authority, whether it should be limited to doctrines necessary for salvation or whether it should be extended beyond them to cover the more mundane aspects of life. In addition there was the question of the reading of the Scriptures, the way in which the Word was related to the actual words of the Bible. And finally and most important of all there was the question of the meaning of the Word, the question of interpretation.

All of these were questions of authority, questions that the reformers could hardly claim had been answered by their initial opposition of the Bible to the Church. They had still to face the fact that for each of these questions the authority of the Church provided an answer extremely effective and most difficult to counter. The Church taught that it alone could authenticate the Bible as the Word of God, that it was the sole judge of the canon, of the extent and scope of scriptural authority, of the relation of the Word to the words, and above all, that it provided the only satisfactory authority for interpretation.

The Roman solution to the question of the authentication of the Scriptures as the Word of God lent credence to the charge of the reformers that Rome placed the authority of the Church before that of the Scriptures. Their answer to Rome was of course an un-equivocal denial of the Roman position. If further answer were needed they could point out as did Calvin that it was obviously not possible to have things both ways: if the Church provided the final authentication for the Scriptures then the Church could hardly claim to prove its own authority from the Scriptures. Either it was the primary authority or the Scriptures were the primary authority. This in the end had to be the final answer for all the reformers. The Scriptures, as the primary and sole revelation of God, must be self-authenticating.

Jewel considered this to be so obvious that he virtually ignored the existence of the question. His creedal statement in the *Apology* concerning their final authority is positive and unqualified, but their authenticity is taken for granted, apparently needing no argument or proof.[1] It is significant that Harding, in his confutation of the *Apology,* at this point, instead of raising the broader question, confined his discussion to the subject of the canonicity of specific books. It was Jewel himself rather than the Roman Catholic who stated the Roman counterview, quoting Eck that " 'the scriptures of God are not authentical or of credit but only by the warrant and authority of the church,' "[2] as if the absurdity of such a statement was obvious to all, obvious even to Harding.

Since Harding apparently preferred to argue the second question, the question of the canon, Jewel from necessity had to develop his answer to it at greater length. In the *Apology* he had stated that "we receive and embrace all the canonical scriptures, both of the Old and New Testament, giving thanks to our God, who hath raised up unto us that light which we might ever have before our eyes."[3] Harding, in his attack on the *Apology,* inevitably confronted Jewel with the old question: "What authority have you to stay yourself by concerning these (books), but only that of the church?"[4] Jewel's answer is definite. "We embrace and reverence every parcel and

---

[1] Jewel, *Apology, Works,* III, 62.

[2] Jewel, *Defence, Works,* III, 247.

[3] Jewel, *Apology, Works,* III, 62.

[4] Thomas Harding, *A confutation of a book intituled An apologie of the Church of England* (Antwerp, 1565), p. 84a; in *Defence, Works,* III, 431.

tittle of the scriptures without exception, not refusing any part thereof that hath been allowed by the ancient catholic fathers of the church of God."[5] Concerning those books which all Christians considered uncanonical, on which, in short, there was general agreement, he felt that the question need not be raised at all. According to Eusebius in his *Ecclesiastical History* the so-called "gospels of Thomas, Bartholomew, Nicodeme, and such others, . . . were wickedly and falsely counterfeited under their names by sundry heretics." The problem of the true and false writings had been solved by the early fathers of the Church for all time. Eusebius had denied the supposed gospel of St. Peter, saying: "We receive Peter and the rest of the apostles as we would receive Christ himself. But counterfeit writings (under their names) we refuse utterly, as having understanding of their sense and meaning; knowing well that we have received no such things delivered by the apostles." "Thus," Jewel concluded, "had the church of God the Spirit of wisdom, whereby to discern the true scriptures from the false."[6]

In the *Institutes* Calvin had considered the question of the canon only in relation to the broader question of authentication. With his customary directness he stated the Roman question in his own terms:

> Who can assure us that God is the author of them? . . . Who can persuade us that this book ought to be received with reverence, and that expunged from the sacred number, unless all these things were regulated by the decisions of the Church? It depends, therefore (say they,) on the determination of the Church, to decide both what reverence is due to the Scripture, and what books are to be comprised in its canon.[7]

Calvin first counters the question with his own question: if it is true, as the Church claims, that it derives its origin from the

[5] Jewel, *Defence, Works,* III, 431.

[6] *Ibid.,* 441–442; *cf.* Article VI of the Thirty-nine Articles of 1571: "In the name of holy Scripture, we do vnderstande those Canonicall bookes of the olde and newe Testament, of whose aucthoritie was neuer any doubt in the Churche." And, concerning the New Testament: "All the bookes of the newe Testament, as they are commonly receaued, we do receaue. . . ." (Philip Schaff, *The Creeds of Christendom,* 3 vols., New York, 1919, III, 489–490).

[7] Calvin, *Institutes,* I, vii, I.

Scriptures, then how can the Church act as a judge between the parts of the Scriptures?[8] Since, to Calvin, this question is unanswerable, he turns to the development of his own positive and fundamental thesis of the authority of the whole Scriptures: the Scripture is self-authenticating, it "exhibits the plainest evidences that it is God who speaks in it, which manifests its doctrine to be divine. And we shall soon see, that all the books of the sacred Scripture very far excel all other writings."[9] Finally, the Scripture "obtains the credit which it deserves with us by the testimony of the Spirit."[10] Later in the *Institutes*, Calvin refers to the Romanist claim that Augustine accepted the canonicity of II Maccabees on the authority of the Church and denies the claim, citing Augustine himself to the contrary and adding evidence from Jerome and "Cyprian" against the canonicity of the book.[11]

In his confutation of the *Apology*, Harding repeated the contention concerning Augustine to which Calvin had referred and Jewel refuted it as Calvin had done, though in somewhat greater detail.[12] The parallel between the passages and the inclusion by Jewel of Calvin's specific authorities suggests an identity of views. Certainly Jewel was in full agreement with Calvin that patristic authority could not be twisted to support either the authority of the Church or the canonicity of II Maccabees. But Calvin's conclusion is a negative one and Jewel's positive, insofar as his use of patristic authority is concerned. "Here (*Institutes* I, vii–ix) there is no indication that a separate canonical problem exists for Calvin. That

[8] *Ibid.*, I, vii, II.

[9] *Ibid.*, I, vii, IV.

[10] *Ibid.*, I, vii, V; *cf.* Article IV of the Gallican Confession of 1559: "We know these books to be canonical, and the sure rule of our faith, not so much by the common accord and consent of the Church, as by the testimony and inward illumination of the Holy Spirit which enables us to distinguish them from other ecclesiastical books upon which, however useful, we can not found any articles of faith" (Schaff, *Creeds*, III, 361). Other Reformed Confessions, including the Scotch of 1560 (Schaff, *Creeds*, III, 460–464), the Belgic of 1561 (Schaff, *Creeds*, III, 386–387), and the Second Helvetic of 1562 (Schaff, *Creeds*, III, 237), also clearly represent Calvin's viewpoint, as the Thirty-nine Articles, in contrast, express a point of view much closer to that of Jewel. See also, Kraeling, *Old Testament*, pp. 35 ff.

[11] Calvin, *Institutes*, III, v, VIII.

[12] Jewel, *Defence, Works*, III, 431–432.

is, he is under no compulsion to *construct* a canon, let us say on historico-critical grounds, nor even to defend the existing canon so far as its accepted composition was concerned."[13] Jewel's repeated citations from the examples of the early Church and the fathers, even his stress upon the possession of the Spirit by the early Church, does not prove that he rejected Calvin's view, to replace it with an alternate view. But it suggests, at least, that he felt the need for a more measurable and demonstrable authority in the determination of the canon.

As Jewel took up the questions, from the initial problem of authentication to the final problem of interpretation, he developed his answers at greater length, devoting more time to each than he had to all of the preceding questions, as if the earlier ones hardly needed proof and the later ones demanded fuller proof and more extended development. Consequently, as he proceeds, his own position becomes increasingly clear. Thus it is with the question of the extent and scope of scriptural authority. In his declaration of belief in the *Apology,* he stated his understanding of the meaning of biblical authority. The Scriptures

be the heavenly voices, whereby God hath opened unto us his will; . . . in them be abundantly and fully comprehended all things, whatsoever be needful for our salvation, . . . they be the very might and strength of God to attain to salvation; . . . the foundations of the prophets and apostles, whereupon is built the church of God; . . . the very sure and infallible rule, whereby may be tried, whether the church doth stagger, or err, and whereunto all ecclesiastical doctrine ought to be called to account.[14]

While he thus clearly places the authority of the Scriptures above

---

[13] E. A. Dowey, Jr., *The Knowledge of God in Calvin's Theology* (New York, 1952), p. 118. Calvin, despite the magnificent orderliness of his thought and the clarity of his expression, at times seems to be subjected to as many and as diverse interpretations as the Scriptures themselves. On the question of the canon, Davies (*Problem of Authority*, p. 143 ff.) states that "Calvin, then, did not think of the Holy Spirit's inner testimony as fixing the canon." Dowey reviews the evidence from both the *Institutes* and the *Commentaries*, together with much of the literature on the subject of Calvin and the canon, and concludes (p. 122) that "it is in the correlation of word and Spirit that the Biblical canon has its existence."

[14] Jewel, *Apology, Works,* III, 62.

all other authorities, he has at the same time defined the extent and scope of their authority with considerable precision. Of particular significance is his use of the word "comprehend," that in the Scriptures all things be "fully comprehended" which are "needful for our salvation." "Comprehended" made its first appearance not as Jewel's word but as Lady Bacon's in the official translation of the Latin *Apology*. Jewel had used the word "continere." The fact that it was translated in a particular way in the official edition does not indicate necessarily that Jewel fully accepted it.[15] In quoting the passage in *The Defence of the Apology*,[16] however, he himself used the translation "comprehended" in preference to several other possible and more literal translations, especially "contained." This is of particular importance when we remember the distinction which Hooker later made between the two words, "contained" and "comprehended" in his discussion of the same problem. Hooker stated specifically that all the essentials of salvation were not to be found *contained* in the Scriptures in the sense that they "do import setting down in plain terms." They are rather *comprehended* "in such sort that by reason we may from thence conclude all things which are necessary."[17]

Hooker, of course, was writing with the Puritans in mind, combating their insistence upon literal interpretation of the Scriptures. Jewel faced no such problem. In neither the *Apology* nor *The Defence of the Apology* was the possible challenge of Puritanism to the English Church recognized at all. Jewel's concern was entirely with the threat from Rome. Yet he reached a conclusion almost identical with that of Hooker. Hooker's insertion of the word "reason" was a step which Jewel presupposed if he did not take. Hooker merely implemented Jewel's solution.

So far we have been concerned with the idea of comprehension. The second half of the phrase is just as important. In the Scriptures are "comprehended all things, whatsoever be needful for our salva-

---

[15] Jewel often made changes in quoting the original translation, though rarely important ones.

[16] Jewel, *Defence*, *Works*, III, 429 and ns. 15 and 19. In quoting this particular passage, Jewel made several changes in the interest either of style or of scholarly accuracy.

[17] Hooker, *Works*, I, xiv, 2.

tion." A clear distinction is to be made here between comprehending "whatsoever be needful for our salvation," and the comprehension of "all doctrine." The Scriptures are rather the rule, the *certissimam normam*,[18] "whereby all truth and catholic doctrine may be proved, and all heresy may be disproved and confuted."[19] That Jewel had this distinction, this measure of comprehension, clearly in mind is shown by a later passage in *The Defence of the Apology:* "We know well enough that the same word which was opened by Christ, and spread abroad by the apostles, is sufficient both to our salvation, and also to uphold and maintain all truth, and to confound all manner of heresy."[20]

All truth, by which is meant sound doctrine as opposed to heresy, is not necessarily contained in the Scriptures. Although the Scriptures are the basis of truth, the ultimate test of the truth, the letter of the Scriptures is not the limit of the truth.[21] The essentials of salvation are comprehended in the Scriptures, but the way is left open for the development of those things not essential to salvation, with scriptural authority, it is true, but of a nature which might be called derivative, and possessed of a freedom denied the essentials themselves.[22]

As for the essentials of doctrine, it was certain, Jewel stated, that in the early days of the Church the fathers and bishops had "no doubt but that our religion might be proved out of the holy scrip-

---

[18] Jewel, *Apologia, Works,* III, 12.

[19] Jewel, *Apology, Works,* III, 62.

[20] Jewel, *Defence, Works,* III, 601.

[21] See below, p. 154.

[22] That this is not the extension of the meaning of a merely incidental passage beyond its original intent is proved, I believe, by the peculiar history of the passage itself. In the Latin *Apology,* in its original form, it reads: "Nos quidem illud verbum quod a Christo patefactum, et ab apostolis propagatum est, scimus et ad salutem nostram, et ad omnem veritatem propugnandam, et ad omnem haeresim convincendam esse satis" (*Works,* III, 16).

In the official translation of the *Apology,* the passage reads: "We know well enough that the same word which was opened by Christ, and spread abroad by the apostles, is sufficient, both our salvation and all truth to uphold and maintain, and also to confound all manner of heresy" (*Works,* III, 67, and n. 12). Jewel clearly intended *propugnandam* to refer to *omnem veritatem* and not to *salutem,* and corrected Lady Bacon's translation accordingly.

tures. Neither were they ever so hardy to take any for an heretic, whose error they could not evidently and apparently reprove by the self-same scriptures."[23] If an angel himself were to preach that which is clearly contrary to the Scriptures, it is not to be received.[24] The Scriptures are the "bounds" of the Church of God,[25] and "the right and only way of building God's house is to lay the foundation thereof upon the everlasting word and will of God."[26]

The view that the Scriptures comprehend all things necessary for salvation and are the rule by which right doctrine is to be proven is incomplete in itself since it gives no indication of the direction of transition from the Scriptures to doctrine. What is the nature of the relation? How are the Scriptures to be studied as the source of doctrine? Obviously a literal reading is out of the question. Of this Jewel had no doubt. Literal interpretation was condemned not only by the evidence of history but by the Bible itself. In his treatise on the sacraments he pointed out that it was "by taking the bare letter" of the law that "the Jews found matter to put Christ to death." "We may not take the letter in all places of the scripture as it lieth. The scriptures stand not in the reading, but in the understanding."[27] To follow literally even the actions of Christ himself, Jewel declared, would be to show a poor appreciation of his teaching and result in a travesty of Christian action. Rather, "we ought to do that thing that Christ *both* did himself, *and* also commanded us to do, *and* was afterward practised by the apostles and holy fathers, that had the spirit of understanding, and knew Christ's meaning."[28]

Literal-mindedness in the study of the Bible, Jewel stigmatized as a kind of superstition, as an approach which had even led to heresy. To say that "the word of God, only because it is written or spoken, is available of itself without understanding, . . . is a superstitious and a Jewish kind of folly."[29] Never "was there any heresy so gross,

---

[23] Jewel, *Apology, Works*, III, 57.

[24] Jewel, *Defence, Works*, IV, 772.

[25] Jewel, *Thessalonians, Works*, II, 819.

[26] Jewel, *Defence, Works*, IV, 1058.

[27] Jewel, *A Treatise on the Sacraments, Works*, II, 1112.

[28] Jewel, *Reply, Works*, I, 127. My italics.

[29] *Ibid.*, I, 327.

but was able to make some simple shew of God's word."[30] Jewel's attack in these passages upon the *literal* reading must not be construed in any way as a defense of medieval interpretative methods. Like the humanists and the reformers before him, Jewel stressed the *natural* sense, the nonallegorical. His opposition here is to *literal* in the sense of *verbal*.[31]

In place of the mere words, Jewel stressed their "sense and meaning," in Jerome's phrase, "the very pith and substance of the scriptures."[32] "That the substance of the scriptures standeth in the right sense and meaning, and not only in the naked and bare words, it is true and generally granted without exception, and needeth no further proof."[33] The Word of God, though it is in the words, must not be identified with the words. In Jewel's thought it is equated with the sense and meaning of the Scriptures, with the substance of the Scriptures. "God's word written in paper is a creature corruptible, and shall consume and perish, as other corruptible creatures do: 'but the word of God' which we speak of 'endureth for ever.'"[34]

Jewel's statements concerning the nature of the Word are not to be interpreted in Luther's sense of *the Gospel*, which was "in essence 'that which Paul preaches,'"[35] the Gospel which through faith appealed directly to the souls of men.[36] And since Jewel did not share Luther's belief in a Gospel defined *a priori*, he could hardly follow Luther in judging the Scriptures by such a standard. He looked upon the Scriptures rather as a foundation, a norm to which he could turn to prove right doctrine. This is the primary use to which he puts the Scriptures throughout his works. We see the particular bent of his approach quite clearly for instance in his discussion of the *Apocrypha* when he observes that these books are not "such as may be alleged in proof of faith"; they cannot be used

[30] *Ibid.*, II, 563.

[31] See Calvin: *Commentaries* (Philadelphia, 1958), Introduction, p. 28.

[32] Jewel, *Reply, Works*, I, 447.

[33] Jewel, *Defence, Works*, III, 242.

[34] *Ibid.*, III, 434.

[35] Davies, *Problem of Authority*, p. 56.

[36] T. M. Lindsay, *A History of the Reformation*, 2 vols. (New York, 1906–1907), I, 458–459.

"'to prove ecclesiastical doctrine,'" or alleged "in confirmation of doctrine."[37] It is difficult to believe that Luther's concern would have been with *proof* of faith, or with the confirmation of doctrine. As Lindsay has said, the early reformers admitted that it would be "a good thing to put text to text and build a system of Protestant divinity to which their intellects could assent; but it was not essential."[38]

Jewel was much closer to Calvin than to Luther at this point for, unlike Luther, Calvin did not "hold some other theological criterion higher than the canon itself."[39] We would therefore expect to find that Jewel was likewise closer to the Swiss reformer in his teaching concerning the relation of the Word to the words. Here, however, we are faced with the problem of the literal reading of the words, the verbal infallibility long identified with Calvin and Calvinism. The Puritans and later Calvinists, together with many modern students of Calvin, have interpreted him as an extreme literalist, and on the basis of evidence that is very hard to controvert.[40] But a very strong case can be made for an entirely different view, especially when the evidence is confined rigidly to Calvin himself as opposed to his followers. This view holds that for Calvin it is the Word that God has dictated, not the words, that the Word rather than the words constitutes the substance of the Scriptures.[41]

Throughout his written works Jewel consistently held this distinction between the Word and the words. Only in his posthumous works, treatises based on his unpublished sermons and put together by his executor, John Garbrand, did he tend to overemphasize the importance of the letter of the words, and even here it was not in terms of the Word or of basic doctrine.[42]

[37] Jewel, *Defence, Works*, III, 433.

[38] Lindsay, *Reformation*, I, 458.

[39] Dowey, *Knowledge of God*, p. 104.

[40] See especially Hunter, *Teaching of Calvin*, pp. 85 ff.

[41] Dowey, *Knowledge of God*, p. 100. In his treatment of the subject, Dowey reviews at length the conclusions of the differing authorities in addition to the evidence from Calvin's own writings for both points of view.

[42] It might be argued that since these works, *A Treatise of the Holy Scriptures* and *An Exposition upon the Two Epistles of St. Paul to the Thessalonians*, were not, in their final form, Jewel's own, they possibly represent the ideas of the editor

In general the emphasis in these treatises, as in the other works, is on the value of the Word rather than upon the value of the words. However, in discussing the profit which people can gain from reading the Scriptures, Jewel declared that there was "no sentence, no clause, no word, no syllable, no letter, but it is written for thy instruction. . . . the whole word of God is pure and holy: no word, no letter, no syllable, no point or prick thereof, but is written and preserved for thy sake."[43] One could hardly go further in stressing the importance of the letter. The passage, however, must be read in its context, that of a didactic sermon. Moral precept follows moral precept and edifying example edifying example. The Bible is put to very different use here. Taken literally it becomes a rich storehouse of precepts, of heroic stories, of sacrifice, of God and his people—a source of comfort to all who would read. Jewel's use of the Bible in this sermon is not to be confused with the extreme literal-mindedness which later grew up among the Puritans and with which we are familiar today in the fundamentalist churches. All the passages which he suggested be taken literally are so simple and straightforward that in fact no contradiction could be suggested between the letter and the spirit.

Moreover, Jewel's purpose in these sermons was "to allure the people to read."[44] If they would not become familiar with the Bible, of what avail would it be to attempt to prove doctrine from it? The people must necessarily know the basis of proof. To stress the literal simplicity and obviousness of certain passages for this purpose is not to predicate the literal interpretation of the whole Bible. Finally we should remember that the Word is in the words. The very letters

---

more than they do Jewel's. According to Garbrand, these works were "gathered out of certain sermons, which . . . Jewel preached at Salisbury" (*Works*, IV, 1162 and II, 816). They should obviously not be considered in the same light as Jewel's major works. The arranging of material from sermons into systematic treatises would tend to distort it, particularly if the reader did not keep in mind that it was material presented orally to a congregation in a provincial town, and not intended by the author to be read by the learned world. If these qualifications are kept in mind, however, it is possible to accept them and their teaching as not fundamentally contradictory to Jewel's other work.

[43] Jewel, *Holy Scriptures, Works*, IV, 1175.
[44] Jewel, *Apology, Works*, III, 92.

of the words, Jewel wrote, are the sole source from which men can draw the inner message of the Word. The letter might kill, but a spirit entirely unrelated to the letter would be equally deadly. In sum, according to St. Basil:

'We may become like unto God, as far forth as the weak nature of man can bear. But this likeness cannot be without knowledge; neither this knowledge without doctrine. And the beginning of doctrine is speech; and the parts of speech be words and syllables.' The resolution hereof is this: The people, without understanding the particular words and syllables, cannot know the speech: not knowing the speech, they cannot attain this doctrine; and without this doctrine they cannot be like unto God.[45]

As a corollary Jewel wished to make the Bible more easily available to the people through inexpensive vernacular versions. In this he was following the path marked out by Erasmus and broadly cleared by Tyndale and Luther rather than the limited way of Tudor Anglicanism.

The record of the Tudors in the popularizing of the Scriptures was by no means as good as the Tudors themselves would have had us believe. Certainly Henry VIII, who boasted the loudest, deserves no credit.[46] During the reign of Edward more was accomplished but not nearly as much as we might expect.[47] The reign was brief and hectic, and was followed by five years of reaction. With the Elizabethan settlement we might anticipate a more liberal policy, but until some years after Jewel's death neither the government nor the Church made any real effort actually to popularize the Scriptures.[48] Nor does there seem to have been much concern expressed

[45] Jewel, *Reply, Works,* II, 670.
[46] Dixon, *History,* II, 134, 264. The Great Bible of the reign was in no sense a popular edition. Whatever pretence of popularization of the Scriptures was connected with it disappeared with the fall of Cromwell and the reaction expressed by the Statute of Six Articles.
[47] Dixon, *History,* II, 424, 430. It was ordered that Erasmus' *Paraphrases of the New Testament* be placed in every parish church, and the old injunction requiring that Bibles be placed in the churches was renewed.
[48] Archbishop Parker adopted from the first a very well-defined policy of compromise toward English translations: that of allowing to be printed in England only those Bibles intended for use in the churches. These were too costly for popular consumption

during the early years of Elizabeth for the lack of inexpensive vernacular versions. In this respect Jewel was exceptional. In his writings and in his sermons, he insisted that the people be made familiar with the Scriptures, that they have them in their homes as well as in their churches, since all men are equally the rightful inheritors of the Word of God, whether they be learned or unlearned, rich or poor. In the Scriptures, he wrote, God speaks to all of them, regardless of their place in life or their attainments. He pointed out that Chrysostom had considered it as important for the laity to have the Scriptures as for the priests themselves to possess them. The layman's need for defense against worldly evils was actually greater.[49] "The old fathers," he wrote in the *Apology*, "exhort the people to read the scriptures, to buy them books, to reason at home betwixt themselves of divine matters; wives with their husbands, and parents with their children."[50]

The Scriptures therefore must be translated into the language of

---

and no cheap editions were printed at all. The most important translation of the early years of the reign, the Geneva version, was not printed in England during Parker's lifetime. John Bodley was given license to print but evidently his final version failed of Parker's approval and never went to press (A. W. Pollard, *Records of the English Bible* [London, 1911], pp. 27–28). In 1562 the Great Bible was revised and reprinted. And in 1566 the Bishop's Bible, published under the aegis of the Archbishop, appeared. But it was not intended for popular use. It was costly; it lacked the interesting commentaries of the Geneva and preceding versions; and it was inferior to the Geneva version from a literary standpoint, lacking especially the uniformity so marked in the Bible of the exiles. It is difficult not to agree with Pollard (p. 43) that "it seems certain that the Archbishop cared little for providing Bibles for private reading. He saw and met the need of suitable editions for the service of the church but . . . he did not 'trust the people' with cheap editions of the Bible. . . ."

In May 1575 Parker died. In June, in fact only three weeks later, permission was given for the printing of other editions. In the next year appeared the Geneva Bible of Barker. This was the first of many editions of the Geneva version printed during the reign (H. W. Hoare, *The Evolution of the English Bible* [London, 1902], p. 212). It is strange that in these formative years of the English Church no effort was made by the authorities to provide the people with a cheap Bible that reflected better than the Geneva Bible the *via media*. It is highly significant that the first cheap edition of the Bishop's Bible was printed after Whitgift became Archbishop. In the meantime, at first because of Parker's evident lack of faith in popular editions, and afterwards because Grindal was apparently not averse to the Geneva version, the latter became the English Bible and was not replaced until after 1611.

[49] Jewel, *Reply, Works*, II, 671–675.
[50] Jewel, *Apology, Works*, III, 86.

the people. Jewel had no patience with the claims made by Romanists in general and by his opponent in particular that the Latin tongue in and of itself should be considered of especial virtue and fitness for the treatment of religious matters. He had a humanistic regard for the Latin and the Greek and made use of them throughout his work, "for the reading of old commentaries and the ancient doctors, and so for meditation and study of the scriptures," but he denied to these languages any qualities inherently superior to the vernacular.[51]

Harding argued that the possession by the people of the Scriptures in the vernacular had led to many heresies.[52] Jewel as positively contended that the Scriptures were the most potent weapons with which heresy was to be combated.[53] Furthermore, he pointed out, it was quite wrong to restrict the reading of the Scriptures to the learned, as Harding would do, for it was with the learned rather than with the ignorant that sects and heresies, so-called, had originated.[54] The people, deprived of the Scriptures, are then quite helpless to decide whether these teachings be erroneous or not.

Jewel was extremely critical of the Vulgate. "The worst translation that this day is commonly used, either in the English, or in the French, or in the Dutch tongue," he asserted, "is far better and truer than the old common translation in the Latin."[55] He cited the work of Budé and Erasmus and Valla in proof that the Vulgate contains "errors, so open and so gross that a very babe may soon espy them." Yet the Roman Church has consistently upheld this old translation and finally in the Council of Trent has decreed anathema to any one who presumes " 'by any manner of colour to refuse' " it.[56]

Jewel did not discuss or express a preference for any one of the various vernacular translations. His statements concerning them, however, display in general an unusually liberal point of view. He did not claim for any one of them the perfection and absolute authority that the Romanists claimed for the Vulgate. As a scholar

[51] Jewel, *Reply, Works*, II, 695; I, 316.
[52] Thomas Harding, *An answere to maister Juelles chalenge augmented with certaine quotations and additions* (Antwerp, 1565), 196; Jewel, *Reply, Works*, II, 681.
[53] Jewel, *Apology, Works*, III, 68.
[54] Jewel, *Reply, Works*, II, 688.
[55] Jewel, *Defence, Works*, III, 158.
[56] *Ibid.*, IV, 907.

trained in the humanist tradition he had emphasized the errors in Jerome's Vulgate. He did not depart from this attitude in discussing other translations. They too, he admitted, might possibly contain errors, although not as gross nor as numerous as those in the Vulgate.

> I know there are some that lay it unto our charge, . . . that we use the word of God deceitfully: they find fault with our translations of the scriptures. They spare not to say, there be a thousand faults in the new testament. Yet would they never set down five hundred, or one hundred, or fifty, or twenty-five, or five.
>
> If there be errors in the translation, I know they were men which translated it, and might err like men. May no translation be allowed that is not altogether perfect? [57]

It is a conditional statement. No specific errors are admitted. But errors are not denied and, the possibility of their existence being admitted, they are excused on humanistic grounds. The Scriptures were translated by men and men may err.

The situation in brief, Jewel declared, was this: The Romanists have described the vernacular translations as faulty and inaccurate. But they do no more than make general accusations. They have neither pointed out the specific errors in the translations available nor offered a translation of their own.[58] From Jewel's point of view this was sufficient answer, and we must agree that until the Rheims-Douai version appeared it was a very telling one. There was little need for him to develop the point further.

[57] Jewel, *Thessalonians, Works,* II, 830–31.

[58] Jewel, *Reply, Works,* II, 695–96. The accusation that Rome had withheld the Scriptures from the people was one made by most of the critics of Rome. Cardinal Gasquet in his book of essays (F. A. Gasquet, *The Old English Bible and Other Essays* [London, 1897], pp. 87–155) attempted to disprove it in regard to England but only succeeded in proving that the English Church before the Reformation had not forbidden the publication of translated Bibles. He admitted that the Church strictly forbade translations without official sanction. He was unable, however, to cite an instance of sanction being given a printed English Bible before the Rheims-Douai version. Hence, while the Roman Church, in England, at least, has perhaps been unjustly accused of prohibiting translations and of punishing translators, the fact remains that she reserved an effective right of censure and did nothing toward promoting a translation, in Jewel's words, "nor hath devised any other translation of her own" (Jewel, *Reply, Works,* II, 671).

Chapter XI

Interpretative Authority

The Reformers and Interpretative Authority

The problems faced by the reformers in the development of doctrine were in many ways more complex and for that reason more difficult of solution than the more basic problem of the identification and authentication of the Scriptures as the Word of God. Doctrinal differences reflected in every instance differences in interpretation of the Scriptures. The crucial question at issue therefore was not the authority of the Scriptures but the authority for their interpretation.

The Church of Rome had solved the problem of interpretation and the formulation of doctrine by citing its own authority,[1] just as it had cited its own authority in the authentication of the Bible. For the Church this was an obvious and effective solution. It would be difficult indeed to posit a more unanswerable authority for interpretation than an institution whose source of authority was the continuing grace of God.

As the reformers developed their own doctrinal systems they tended, as had Rome itself, to solve the problem of interpretative authority as they had solved the prior question of the validity and the authentication of the original revelation. Their solutions, however, differed from one another. Neither were they formulated immediately nor always as simply and clearly as the Roman solution.

At the center of the problem of interpretation was the question of the objectivity of the interpretative authority. In the very early

[1] "Canons and Decrees of the Council of Trent" in Schaff, *Creeds,* II, 83.

stages of the Reformation the overpowering need for objective authority was not deeply felt, again reflecting the attitudes of the reformers to the prior problem. So it was with Luther after his initial attack on the papacy and so it was with Zwingli in the beginning of his ministry at Zurich. The factor that brought the problem into the foreground and forced the reformers to deal with it was the challenge of radical Protestantism in its various and widely differing forms.

However much the Anabaptists may have differed among themselves on specific teachings, doctrinal, social, or political, they shared a belief in the validity of individual revelation as an authority in addition to or even replacing the authority of the Bible. The same authority was obviously valid for scriptural interpretation. By no stretch of the imagination could it be called objective. Hence the diversity of belief amongst the Anabaptists themselves. To the defenders of the institutional Church such was the logical consequence of the denial of its authority. There could be as many varieties of Protestantism as there were individuals.

The reformers deeply resented such a conclusion. They made as sharp a distinction between themselves and the Anapabtists as they did between themselves and Rome. In fact they liked to point out that the Roman apologists were guilty of the same basic error as the Anabaptists in that they replaced the original revelation by a new revelation every bit as human as that of the Anabaptists, that is, the revelation of the Church in the person of the pope.

The initial result of the attack from the left was the reinforcement in the early reformers of the biblicist character of their teaching. Just as Luther turned again and again to the authority of the Bible in his conflict with the representatives of Rome at Augsburg and at Leipzig, so he emphasized biblical authority against the Anabaptists. The focussing of the controversy upon biblical authority, however, did not do away with the question of individual revelation. Within the compass of biblical authority itself, that is, in the area of interpretation, there was ample room for the development of individual revelation. It was here that objective authority was so vitally necessary.

It can hardly be said that Luther solved the problem. His own interpretation of the Bible, however objective he believed it to be, however acceptable it may have been to his followers, and however appealing and convincing it has been to many others, was in the last analysis subjective. Although he had found the answer to his own deep spiritual struggle in the Bible, the key to his answer was actually that part of the Bible which he believed to be its heart, the Pauline writings, and most specifically, in what he believed to be the core of Paul's teachings, "the message of salvation through Jesus Christ that Paul preached."[2] This to Luther was the Gospel, this was the "principle of authority" to which he always turned, not only in his judgment of the comparative validity of the books of the Bible but in their interpretation as well. "Luther interpreted the Scriptures by the Gospel, not the Gospel by the Scriptures."[3] From Luther's point of view there was no need to go futher. The Bible, so understood and interpreted, constituted a body of objective truth. But to anyone who might not follow Luther, the authority for interpretation must appear altogether subjective.

Is it possible to argue that Luther made use of supplementary authority to bolster his interpretation and thus lend at least an element of objectivity to it? His knowledge of the corpus of patristic writings was profound and in the great debates that set the stage for his final break with Rome he drew heavily upon the patristic arsenal for ammunition against Cajetan and Eck. Furthermore Luther's debt to Augustine was tremendous. It was Augustine who provided the initial guidance to the Pauline solution[4] and throughout his life Luther turned again and again to Augustine for guidance.[5] Even so, in the final analysis, the fathers, including Augustine, played an entirely secondary role in interpretation, such a secondary role in fact, that it would be incorrect to characterize them as interpretative authority. Luther himself was quite clear on this point. Helpful though they might be to the student,[6] useful though they certainly were in controversy, they had no more authority in scriptural inter-

---

[2] Kraeling, *Old Testament*, p. 11.

[3] Charles Beard, *The Reformation of the Sixteenth Century* (London, 1907), p. 127; Martin Luther, *Works*, 6 vols. (Philadelphia, 1915–1932), VI, 478–479.

[4] E. G. Schwiebert, *Luther and His Times* (St. Louis, 1950), pp. 157–163.

[5] R. H. Bainton, *Here I Stand* (New York, 1950), pp. 238, 298, 303.

[6] Martin Luther, *Letters of Spiritual Counsel* (Philadelphia, 1955), p. 112.

pretation than they had independently of the Scriptures. " 'If one pauses at some individual passage (of the Bible) and seeks help for its interpretation in the patristic books, one has nothing but sorry patchwork in one's hands,' " [7] he wrote Spalatin. And in his *Answer to Emser* he declared that he would take his stand with Paul to believe that "the Scriptures need no man's interpretation"; that it was a new papal discovery "that one must arrive at the meaning of the Scriptures not through the Bible itself but through patristic interpretation." [8]

Since Zwingli differed so radically from Luther on important doctrinal questions we would expect to find basic differences also in his handling of the problem of authority for doctrine. Differences there were, but differences in their basic approach to the problem rather than in the results, the conclusions reached in terms of interpretative authority.

Zwingli did not rely on a simple principle of authority as Luther relied on the Pauline doctrine of salvation. For Zwingli the Scriptures comprised a totality so inherently harmonious and unified that he felt no need for an a priori principle by which they were to be explained. The clarity of the Word in the Scriptures is self-evident to the penitent and faithful recipient of the Holy Spirit. [9] There is no need of a human interpreter. In his sermon, *Of the Clarity and Certainty of the Word of God,* Zwingli declared that "when the Word of God shines on the human understanding, it enlightens it in such a way that it understands and confesses the Word and knows the certainty of it." It can only come from above. "No other man can attain it for us. The comprehension and understanding of divine doctrine comes then from above and not from interpreters, who are just as liable to be led into temptation as Balaam was." [10] Zwingli's only concession to the view that the Scriptures may not be altogether clear is the admission that a particular passage may be obscure. In such a case, however, the meaning is to be elucidated by

[7] Kraeling, *Old Testament,* p. 10, from a letter of Luther to Spalatin.

[8] R. H. Fife, *The Revolt of Martin Luther* (New York, 1957), p. 606, from Fife's paraphrase of Luther's "Answer to the Superchristian Book of Goat Emser."

[9] G. W. Bromiley, *Zwingli and Bullinger* (Philadelphia, 1953), p. 55.

[10] *Ibid.,* pp. 75-79.

the aid of another passage from the Scriptures. "If I do not correctly understand the Scripture, I undertake to allow myself to be better instructed, yet only from the aforementioned Scripture."[11]

It is in the light of statements such as these that we must read his oft-quoted letter to Francis I in which he declared: "We teach not an iota that we have not learned from the divine Oracles; and we assert nothing for which we cannot cite as guarantors the first teachers of the Church, prophets, apostles, bishops, evangelists, Bible-expositors."[12] As a matter of fact, the distinction which Zwingli makes in the passage itself is a fair measure of the subordinate position to which he relegates all interpretative authorities.

Calvin is the heir of the earlier Reformed theologians and his work represents the culmination of Reformed theology. While he owes much both to his predecessors and to his contemporaries, he moves beyond them to a point where in the end Reformed theology becomes virtually the theology of Calvin. It would be false to conclude, however, on the basis of the position he now holds in the history of Reformed theology, that he overwhelmed and dominated his contemporaries. Calvin, for instance, owed more to Bucer than Bucer owed to Calvin.[13] And certainly the *Consensus Tigurinus* was as much Bullinger's as it was Calvin's.[14] But the fact remains that the *Institutes* is the masterpiece of the whole vast literature of Reformation theology, its unrivaled formal synthesis. Calvin's *Commentaries* is the *Encyclopédie* of the Reformation. Only Bullinger's *Decades* can be compared with it in the weight and comprehensiveness of its authority. Finally, and equal in significance and importance to his writings, is his other masterpiece, the city of Geneva. As a capital of Reformed Protestantism and a model for Christian society, it, like the *Institutes,* had no rival. The Anglican bishops and their Queen might prefer the city of Bullinger and Gualter, but to the Reformed Churches of the continent Geneva was the city par excellence, whether under Calvin or, during the later half of the

[11] McNeill, *Calvinism,* p. 73, from Zwingli's Sixty-Seven Conclusions of 1523.
[12] McNeill, *Calvinism,* p. 75.
[13] Calvin: *Commentaries,* p. 54, n. 3.
[14] McNeill, *Calvinism,* p. 198 ff.

century, under his successor, Theodore Beza. It is only natural therefore that in the end the study of Reformed Protestantism should tend to become the study of Calvin. And similarly any study of modifications or departures from Reformed theology has tended to take its point of departure from Calvin.

Although such a situation is altogether natural, it is nonetheless unfortunate, both for an unbiased treatment of Calvin himself and for a proper assessment of the relative importance of the other leaders during the period of the Reformation itself and later. Calvin has become the obvious whipping boy for those who are not of the Reformed tradition and who have come to resent the dominance of the Reformed teachings under their Calvinist label in the decades and centuries following his final return to Geneva. This in turn has led to a reaction on the part of Reformed theologians. In their defense of Calvin they have refused to see flaws in his character and, even more emphatically, have closed their eyes to the existence of flaws in his theology, especially flaws which might suggest either incompleteness or inconsistency.

Equally important and, for the historian doubly unfortunate, as a result of the overwhelming shadow cast by Calvin, has been the denigration of the other reformers to the point where all have tended to become pale satellites of the great Frenchman. Bucer, for instance, has actually been described as a disciple of Calvin.[15] These men, on the Continent and in England, were equals, all working on common problems, in most cases on friendly terms with one another. Conclusions were reached on the basis sometimes of consultations, sometimes as the result of direct influence of one on the other and at times, doubtless, by steps quite independent of one another.[16]

The English reformers have suffered not only from the shade

---

[15] C. W. Baird, *Eutaxia* (1856), p. 194: " 'We may fairly claim the Liturgy of Cologne as the fruit of the Calvinistic Reformation, for Bucer, who had the chief hand in it, was a disciple of Calvin.' " Quoted by Horton Davies, *The Worship of the English Puritans*, p. 26.

[16] McLelland has stressed, for instance, the close relation of Bucer, Calvin, and Martyr to one another on the central problem of eucharistic doctrine (*Visible Words*, pp. 272–281).

cast by Calvin but by the shade of the continental reformers in general. Professor Dugmore complains with justice of an all-too-common point of view which does not make allowance for the possibility that a Ridley or a Cranmer reached solutions to problems without reference necessarily to outside influence, and in a thoroughly English fashion.[17] At times, the English leaders were deeply influenced. But so also was Calvin himself.

On the question of interpretative authority, Calvin represents, as he does in so many areas, the final development and statement of Reformed thought. His solution differs from Zwingli's largely in its completeness. It is as if Calvin finished a task which Zwingli had begun. The key to Calvin's solution is to be found in his statement concerning the broader problem of the authority of the Bible itself and the authentication of the Bible as the Word of God.[18] Authority is in the Scriptures themselves which are self-authenticating, and concurrently in the heart of the believer, through the testimony of the Holy Spirit. This statement is far more comprehensive than it appears at first, for it includes Calvin's answer to the question of interpretation as well. To say that the Scriptures are their own authority and are self-authenticating is to say at the same time that the message is likewise possessed of its own authority and is self-authenticating. To say that the authority of the Bible is concurrently recognized in the heart of the individual through the testimony of the Spirit is to say also that its message is so recognized and understood. There appears to be no need for further interpretative authority. All that is required in the construction of dogma is a clear exposition of God's will in terms of specific doctrines. Calvin's life work, the *Institutes* and the *Commentaries,* supplied this need. Togther they constitute the *Summa Theologica* of Protestantism.

As a *Summa,* however, Calvin's works are far more than simple exposition. In his development of doctrine in the *Institutes* and in his line-by-line examination of the Bible in the *Commentaries,* Calvin makes use of all the devices of the advocate and the teacher, drawing heavily on the literature of the past, pagan as well as

[17] Dugmore, *The Mass,* pp. vii–viii.
[18] See above, pp. 148–149.

Christian. Patristic literature occupies a major place and, as with Luther, Augustine stands preeminent. The same question arises therefore which arose in the case of Luther; that is, do the early Christian writers, and Augustine in particular, function as interpretative authority in any sense of the term? Does Calvin, despite statements which appear to preclude any need for further authority in interpretation, suggest in practice that such authority is either necessary or desirable? The fact that Calvin's work contains an overwhelming number of references to Augustine proves very little in this respect. It is a question rather of the use to which Calvin puts the evidence he culls from the fathers and his attitude towards their opinions.

Since Rome and her apologists accepted the writings of the fathers as part of the orthodox Christian tradition, Calvin, like Jewel, delighted in citing evidence from their writings against current Roman teaching and practice, and conversely, in answer to the accusation of novelty directed against the reformers, to show identity between Reformed and patristic teaching and practice.[19] Calvin stresses agreement with patristic teaching almost as a matter of course in his exposition of doctrine and the explanation of scriptural passages. Reference after reference to Augustine (and somewhat less frequently, to Chrysostom, Jerome, Ambrose, and others) is introduced by phrases such as: "Augustine correctly and judiciously observes," "It is judiciously remarked by Augustine," "This is concisely and beautifully represented by Augustine, when he says," "as Augustine excellently observes," "Augustine, indeed, properly observes,"[20] "Augustine writes truly," and "Augustine is correct when he says."[21] Such statements do indicate the high opinion in which Calvin held Augustine. But they have nothing to do with interpretative authority, however effective they may be as

---

[19] "I ask you to place before your eyes the ancient form of the Church as their writings prove it to have been in the ages of Chrysostom and Basil among the Greeks, and of Cyprian, Ambrose and Augustine among the Latins; and after so doing, to contemplate the ruins of that Church which now survive among yourselves" (Calvin, *Theological Treatises*, p. 231); *Institutes*, I, xi, XIII; IV, xiii, IX; I, xi, VI.

[20] *Institutes*, IV, i, XIV; III, xxii, I; III, xiv, XX; I, xiii, XV; II, i, IV.

[21] Calvin: *Commentaries*, pp. 391, 334.

rhetorical devices to reinforce the personal authority of the writer.

At other times, however, Calvin uses phrases that serve more than a mere rhetorical purpose. As an advocate he makes generous use of patristic evidence to corroborate and support a position he has taken, introducing his evidence with the statement: "as his words will perhaps have more authority than mine," or "but for further confirmation . . . I will cite a passage from Augustine."[22] Throughout his extensive treatment of sacramental doctrine in the *Institutes* in particular, he makes full use of Augustine in this fashion not only to prove the novelty of Roman teaching but to emphasize agreement between Augustine's teaching and his own.[23]

In several instances of scriptural exegesis and the development of particularly difficult points of doctrine in the *Institutes,* Calvin appears to lean quite heavily upon the fathers, especially upon Augustine.[24] Here the suggestion of the interpretative authority of the fathers is perhaps strongest. In these instances, however, it is possible to interpret Calvin's position as that of a man who is explaining a point of view that he has reached by other means. At no time does he cite patristic authority as proof that the doctrine is true, and only rarely that a father provided the means whereby he, Calvin, was brought to believe it to be true.[25]

Positive evidence, when it is available, is always preferable to negative evidence, significant though the latter may be. And the freedom with which Calvin rejects patristic interpretations together with the cavalier manner he displays at times even toward Augustine makes it quite obvious that however useful patristic literature may be, it is not to be regarded as interpretative authority, even in a subsidiary sense.

On the subject of the relation of the Persons in the Trinity to one another, Calvin found grave inconsistencies, not only among the fathers but even within the writings of a particular father.[26] On the doctrine of election, so central to his own thought, he declared that

[22] *Institutes,* III, xxiii, XIII; II, xvi, IV.

[23] *Ibid.,* IV, xiv, XVII–XIX.

[24] *Ibid.,* III, xxiii, I; III, xxiv, I.

[25] *Ibid.,* II, viii, L.

[26] *Ibid.,* I, xiii, V.

"such are the variations, fluctuations, or obscurities of all the fathers, except Augustine, . . . that scarcely any thing certain can be concluded from their writings."[27] He freely took issue with Jerome.[28] He characterized an interpretation of Chrysostom as an "evasion."[29] Augustine himself was not free from serious criticism. His speculation concerning the soul as a mirror of the Trinity, Calvin declared "far from solid," his interpretation of the meaning of the baptism of John, "that subtlety," his exposition of a passage from John 1, irrelevant, and his "subtle reasoning" concerning a passage from Hebrews 1, "frivolous."[30]

Calvin does not give specific consideration to the problem of patristic authority in the *Institutes*. The multitude of references to the fathers are all incidental to other questions. But in a discourse at the Colloquy of Berne, delivered the very year that saw the first publication of the *Institutes,* he summarized his position quite clearly. In answer to the Roman accusation that he and his colleagues, Viret and Farel, had condemned the "holy doctors of antiquity," he replied that

those who make parade of according them great reverence often do not hold them in such great honour as we; nor do they deign to occupy their time reading their writings as we willingly do. . . . But we have always held them to belong to the number of those to whom such obedience is not due, and whose authority we will not so exalt, as in any way to debase the dignity of the Word of our Lord, to which alone is due complete obedience in the Church of Jesus Christ. . . . We, who have to teach the people of Jesus according to his will and ordinance, do not wish to instruct it in human doctrines, but in celestial wisdom which has been committed to us for faithful transmission. . . . We do them (the fathers) such honour as may according to God be accorded to them, while we attend to them and to their ministry, to search the Word of God, in order that, having found it, we should with them listen to and observe it with all humility and reverence, reserving this honour for the

[27] *Ibid.,* II, ii, IV.
[28] *Ibid.,* II, vii, V: "What was the opinion of Jerome, I regard not; let us inquire what is truth."
[29] *Ibid.,* III, xxiv, XIII.
[30] *Ibid.,* I, xv, IV; IV, xv, VII. Calvin: *Commentaries,* pp. 114, 178.

Lord alone, who has opened his mouth in the Church only to speak with authority.[31]

As Dr. Dakin paraphrases Calvin: "With the conviction of the truth of Scripture and of its divine origin there comes also by the agency of the same Spirit the ability to understand and receive the truth."[32] Such ability is sufficient. There is no need for further authority.

For the Protestants of the sixteenth century and indeed for many Protestant theologians of the twentieth century, Calvin's answer was the final answer to the problem of interpretation, providing an authority as objective as that of the Church itself. In a sense it was just as objective, since in the last analysis, the authority of the Roman Church must rest on the "initial act of personal submission" of the individual believer, an authority no less objective nor more subjective than the "inner testimony of the Holy Spirit" of Calvin. In this sense it can be argued convincingly that John Fisher gave his life for a truth which was as much a matter of individual faith as the truth for which the lowliest Anabaptist died.

The historian must note, however, that for many, both in the sixteenth century and later, the institution of the Roman Church did offer an interpretative authority that seemed less individual, and that could be considered more objective and external.[33] Thus, despite the incredible achievement of Calvin in providing an answer that satisfied many Protestants, the need continued to be felt for an authority which possessed the kind of objective authority associated with the institutional Church.

Dr. Dakin argues that Calvin, in seeking an authority to replace the authority of the papal Church, avoided the two extreme solutions commonly ascribed to Protestantism, that is, on the one hand the mere substitution of "the Bible for the Pope, thus setting up

---

[31] Calvin, *Theological Treatises*, pp. 38–39.

[32] Dakin, *Calvinism*, p. 181.

[33] Davies (*Problem of Authority*, p. 59) defines "external authority" as "an authority which, after the initial act of personal submission, expresses its decrees and dogmas from a position entirely outside the individual." It is in this sense that the terms *external* and *objective* are used here.

another purely external authority," or, on the other hand, offering "a purely subjective authority, making human reason or some sort of intuitive feeling the final arbiter." For Calvin, Dakin concludes: "There is no authority in religion apart from the Bible, but also there is no authority in the Bible apart from the Holy Spirit speaking in the heart."[34] We must observe with Dakin, however, that while Calvin avoided the two extremes—straight biblicism with the Bible as an authority comparable to the objective authority of the Church or the pope, and the subjective authority of human reason or intuition—"he opened the way for both developments."[35] Inevitably these solutions, rather than his own came to be increasingly stressed in the years after his death, not so much with reference to the authority of the Bible itself or its authentication as God's Word, but in regard to its meaning and its interpretation.

Jewel, like Calvin, avoided the two extremes. In his work the teachings of the early Church and the fathers became a positive element in interpretative authority. He thus moved in a direction altogether different from that of the Puritans, in whose hands the biblicist element in Calvin's teachings became paramount. At the same time Jewel avoided the opposite extreme of interpretation by individual inspiration or individual reason. In contrast to these alternatives, however, Jewel's development of a positive interpretative authority can hardly be described as implicit in Calvin. Calvin's use of patristic evidence simply does not open the door to such a development. Here, as in the development of eucharistic doctrine,[36] Jewel is of another tradition and his immediate progenitor is Thomas Cranmer. That is not to suggest that Jewel, any more than Cranmer, sought to emphasize a difference between his teachings and those of the continental reformers. Certainly in his devotion to the concept of Protestant unity he was as consistent as were Bucer and Calvin, indeed as was Cranmer himself. Nor is there any evidence of his

[34] Dakin, *Calvinism*, p. 180.

[35] *Ibid.*, p. 184.

[36] In his analysis of Jewel's eucharistic doctrine, Dugmore concluded that Jewel, despite the influence of continental Protestantism in its Tigurine form, belongs definitely to the central Anglican tradition, "the Augustinian realist-symbolist tradition of Ratramn, Frith, Ridley and Cranmer" (*The Mass*, p. 232).

awareness of a fundamental difference at this point. Calvin's use of patristic literature appeared to provide an excellent precedent and the difference in its use could be viewed as a difference in degree, which it was not, rather than the difference in kind, which it was.

Cranmer's writings are neither as extensive nor as comprehensive as Calvin's or Jewel's. His formal work is confined almost entirely to the subject of eucharistic teaching and even the records of his disputations and trials are largely concerned with the same subject. As with those portions of Calvin's works concerned with the Mass, Cranmer's are heavily weighted with citations from patristic literature, and patristic evidence is used at every turn to buttress a stand he has taken. Cranmer, however, does not stand over the witnesses he cites and pass judgment upon them as does Calvin. The reader has the feeling throughout that for Cranmer, the fathers, with Augustine always in the van, are the solid support upon whom he leans and toward whom he looks for guidance, that he would never criticize them for oversubtlety, or describe their words as irrelevant, or even use such favorable critical phrases as "Augustine is correct," or "Augustine *truly* says." It could be argued of course that Calvin and Cranmer are using patristic evidence for different purposes, Cranmer being on the defensive, always less sure of his own mind and, insofar as his worldly position was concerned, either uncertain of support or certain that he was wholly without support. But this is an explanation for a difference—it does not explain away the difference—and as an explanation for the difference it only throws into bolder relief the contrast between the ever-present insecurity of both Cranmer and Jewel and the security of John Calvin with his tremendous resources of inner strength and certainty and, after 1555, his unquestioned position and authority in Geneva.

Cranmer does not rest content with the citation of mere corroborative evidence nor with the citation of isolated passages from individual fathers. He placed great stress upon their agreement, the solid and unanimous support he found in their writings. He cites the "consent of all the old doctors of the Church," and declares concerning the Roman doctrine of the Mass, that "all the old Church of Christ believed the contrary, and all the old authors wrote the contrary," that "not one of them maketh" for the Roman error.[37] In his *Answer to Gardyner,* he recalled that after "I had alleged for the proof of my purpose a great many places of old authors, both Greeks and Latins, I provoked the papists to say what they could to the contrary. Let all the papists together, said I, show any one authority for them, either of Scripture or ancient author, either Greek or Latin, and for my part I shall give them place."[38] Almost certainly, as Dr. Bromiley suggests, this was the germ of Jewel's greatly extended challenge of 1559.[39]

In *A Confutation of Unwritten Verities,*[40] Cranmer expressed his conviction that "every exposition of the Scripture, whereinsoever the old, holy, and true Church did agree, is necessary to be believed."[41] We must conclude with Bromiley that for Cranmer the fathers are the "first interpreters of Scripture," and that he allows them "a firm subsidiary authority."[42]

Jewel and the Interpretative Authority of the Fathers.

Throughout the whole discourse of this Apology, in the defence of the catholic truth of our religion, next unto God's holy word, (we) have used no proof or authority so much as the expositions and judgments of the holy fathers. We . . . give God thanks in their behalf, for that it hath pleased him to provide so worthy instruments for his church.[43]

Patristic literature, in every respect equal in authority to the decrees of early councils, was at the same time almost entirely free

[37] Cranmer, *Defence of the True and Catholic Doctrine, etc.,* in *Remains,* II, 360, 365, 438.

[38] Cranmer, *Answer unto . . . Stephen Gardyner, Remains,* III, 184.

[39] Bromiley, *Thomas Cranmer,* p. 23.

[40] The *Confutation of Unwritten Verities,* as published in 1558, is not Cranmer's own but rather a work based on materials which were his. Jenkyns, the editor of the 1833 edition of the *Remains,* believed that "it cannot safely be quoted as evidence of Cranmer's tenets," but Bromiley is convinced that the material is Cranmer's. The general agreement of the work as published, with Cranmer's known works on the one hand and with Jewel on the other is so pronounced that its mere existence, even as an anonymous pamphlet, would be significant as evidence of the existence of a tradition that Jewel was to carry on. See Cranmer, *Remains,* IV, 144, and Bromiley, *Thomas Cranmer,* p. 15.

[41] Cranmer, *Remains,* IV, 229.

[42] Bromiley, *Thomas Cranmer,* p. 22.

[43] Jewel, *Defence, Works,* III, 225.

of the limitations which made the conciliar decrees of so little practical value in scriptural interpretation. In contrast to the decrees of a few councils the writings of the fathers seem to the student almost limitless, both in mere quantity and in the extent of the subject matter covered. One has only to consider the titles of Augustine's works to realize the range of subjects. Furthermore, not one of the fathers was, in the sense of an Albertus or an Aquinas, a systematic thinker. Most of them wrote for an occasion—usually controversial. Not one of them, not even Augustine, wrote anything approaching a clearly definitive work. Hence all of their writings, from those of the Hellenistic, mystical, and at times heretical, Origen, to those of the orthodox, practical Ambrose, from the works of the Alexandrian theologian-bishop, Athanasius, to those of the Roman legist, Gregory the Great, present to the scholar one vast body of unsystematized and even contradictory teachings.

Moreover, this great body of literature had been made easily available to the sixteenth-century scholar by the work of the humanists. The sixteenth-century controversialist who could not cite a line or two from a father to prove the rightness of his position was rare indeed. It is almost is if anyone might venture into this great repository of teachings and adduce therefrom a basis of proof for any doctrine. Such an observation however is not applicable to Jewel. The very procedure which Buckle criticized in his writings, the piling up of evidence on evidence, as if quantity alone was sufficient proof, provided a strong safeguard against the possible misapplication of isolated passages. When numerous passages were cited from different works of an author, when additional passages were cited to the same effect, almost in the same words, from other fathers, both Greek and Latin, the reader could not but agree that Jewel had managed to come very close to the original patristic meaning; that he was not forcing the patristic words into a sixteenth-century mold.

At the same time, the patristic writings, far more than the brief decrees of the councils, gave Jewel the opportunity to present a detailed and reasonable analysis of a problem. The writings were the work of men about whom some facts were known, the product of periods historically clearer than apostolic times. They therefore lent themselves readily to the type of historical and textual criticism in which he excelled. The fathers represented a congress before which a problem could be presented, considered, and argued, the verdict being reached by a process of reason. With their writings it was possible to compare passage with passage and cause with cause.

From the primary question of the canonicity of the Scriptures themselves to the quite current question of the organization of the Church, Jewel relied upon patristic authority. His answer to the question of the canon was that it had been settled once and for all by the early Church in the persons of the fathers.[44] In these more recent times, he asserted, we have formed "our churches" upon the pattern of the Church of the fathers. It is to the example of their lives that we have endeavored to conform our own.[45] Jewel made it one of his major objectives to prove conformity with the great patristic leaders beyond the slightest doubt; to make the agreement absolutely clear and certain in the minds of his readers. On every point, on virtually every page, he stressed this basic agreement. These doctrines which we hold, he declared, "be cases, not of wit, but of faith; not of eloquence, but of truth; not invented or devised by us, but from the apostles and holy fathers and founders of the church by long succession brought unto us." Nor should we be accused of devising them: we claim only to be "the keepers; not the masters, but the scholars. Touching the substance of religion, we believe that the ancient catholic learned fathers believed: we do that they did: we say that they said . . . marvel not . . . if ye see us join unto" them.[46]

Since the early sixteenth century, Roman Catholic writers have argued that in doing away with the control of the Church over doctrine and the interpretation of the Bible, the reformers set in motion centrifugal forces which would end only in complete and unchecked individualism. In the main, it was by means of patristic authority that Jewel sought to disprove the existence of these forces in the Anglican Church. It was a large undertaking, for Harding

[44] See above, pp. 147–148.
[45] Jewel, *Defence, Works*, III, 191.
[46] Jewel, *Reply, Works*, II, 810.

recognized the Protestant weakness and attacked at this point ably and with great force. Nowhere did he state his case better than in his confutation of the *Apology*. There he pointed out that:

Forasmuch as the scriptures, wherein God speaketh unto us, be in sundry places not most open and plain to human senses, and many by mistaking them be deceived; were it not well done of you . . . to follow the judgment of the catholic church represented in general councils? Yea, we say boldly, that surer it is in points of faith to lean to the exposition of the fathers agreeing together, and to follow the tradition of the church, *than to trust yourselves, or to the letter of the scriptures, scanned only by your own wits.* For the church is promised to be led into all truth by the Holy Ghost. Ye cannot say any such promise hath been made to your particular company. Therefore it were not fondly done, as ye say, but wisely, say we, if ye tried and examined your doctrine, which ye pretend to be according unto the scriptures, by the rule of ecclesiastical tradition. . . .[47]

It is a clear challenge, incisive and complete. Small wonder that Bishop Parkhurst protested the order placing the *Defence* in the parish churches for the layman to read. Harding has drawn to his side both conciliar and patristic authority by identifying them with the tradition of the Roman Church, leaving the Church of England only its "own wits." It was an alignment which Jewel would never for a moment admit. He would no more allow that the Church of England relied upon individual wit and inspiration alone than he would have admitted Harding's premise that the Church of Rome possessed the true tradition. Believing that the collective, institutional, and indeed objective authority of the Roman Church could not be replaced, at least in kind, with the authority of special revelation, he claimed for the Church of England the authority of the older tradition of the fathers. The patristic tradition was objective and substantial. It led neither to Rome nor to anarchy.

In his answer to Harding's charge Jewel flatly reversed the charge

[47] From Jewel's *Defence*, *Works*, IV, 900–901. The italics are mine. Harding's original statement is here quoted verbatim except for the insertion of several commas and the capitalization of "Holy Ghost." Ayre, the Parker Society editor of Jewel's *Works*, followed the 1611 edition of the *Works* in changing "your" to "our," despite Harding and despite Jewel's own use of "your" in editions previous to 1611 (Harding, *Confutation*, pp. 274a–274b; Jewel, *Defence*, *Works*, IV, 901, n. 12).

to insist that Rome, not its critics, had substituted the judgments of men for the authority of patristic tradition. "And therein," he protested, "we find you the more blameworthy, . . . for that having without cause renounced the judgment and orders of the primitive church and ancient fathers, . . . yet nevertheless ye evermore make vaunt of your antiquity, and fray the world with a vizard of the church and a shew of old fathers." It is "as if a poor summoner, that had lost his commission, would serve citations by the virtue of his empty box."[48] Rome has in fact "forsaken the fellowship of the holy fathers."[49] In contrast, we of the Church of England "take them and embrace them as the witnesses of God's truth."[50] We do "allege against you the manifest and undoubted and agreeable judgments of the most learned holy fathers; and thereby, as by approved and faithful witnesses, we disclose the infinite follies and errors of your doctrine."[51]

Such witness of the "agreeable judgments" of the fathers, it should be noted, has to do with the exposition and interpretation of the Scriptures, not with independent patristic authority. Throughout his works, Jewel carefully distinguished between the fathers considered as interpreters of the Scriptures and the fathers as original authority for doctrine. Their place, he maintained, was that of "interpreters of the word of God." While they were "instruments of the mercy of God and vessels full of grace," while "we reverence them, and give thanks unto God for them," recognizing them as "witnesses unto the truth" and "worthy pillars and ornaments in the church of God, . . . we may not build upon them: we may not make them the foundation and warrant of our conscience: we may not put our trust in them. Our trust is in the name of the Lord."[52]

Jewel did not believe that in maintaining such a point of view he was belittling their authority or showing disrespect for their judgment. He was rather following their own teaching and example.

---

[48] Jewel, *Defence, Works*, IV, 901. [49] *Ibid.*, III, 229.

[50] *Ibid.*, IV, 901.

[51] *Ibid.*, III, 229.

[52] Jewel, *Holy Scriptures, Works*, IV, 1173. Jewel was in complete agreement here with Peter Martyr who had written in regard to the problem of patristic authority versus the authority of the Scriptures: "We are called Theologians, and such we would be accounted: let us answer to the name and profession—unless instead of *theologi* we would be *patrologi!*" (McLelland, *Visible Words*, p. 267).

The fathers themselves, he said, would not have us accept their pronouncements as equal to those of God. They were themselves seekers after truth and always proved the rightness of their conceptions and the teachings of their fellows by consulting the Scriptures. "We allow the ancient fathers the same credit that they themselves have ever desired."[53] In the words of St. Augustine:

'We receive not the disputations or writings of any men, be they never so catholic or praise-worthy, as we receive the canonical scriptures; but that, saving the reverence due unto them, we may well reprove or refuse some things in their writings, if it happen we find they have otherwise thought than the truth may bear them. Such am I in the writings of others; and such would I wish others to be in mine.' Likewise he writeth to St. Hierome: . . . 'I reckon not, my brother, that ye would have us so to read your books as if they were written by the apostles or prophets.'[54]

Only the Scriptures themselves, according to Jewel, had the complete authority of the divine. He revered the fathers above ordinary men, as true saints of the Church, but for him their greatness remained the greatness of men. Though they were close to the age of the apostles they lacked the complete knowledge and inspiration of those who had known Jesus.

The interpretative authority of the patristic writings, as Jewel conceived it, was neither rigid nor absolute. A particular teaching was not authoritative in and of itself merely on the grounds that it was patristic. To begin with, since their primary function was the interpretation of the Scriptures, the greatest care must be used in studying patristic interpretations against the background of the scriptural passages interpreted. Their conclusions, to be accepted, must be subjected to reasonable demonstration and proof. According to St. Augustine, Jewel noted, teachings are to be received not because of those who held them but because their proponents are "able to persuade" the student "either by other canonical writers or else by some likely reason."[55]

These principles Jewel applied consistently and skilfully in his

---

[53] Jewel, *Defence, Works,* III, 176; Cranmer had developed this point at length in his *Confutation of Unwritten Verities (Remains,* IV, 173–91).

[54] Jewel, *Defence, Works,* III, 176.

[55] *Ibid.,* III, 227.

own handling of the patristic exegesis, giving the method he advocated the all-important support of example. He brought to the specific case a sound knowledge of the literature and its historical background and an unusual fund of commonsense. As a trained scholar he insisted that the fathers be examined as far as possible in their own writings, that they be accepted as authoritative guides only at first hand, not in quotations taken second- or third-hand from later authors. He particularly objected to the citation as authority of passages which were to be found only in such compilations as those of Gratian and Peter Lombard.[56] Such passages, he claimed, were in most cases either misquoted or taken out of their original context or, worse still, quite without any foundation whatsoever in the original works.

Jewel was equally sceptical of the genuineness of certain works long accepted simply because they carried the name of a patristic author. His analysis of several such writings is historical criticism in the best tradition of Valla and Erasmus. For instance, in the case of a piece cited by Harding as a contemporary life of St. Basil, Jewel noted that since the actual author of the work discussed events which occurred centuries after Basil's death, he could hardly have been a contemporary of Basil. Equally damning, Jewel observed, was this very late author's flat contradiction of so much that is generally accepted about Basil on the authority of indisputably trustworthy contemporaries, Gregory of Nazianzus, and his own brother, Gregory of Nyssa.[57]

It was not enough that a work be accepted as genuine. Consonant with his historical point of view Jewel demanded that the circumstances surrounding the composition of a particular work be carefully reviewed. It must be understood in relation to the author's life and the period in which he lived. As he wrote concerning a disputed passage from Tertullian, "I will first open the occasion of the writing and then lay forth the words. That done, I doubt not but the sense will stand clear and easy of itself."[58] To investigate the background

---

[56] Jewel, *Reply, Works*, II, 603.
[57] *Ibid.*, I, 189–191; *Defence, Works*, III, 311.
[58] Jewel, *Reply, Works*, II, 601.

of a work, to "resolve . . . words into their causes," he declared in another instance, is an "infallible way of understanding."[59]

In addition, great care should be taken to consider the relative value of an author's known works. Jewel pointed out, for instance, that those works of Augustine written before he was baptized were not to be accepted without qualification, especially when in later writings Augustine completely and unmistakably denied those things which he had taught in the earlier work.[60] In a very broad sense it was necessary to study the works of an author as a whole. The most valid and trustworthy way to make clear the meaning of a disputed passage would be to seek in the author's own works, comparable passages, instances where the words or phrases which were the occasion of dispute were used in a clearer context.[61] Still further light might be thrown on a subject by seeking comparable passages in contemporaneous authors.[62]

Jewel viewed the fathers at all times as men, not as divine oracles whose words were to be taken with complete literalness. As preachers and controversialists themselves, he pointed out, they used extreme figures of speech, rhetorical devices which were not meant to be taken literally. "In the sway of disputation," he stated, the holy fathers used "oftentimes to enlarge their talk above the common course of truth," not only for controversial purposes but with the end in view of bringing the people to a realization of higher things.[63]

Thus, for instance, Jewel argued concerning a passage from Chrysostom quoted by Harding in support of transubstantiation. Chrysostom, he wrote, in this place "inflameth his speech with rhetorical amplifications and heat of words" only in order to "lift up and enkindle his hearer's minds."[64]

As Colet early in the century had emphasized the necessity of

[59] *Ibid.*, I, 285.

[60] Jewel, *Defence, Works*, IV, 645.

[61] Jewel, *Reply, Works*, I, 349–350.

[62] *Ibid.*, I, 490–491.

[63] *Ibid.*, II, 608. The argument is used here in relation to patristic statements concerning the real presence.

[64] *Ibid.*, I, 487–488. The passage from which this is quoted is an excellent example of Jewel's method and should be read in its entirety.

studying the state of affairs in the church at Corinth and the problems faced by Paul in order to understand the real meaning of the Epistle to the Corinthians,[65] so Jewel stressed the importance of the natural, even mundane, conditions which had qualified the work of a church father. Such a procedure is of course open to the same criticism that Jewel once made of Harding; that he acted as if it were lawful "to examine the old learned fathers upon the rack and to make them speak what him listeth."[66] In all fairness to Jewel, however, this does not seem a just criticism. He presented his point of view in interpretation most persuasively, supporting his arguments by a wealth of example. While he may have erred at times in interpretation, the evidence is there in his own writings and in those of his opponent to be considered by the reader and judged accordingly.

While Jewel's procedure is thoroughly in keeping with the generally accepted methods of modern scholarship, it is rare even today in controversial writings and certainly it was unusual in his own day. Not that he showed complete historical objectivity and his opponents none at all. Jewel was just as much a controversialist as those who entered the lists against him. But he was the better scholar. Hence he was able to make use of sound historical method even in controversy. This is not the place to attempt an assessment of Jewel's ability as a historian of the early Church. The question could not be settled finally in any case since so much of the data is still in dispute; but when allowance is made for the limitations of historical study in the sixteenth century, Jewel's conclusions do not appear to differ markedly from those of the more moderate Roman Catholic scholars like Duchesne. Without question Jewel himself was honestly convinced of the rightness of his own conclusions; he believed patristic authority to be valid authority: on patristic evidence he judged the Church of Rome guilty of denying its early heritage. That he could prove this in open controversy with an able opponent backed by the full resources of Louvain must in itself have been singularly convincing to him. Not once in all of his writings was he forced either to avoid a challenge or to admit that the teachings

[65] Frederic Seebohm, *The Oxford Reformers* (London, 1911), pp. 78–83.
[66] Jewel, *Reply, Works*, II, 602.

of the fathers went against him. It was a heartening achievement.

Jewel was too familiar with the corpus of patristic literature not to recognize that despite the most careful and painstaking textual and historical scholarship, the very characteristic of the literature which appealed most to him as an apologist and controversialist, its tremendous range and variety, could be a source of grave weakness. As a matter of fact, scholarship tended to underline the contradictions rather than to blur them. The more careful the scholar the more apt he was to find some nugget of patristic wisdom to support his own particular point of view—only to a slightly less extent than with the Bible itself and to a much greater extent than with the decrees of the early councils. To avoid this danger, to insure stability and trustworthiness in his chief source of interpretative authority, Jewel insisted that even the most carefully verified teachings of the fathers be further tested.

First of all, patristic teaching, to be regarded as valid authority, must represent a general agreement among the fathers, not an isolated opinion maintained by an individual father. Secondly, as a corollary, the fathers must be certain in their conclusions. And finally, they must regard the particular teaching as essential to Christian doctrine, not a matter of choice, regardless of their agreement and certainty.

The determination of whether or not the fathers were in agreement upon a specific point of doctrine plays a major part in Jewel's patristic exegesis. Here he had full opportunity for the examination of a body of evidence, for reasonable analysis and demonstration, for the "exercise of judgment," in which he took such pride. And for the procedure he was able to cite good precedent. In the early Church, he noted, the bishops themselves always consulted one another on doubtful points and were sure of the rightness of their teachings only when they had considered the judgment of their fellow bishops. They neither wished nor expected to be accepted on their individual authority alone.[67] Furthermore, "the same fathers' opinions and judgments, forasmuch as they are sometimes disagreeable one from another, and sometimes imply contrarieties and con-

[67] *Ibid.*, I, 382.

traditions, . . . alone and of themselves, without farther authority and guiding of God's word, are not always sufficient warrants to charge our faith. . . . thus the learned catholic fathers themselves have evermore taught us to esteem and to weigh the fathers."[68]

It is for this reason that on every important question considered in his longer works there is such a plethora of patristic evidence. No single characteristic of his procedure is more marked than this. The congress of fathers before whom each question was debated was always a large one and always unanimous in its vote. While he had challenged his opponents to cite one passage from one father in support of their views, and had been able to counter and to dismiss all such evidence, his own proof never rested on so slight a basis. Jewel was not content with one citation. Agreement upon the particular point by a large number of fathers must always be shown. And except where he felt there could be no shadow of a doubt, agreement was demonstrated by a score of citations. Trying though the method may be to the modern reader with its endless quotations and its repetitiousness, by means of it Jewel does succeed in driving his points home, in making good his contentions, through the sheer cumulative weight of the evidence.

Jewel's treatment of patristic authority in relation to the doctrine of clerical celibacy provides an excellent illustration of his method, involving as it does both the question of the general agreement of the fathers and the necessity of their having considered the particular doctrine essential.[69] The argument that Jewel had to meet was not especially involved. Harding[70] had made a fairly successful effort to confine himself to the single point of condemning the marriage of those who had taken vows. He carefully avoided any discussion of the institution of marriage itself as well as that of the question of married men becoming priests. Within these carefully circumscribed limits he presented an impressive case backed up with a large amount of patristic evidence. Jewel refused to accept his first premise on the grounds that the English priests were not votaries.

[68] Jewel, *Defence, Works*, III, 239.

[69] *Ibid.*, III, 385 ff.

[70] Harding, *Confutation*, pp. 73b–76a; in *Defence, Works*, III, 386 ff.

Harding, his chief basis of argument facing destruction, amended his statements to contend that the vows need not be spoken but were rather taken for granted in ordination according to the custom and constitution of the Church. This Jewel also refused to admit, and so the argument was removed from the fairly certain and, indeed for Jewel, dangerous grounds of the breaking of holy vows, to the far more debatable question of Church usage, where the answer would be uncertain, as far as the practice and teaching of the early Church was concerned. It would be a poor scholar who could not adduce evidence either for or against clerical celibacy, the problem of broken vows being excluded. Jewel further emphasized the element of uncertainty when he insisted that if the only authority for vows is the force of the constitution of the Church, then that is a matter in no way final, since such laws can always be changed.[71]

Although Jewel may have regarded the question as simple, he was not content to settle it on mere legalistic grounds. Indeed, it was imperative that he answer the contention of Harding that the early Church and the fathers were against a married clergy. His first aim in dealing with the problem as a whole seems to have been to render as obscure as possible the distinction between clerical marriage and marriage in general. In so doing, he was able to depict the Roman Church as inimical to the institution of marriage itself and thus arouse serious qualms in the mind of the average married lay reader. "He that condemneth marriage in a few," he protested, "must . . . be called a condemner of marriage." Of such sort are the bishops of Rome.[72] Jewel's purpose in confusing the two problems was more subtle and more fundamental to his argument than any such extreme statement would indicate. He was able to show that many of the authorities cited in favor of sacerdotal celibacy were in fact opposed to matrimony itself. Hence he could avoid the problem of proving debatable doctrine in the face of admittedly genuine patristic evidence and, instead, show that this evidence could be used effectively to deny a doctrine which was universally accepted by the whole of Christendom. In this sense, Jewel granted, "M.

[71] Jewel, *Defence, Works*, III, 428–429.
[72] *Ibid.*, III, 419.

Harding is like to find some good advantage, as having undoubtedly a great number of the holy fathers of his side."[73] For instance, there is the statement attributed to Chrysostom that marriage is no better than fornication. Such a statement, Jewel pointed out, is indefensible upon any grounds whatsoever. "Why . . . defend an open error?" Chrysostom, though one of the greatest of the fathers, was manifestly in the wrong. On the authority of the Scriptures, most clearly, and on the undoubted authority of many of the fathers, marriage was a holy thing. Why not "leave this niceness, M. Harding," Jewel suggested, "and tell us plainly that the conjunction of man and wife is not only an evil thing, but also sin before God." And then compare such teaching with the views of marriage held by St. Paul and St. Augustine.[74]

Jewel's treatment of a citation of Harding's from Origen was of the same order. While he admitted that Origen had forbidden the offering of sacrifices by any one who had not vowed chastity, he pointed out that in this instance Origen plainly meant the continual sacrifice of prayer and that therefore he was not confining his statement to priests but was including the laity as well. Such teaching, Jewel concluded, was not of the general order of the Church in the patristic period, "but one of Origen's particular and known errors."[75]

Against such examples Jewel marshaled a wealth of evidence from the fathers. He pointed out that the apostles approved of marriage and a number of the fathers had themselves been married; that in addition, the eastern Church, whose Catholicism could not be impugned, had never insisted upon the necessity of a married clergy. Celibacy as a positive and certain rule of the Roman Church was fully established only in the time of Gregory VII. Jewel concluded therefore that since biblical authority could not be cited against clerical marriage, since patristic authority was divided on the subject, since the fathers themselves were uncertain and manifestly did not consider the doctrine of clerical celibacy to be an essential doctrine, it could not be justified.[76]

[73] *Ibid.,* III, 387.
[74] *Ibid.,* III, 389.
[75] *Ibid.,* III, 397.
[76] *Ibid.,* III, 390, 396, 423, 426.

The certainty of the fathers concerning a point of doctrine was the test Jewel applied to the problem of purgatory. His discussion of the doctrine which played such a central role in the Protestant revolt is worthy of examination in some detail, both as an illustration of his views concerning patristic certainty and as a good example of his general method in dealing with patristic authority itself. He acknowledged that clear evidence of a belief in purgatory was to be found in the early Church. However, he was able to dismiss much of this evidence summarily.[77] Certain examples, such as the placing of bread in the mouths of the dead he branded as manifestly and admittedly erroneous, both on clear scriptural authority and by the universal practice of the Christian Church itself. He dismissed the testimony of Origen almost as briefly, pointing out from Origen's own works and on the testimony of Augustine that the former had considered such incredible possibilities as that of the evil angels arising from hell through the intervention of Christ, who himself should descend into hell to save them. It was a comparatively simple matter to dismiss Origen. While he was a father of great holiness, the Church itself had never canonized him, he had often bordered on the heretical, and finally had divorced himself altogether from the Catholic tradition. Origen, like Tertullian, was a father who could be most helpful, both in explanation of doctrine and in subsidiary historical exegesis, but never in the final and authoritative manner of the universally acknowledged Catholic fathers.

The doctrine of purgatory was in origin a heathen doctrine, Jewel explained, giving as authority for its existence in pagan times the testimony of Plato and Virgil—a negative but extremely effective argument in the days before modern scholars had shown and the more enlightened Christian Churches admitted the pagan origins of so much that was revered in Catholic teaching and practice.

Concerning the evidence cited by his opponent that Chrysostom and Basil had accepted the doctrine of purgatory, Jewel contended that the passages adduced from their works were authority not for purgatory but for prayers for the dead. This he pronounced a wholly different matter, since such prayers, on the evidence of these fathers and others as well, were offered for the martyrs, the apostles, and

[77] *Ibid.*, III, 560.

for the Virgin Mary herself, not one of whom could possibly have been regarded as lying in purgatory. You yourselves, he exclaimed, pray that you be delivered from hell without necessarily implying purgatory. "By your own doctrine, ye may pray for the dead, and yet never be near of your purgatory."[78]

These arguments, together with his exposition based upon scriptural and patristic evidence that Christ by his sacrifice had cleansed man from the need of purgatory, and that man goes from this life to a greater life in death, constituted Jewel's general answer to the doctrine of purgatory and the Roman Catholic evidence for it. The extremely varied approach here exemplified is typical of his method in controversy. It is in his handling of the evidence cited from Augustine in favor of purgatory, however, that Jewel really comes to grips with the problem. In the *Apology* he had admitted that Augustine "indeed sometime saith there is such a certain place" as purgatory. "Sometime he denieth not but there may be such a one." However, "sometime he doubteth; sometime again he utterly denieth it to be at all."[79] According to his oft-repeated axiom that the first authority in all things must be the Scriptures, Jewel first cited a wealth of scriptural evidence which seemed to him in no sense clear authority for purgatory; rather indeed, implying its non-existence.[80] That having been done, he proceeded to a detailed examination of the passages quoted by Harding from Augustine. In these quotations, Jewel affirmed, are always to be found such phrases as: " 'it may be a question:' 'perhaps it is true:' 'as much as I think:' 'I cannot tell:' 'I could never attain to the knowledge of it.' " Augustine, he declared, was plainly in doubt concerning this question. "Therefore undoubtedly he took it neither for an article of the christian faith (for thereof it had not been lawful for him to doubt) nor for any tradition of the apostles." Furthermore, Jewel argued, Augustine had made himself quite clear when, in discussing the Catholic belief in heaven and hell, he had concluded, " 'as for any third place, we utterly know none, neither shall we find in the holy

---

[78] *Ibid.*, III, 561.

[79] Jewel, *Apology, Works*, III, 65.

[80] Jewel, *Defence, Works*, III, 565–567.

scriptures that there is any such.'" "If these words make not against your purgatory," Jewel exclaimed, "yet truly in any appearance they make but slenderly for your purgatory." To his own satisfaction, Jewel had thus established two important points, the doubt of Augustine, and the lack of scriptural foundation, the latter, it should especially be noted, on the authority of Augustine himself.

Jewel's argument may be summed up as follows: since the fathers were uncertain concerning the doctrine of purgatory, they are not to be cited as authority for it. As Augustine, in these matters, was "but a doubtful judge," he is not to be followed. For "a doubtful judge, so far forth as he doubteth, is no judge."[81] The Scriptures do not clearly set forth this doctrine; the fathers were neither certain concerning it nor in agreement upon it; therefore, the doctrine is not to be considered a necessary part of Catholic dogma.

Jewel's treatment of patristic literature suggests at times a faith in patristic authority more basic than either the result of a mere counting of heads or the most convincing historical analysis would seem to justify. It is true that he never departed from the view that as individuals the fathers were but men. They had not received as individuals the special revelation from God which set the apostles as individuals apart from other men. As a group, however, Jewel did regard them as set apart, as superior to other men. The "consent of the fathers" appears to have had for him deeper meaning than the mere numerical sum of the views of the individual fathers. Consent, agreement among them, was an instrument through which God had chosen to instruct his Church. The fathers, not merely an Augustine or a Basil or a Jerome, were "'inspired from heaven,'"[82] he wrote. The fathers "had the spirit of understanding and knew Christ's meaning."[83] The proof of the rightness of their interpretation of Christ's meaning was their agreement among themselves on the point in question. In a passage in the *Reply*, Jewel seems almost to have identified this agreement with the Spirit itself. In answer to a very personal attack which had been made upon his own belief, he

[81] *Ibid.*, III, 565.
[82] *Ibid.*, III, 238.
[83] Jewel, *Reply, Works*, I, 127.

declared: "Only the faith of Christ, and the truth of God, I cannot deny. Or with this faith, or for this faith, I trust I shall end. I cannot withstand the Spirit of God. I cannot say the consent of all the ancient catholic fathers was an heap of errors and a link of heresies." [84]

Unlike his predecessors, Jewel did not cite individual fathers merely because it suited his purpose to buttress his primary argument with supplementary evidence. He chose to rest his case squarely on patristic support. In contrast to the great apologetic and controversial works of his predecessors, Jewel's challenge sermon and the *Reply to Harding* are constructed specifically in terms of patristic authority, and the *Defence of the Apology,* though different in outline, is indistinguishable from the earlier work both in its argument and its handling of evidence.

Jewel presented no complete and systematic statement of a theory of scriptural interpretation. His views emerge as we study the apologist and controversialist in action. Although he wrote no systematic theological treatise, the basic principles of his thinking, whether reflected in his sermons and the early challenge controversy or more explictly stated in the carefully constructed *Apology* and its defense, remain singularly consistent and logical.

That he failed to present his views in systematic form was the result not so much of the controversial nature of his labors and certainly not from any dislike of order, as it was of the character of the age in which he wrote. In the first decade of the reign of Elizabeth a complete and finished solution such as that which Hooker was later to formulate would have been out of place. To the Puritans it would have seeemd blasphemous. To the conservative and Catholic-minded it would have appeared pointless. Before Hooker's solution could make an effective appeal, the Church must stand in clearer outline than did the Church of England of the fifteen-sixties. The same practical objection, though in lesser degree, would hold for a formal and systematic expression of Jewel's solution. Because of the great influence of the small group of extreme Protestants in England, and the need of continental Protestant

[84] *Ibid.,* I, 100.

support, it was necessary at all times to emphasize as much as possible not only the finality but the completeness of biblical authority. Even had he wished to do so, to have granted actual authority to the teaching and practice of the early Church, before a successful attempt had been made to dissociate it entirely from the Church of Rome, would have seemed to many Protestants, and with some justice, an invitation to Rome.

To the conservative majority in England the emphasis placed by Jewel on the interpretative authority of the early Church would naturally have an appeal. Jewel therefore stressed it as much as he possibly could without antagonizing the more Puritan-minded. It was an extremely delicate task. He must not offend the extremists, he must attempt to win over the Romanists and waverers, and yet in keeping with his own intellectual honesty, he must evolve a solution which was a solution and no compromise. Finally, having in his own mind worked this out he had to present it and the evidence for it so well that in time his way of thinking would become a way of thinking for a large group of Englishmen. This was not to be achieved by setting forth an elaborate and dogmatic system upon which agreement could not possibly be reached for many years. It was far more effective to teach by example, to prove the particular case in point, and trust that in time the underlying and unexpressed principles of such teaching would provide the basis for the natural evolution of theory and system. Such a method was thoroughly in keeping with the temper of Elizabeth and her England.

Chapter XII

The Church

The Church Catholic

The method which Jewel evolved to prove right doctrine is incomplete without its corollary, an agency which can implement the method and give definite and concrete form to doctrine. Such an agency in the nature of things is the Church, specifically, for Jewel, the Church of England. So far we have been concerned with Jewel's concept of the Church only obliquely, with reference to the "early Church" and its doctrinal relation to modern churches, and not at all, with his concept of the Church as such. Therefore, before taking up the subject of the Church of England, we must consider the Church in its broader aspects, the Church Catholic and the relation of the Church Catholic to the particular churches.

In his treatment of Catholicity and his stress upon the ecumenical character of the Church Catholic, Jewel represents the full development of two major traditions of Reformation Christianity, traditions all too frequently ignored or lost sight of by historians of the Reformation, the conviction of the leading reformers from Luther to Calvin that the reformed Churches "were the perpetuators of the catholic church of which Rome had become the betrayer,"[1] and the devotion of many of them, especially Bucer and Cranmer and Calvin, to the concept of ecumenical Christianity.

The Church Catholic, as Jewel understood it, was truly universal

---

[1] McNeill, *Unitive Protestantism,* p. 63; ch. ii, *passim.*

[2] Jewel, *Apology, Works,* III, 59.

and all-embracing.[2] "The church of God hath been ever from the beginning, and shall continue unto the end, and over spreadeth all the parts of the world, without limitations of time or place."[3] The Church so conceived, has such breadth, such comprehensiveness,[4] that the mind cannot grasp it in concrete terms at all. At times, in fact, it is difficult to distinguish the Church in its visible manifestation from the Church invisible. The sole bond of the Church, wrote Jewel, is Christ himself. He alone is prince of this kingdom, He alone is head of the Church.[5] Jewel, however, was clearly thinking in terms of a visible Church for, "the church of Christ, which containeth the churches through all the world, is joined together in the unity of the Spirit, and hath the cities of the law, of the prophets, of the gospel, and of the apostles. This church goeth not forth, or beyond her bounds, that is, the holy scriptures."[6] The Church is exalted, in a sense it is unlimited, yet at the same time it is strictly circumscribed. It cannot dictate the articles of faith nor control the sources of authority. Its authority is only of the Word. " 'We believe that there is a holy church' " Jewel quoted Augustine, " 'but we believe not *in* the holy church,' for the church is not God, nor is able of herself to make or alter any one article of the faith." Thus the Church having acknowledged the validity of the scriptural law must submit herself to that law. Its authority is not "over and above the scriptures."[7]

In so broadening and at the same time limiting the concept of the universal Catholic Church, Jewel had two aims. The first of these was primarily negative. Of the foundations of Roman supremacy, one of the most basic was its narrowed concept of Catholicity, that is, that Catholicity was only within the confines of the Roman jurisdiction. Of comparable importance was its actual, if not theoretical independence of the original revelation as a source of authority. By broadening the concept of the Church Catholic and at the

[3] Jewel, *Defence, Works*, III, 190.
[4] *Cf.*, Jordan, *Toleration*, I, 85.
[5] Jewel, *Apology, Works*, III, 59.
[6] Jewel, *Thessalonians, Works*, II, 819.
[7] Jewel, *Defence, Works*, III, 434, 442.

same time limiting its power by scriptural law external to it, Jewel removed the very foundation stones of the Roman structure. At the same time he attained a vital positive objective. A broadened concept of Catholicity made provision for the existence of particular churches and thus justified the use of the term "Catholic" by the Church of England and the other non-Roman communions.

In making his case against the Roman appropriation of Catholicity Jewel returned to a basic thesis: that the Roman Church was but the Roman curia and that the curia was in essence the pope. "The two principal grounds" of Harding's whole work, he asserted in his preface to the *Defence,* are first that the pope " 'as he is the shepherd of the universal church,' " so he can never err, and secondly, that " 'the church of Rome is the whole, and only catholic church of God.' "[8] These two claims, he contended, were inextricably bound up with each other. His own answer was clear. "There neither is, nor can be any one man, which may have the whole superiority in this universal state."[9] Christ alone is head of his Church.[10] He is ever present to assist it, "and needeth not any man to supply his room, . . . there can be no one mortal creature, which is able to comprehend or conceive in his mind the universal church, that is to wit, all the parts of the world, much less able to put them in order, and to govern them rightly and duly."[11]

Since true unity is only in Christ and in the essentials of doctrine and not in a single visible Church, churches may differ in government and in nonessentials and yet remain part of the Church Catholic. Jewel regarded the virtual independence one from another of the great metropolitan sees of the early Church as a precedent. That Antioch and Alexandria, Constantinople and Rome had acknowledged each other only as equals had in no way affected adversely the Catholic truth of the Church. His many references to the Greek Church, his unqualified acceptance of it as Catholic,

[8] *Ibid.,* III, 119–120.
[9] Jewel, *Apology, Works,* III, 59; *cf.* Peter Martyr: Christ "is its Head, and to speak of an earthly Head as well is to create a two-headed monster!" (McLelland, *Visible Words,* p. 127).
[10] Jewel, *Defence, Works,* IV, 751.
[11] Jewel, *Apology, Works,* III, 59.

though it might not be in full agreement with his own Church, followed logically from his belief in particularism.

Again by the example of the early Church, Jewel argued that reformation, to be effective, need not necessarily be uniform throughout the whole Church. He pointed out that many times particular parts of the early Church had undergone reforms without the interference of some broader power or the authority of a general council.[12] Thus, as the concept of the particular Church within the Church Catholic could support the Catholicity of the Greek Church, so it could justify the existence of the differing continental Churches.

On the subject of Roman Catholicity Jewel displayed a moderation quite surprising in one whose views of the papal Church itself were so bitter. It was his belief that the Catholic Church had never ceased to exist in physical form. It is not the Church of Rome, he wrote, with which we contend and find fault. "The name of the church of Rome is catholic; but the errors and abuses thereof are not catholic." We do not attack the Church but the "great corruptions and foul deformities" that have been brought into the Church.[13] It was the point of view of Colet and Erasmus. But Jewel went far beyond the early humanists. They had clung to the institution and attacked the persons who at the time represented it. Jewel had done forever with the institution which the Church had become.

Jewel's concept of the Church Catholic denied the existence and indeed the need of a visible institutional counterpart of the Church Catholic. The visible Church was composed of those who agreed upon the fundamentals of Christian teaching. These teachings, the standards of Catholicity, were to be found in the Bible and in the early Church. The early Church was Catholic. The Church today which is Catholic must therefore agree with the early Church concerning fundamentals. The institutional inheritance upon which the Church of Rome rested its claim to be the one Catholic Church

[12] Jewel, *Reply, Works*, I, 322.
[13] Jewel, *Defence, Works*, III, 222; *cf.* Sykes, *Old Priest and New Presbyter*, p. 180: "It was implicit in Jewel's challenge that the Roman church, stripped of such excrescences and corruptions, held the fundamentals of faith, and was therefore still a branch of Christ's universal church, albeit in present need of purgation and reform. What was implied by Jewel was made explicit by Hooker. . . ."

meant nothing to Jewel. If it could not prove its possession of the doctrinal heritage of the early Church it could not claim for its teachings Catholic authority.

Within his broad concept of Catholicity he envisaged particular churches and accepted others as members in the Church, although he made no attempt to prove their membership. His interest was focussed upon that particular branch of the Church Catholic which was the Church of England. His purpose was to establish a sound basis whereby his Church could be designated a true member of that Church. By succession of doctrine he held it to be one with the Church of the apostles and the fathers, a true Catholic Church.

Doctrinal Succession

If the Church of England is of the Church Catholic, if her faith is Catholic, by what means can it be proven? In the early centuries of the Christian Church, its leaders, faced with heresy and strange prophets, based their authority upon the possession of proofs, written and oral, which had been handed down from the leader of an individual church to his successor. By tradition, these proofs had originated with the apostles and the actual handing down of documents or oral teachings had continued in a direct line to the present. Thus, authority was strengthened a hundred-fold against attacks which it could not meet by logic and dialectic. In time this tradition became that of apostolic succession and the descent became more than a mere handing down from generation to generation of certain objective teachings. In the person of priest or bishop the succession of the visible Church was given sacramental and spiritual meaning.

Jewel did not believe that the test of Catholicity lay in succession of persons, either in the sense of a mere physical handing down from generation to generation of correct teachings or in the more esoteric sense of the spiritual succession from generation to generation signified by the sacrament of ordination. He believed rather that the Catholicity of the Church was to be measured only by the degree of its conformity to the teachings of the early Church, the Church of the apostles and the fathers. Rightful succession lay therefore in the possession of right doctrine, doctrine which had no need of a continuous institution to make it valid. The proof of inheritance is not an unbroken line of succession from the apostles but the identity of modern teachings with apostolic teachings. Thus, to the Roman theory of apostolic succession Jewel opposed a theory of doctrinal succession. In doing so he flatly denied apostolic succession as a basis for doctrinal authority. By doctrinal succession he condemned the errors of the Roman Church and proved to his own satisfaction the Catholicity of the Church of England.

It is small wonder that later Anglicans, stressing the rightful apostolic succession of the Church of England, found Jewel of little help. Keble, in his introduction to Hooker's works,[14] expressed surprise that Jewel and his contemporaries did not emphasize the apostolic episcopal succession and explained their failure on the grounds of their Erastianism. But doctrinal succession was just as difficult to reconcile with Erastianism as was apostolic succession. Indeed, when Erastianism was succeeded by a thorough-going theory of the divine right of kings, it was apostolic succession rather than doctrinal succession which came to be associated with the more extreme theory of the kingship and a major prop of the monarchy. Apostolic succession was ignored in the early decades of Elizabeth's reign for more valid reasons. Keble simply forgot, as the best of Anglican historians have been prone to forget, that the deadly challenge to the Anglican Church was Rome and the forces of the Counter-Reformation, not Puritanism. He vastly oversimplified the problem when he declared that two alternatives were offered those who defended the Establishment—Erastianism and the doctrine of which the "papal supremacy is a perversion and excess," that is, apostolic succession. Keble's own statement, as a matter of fact, points towards an explanation that he overlooked. In 1558 and for many years thereafter the Anglican apologists found it as impossible as had the reformers before them[15] to make an effectively clear

---

[14] Hooker, *Works*, Editor's Preface, I, lxvi–lxvii.

[15] E.g., Calvin, *Institutes*, IV, ii, I–VI; Bullinger, *Of the Holy Catholic Church*, in Bromiley, *Zwingli and Bullinger*, pp. 309–314.

distinction between apostolic succession and its papal "perversion." Apostolic succession in the sixteenth century could only mean the road to Rome.

The problem here must not be confused with the problem of Anglican orders and the sacramental priesthood. Although he never claimed for episcopacy the exclusive prescription of Scripture,[16] Jewel, no less than Matthew Parker, believed the offices of priest and bishop to be essential to the Church and fully justified by the historical precedent of the early Church. The Church of England which Jewel defended was an episcopal Church with an ordained priesthood. Its bishops were canonically elected and consecrated.[17] The ordination of its priests had been and continued to be according to Catholic tradition. He pointed out that any questions which might be raised concerning the proper ordination of Anglican priests would apply equally to the ordination of the English Romanists. In many instances Anglicans and Romanists had been ordained by the same bishops.[18] We need only reverse this point to see that in fact it was the crux of the whole problem. The very evidence which Jewel would present to prove the validity of his own orders also made valid the orders of a Thomas Harding, as it did those of the entire body of the Marian clergy. Concerned as Jewel was to make clear beyond all question the distinction between the teachings of the Anglicanism he professed and the teachings of the Roman Catholicism of a Thomas Harding, he did not believe that orders provided the answer. Succession of place, as he called it, could argue for the other side as eloquently as for his. Apostolic succession, he believed, had been so "perverted" by Rome that it had become wholly Roman. And so he rejected it as a proof of Catholicity.

Harding clearly and ably stated the issue in his confutation of the

---

[16] Keble also expressed his surprise at this failure of the Elizabethans. "It is enough, with them, to show that the government by archbishops and bishops is ancient and allowable; they never venture to urge its *exclusive* claim" (Hooker, *Works*, Editor's Preface, I, lxvii); Sykes, *Old Priest and New Presbyter*, p. 18.

[17] Jewel, *Defence, Works*, III, 330, 334, 339.

[18] "I am a priest, made long sithence by the same order and ordinance, and I think also by the same man and the same hands, that you, M. Harding, were made priest by. . . . Therefore ye cannot well doubt of my priesthood without like doubting of your own" (Jewel, *Defence, Works*, III, 334).

Apology. He denied that the Church of England could show any proof of its "pedigree" and therefore maintained that it could prove no succession. "Shew us," he demanded, "the register of your bishops continually succeeding one another from the beginning, so as that first bishop have some one of the apostles or of the apostolic men for his author and predecessor. For by this way the apostolic churches shew what reputation they be of."[19] In his *Defence,* Jewel made it abundantly clear in what estimate he held such a succession. He admitted frankly that the English Church could not claim direct succession. "If it were certain," he said, "that the religion and truth of God passeth evermore orderly by succession, and none otherwise, then were successsion, whereof he hath told us so long a tale, a very good substantial argument of the truth." But such is not the case. In the words of Jerome, "they not always be the children of holy men that (by succession) have the places of holy men." Although the Pharisees had succeeded Moses, Christ forbade men to obey them.[20]

Succession he held to be unnecessary when the true doctrine was to be known directly. He satirized unmercifully the claims of various Roman apologists to hold, by "ascent and descent," by lineage, and the uses of heraldry, many doctrines and "fantasies" of which there was no record prior to Innocent III.[21] It has come to the point, he exclaimed, that "ye would say, the gospel of Christ, unless it be delivered by you, is no gospel." The true gospel is not that which was delivered from hand to hand but "delivered and received in the scriptures."[22] The argument of those who upheld succession, Jewel declared, might read thus: "though faith fail, yet succession must hold; for unto such succession God hath bound the Holy Ghost." The Church of England, he reflected, lacks this succession and therefore in it "we find not so many idolators, . . . scribes and Pharisees" as can be found where succession is held.[23]

St Paul saith: "Faith cometh (not by succession, but) by hearing; and hearing cometh (not of legacy or inheritance from bishop to bishop,

[19] Harding, *Confutation,* p. 56b; in *Defence, Works,* III, 321.
[20] Jewel, *Defence, Works,* III, 322–323; the parenthetical addition is Jewel's.
[21] *Ibid.,* IV, 783–784.
[22] *Ibid.,* IV, 771.
[23] *Ibid.,* III, 347.

but) of the word of God." They are not always godly that succeed the godly. . . . By succession the Turk this day possesseth and holdeth the four great patriarchal sees of the church. . . . By succession Christ saith desolation "shall sit in the holy place;" and antichrist shall press into the room of Christ.

"Succession," you say, "is the chief way for any christian man to avoid antichrist." I grant you, if you mean succession of doctrine.[24]

Such passages are not unique. The *Defence* in particular is rich in them. The substitution by Jewel of a theory of doctrinal succession for that of apostolic succession, the identification of apostolic succession with mere succession of place with no recognition of intent, as in the startling reference in the passage above to the Turk, was a positive and considered action and thoroughly in keeping with his thought as a whole. On the ground of the invalidity of apostolic succession and the rightness of doctrinal succession he condemned the teachings of the Church of Rome and justified the English Establishment. "To be Peter's lawful successor," he stated, "it is not sufficient to leap into Peter's stall. Lawful succession standeth not only in possession of place, but also, and much rather, in doctrine and diligence."[25]

We think it better to examine and try the grounds of your religion by the word of God, that is one, and uniform, and endureth for ever, than by your touch of Rome that is so uncertain and so mutable, and so often hath deceived us. . . . "If we return to the head and original of the heavenly tradition," which is the word of God, "all human error giveth place."[26]

Jewel admitted the corollary, that the English of his day must therefore have been brought up in darkness. An open break had been made with the institution which for several centuries had been known as the only Church. The break had been essential in order that the Church of England be joined once again with the true Catholic Church of the early centuries. The Catholicity of the English faith rested its proof not upon succession of place or of

---

[24] *Ibid.*, III, 348; the parenthetical additions are Jewel's.
[25] *Ibid.*, III, 201.
[26] *Ibid.*, IV, 1047.

persons but upon the agreement of its doctrines with that of the primitive Church. In the restrained and considered *Apology* Jewel eloquently stated his case for his Church.

We truly for our parts, as we have said, have done nothing in altering religion, either upon rashness or arrogancy; nor nothing but with good leisure and great consideration. Neither had we ever intended to do it, except both the manifest and most assured will of God, opened to us in his holy scriptures, and the regard of our own salvation, had even constrained us thereunto. For, though we have departed from that church, which these men call catholic, and by that means get us envy amongst them that want skill to judge, yet is this enough for us, and it ought to be enough for every wise and good man, and one that maketh account of everlasting life, that we have gone from that church which had power to err; which Christ, who cannot err, told so long before it should err; and which we ourselves did evidently see with our eyes to have gone both from the holy fathers, and from the apostles, and from Christ his own self, and from the primitive and catholic church; and we are come, as near as we possibly could, to the church of the apostles and of the old catholic bishops and fathers; which church we know hath hitherunto been sound and perfite, and, as Tertullian termeth it, a pure virgin, spotted as yet with no idolatry, nor with any foul or shameful fault; and have directed according to their customs and ordinances not only our doctrine, but also the sacraments, and the form of common prayer.[27]

The Church of England

Jewel, like Anglican apologists before him and since, was faced with a difficult and fundamental dilemma when he turned to a consideration of the Church of England itself. He believed the Church to be Catholic and the truth which it professed completely objective and beyond all human authority. Yet the bishops and clergy who constituted the Establishment and had the actual responsibility for the declaration of doctrine, were legally subject to the authority of the state. They were officers of the state, appointed by the state and holding office at the will of the state.

It is of course true that their medieval predecessors from Lanfranc to Warham had likewise been appointed by the civil government.

[27] Jewel, *Apology, Works*, III, 100.

But these men were officers of a Church whose boundaries extended far beyond England's, officers of an institution which possessed authority, in doctrinal matters at least, independent of the civil power in England. As a result, the medieval English churchman always had in reserve the latent support of the whole Church in the West. Though the position of a particular churchman might at times be extremely uncertain and weak, he could, if he chose, bring pressure to bear upon the English government to a degree impossible for Parker or Grindal or Laud.

The problem then was to achieve an independence in doctrinal matters despite an ecclesiastical framework where the practical power lay with the civil government. The Erastian solution which some Tudor Englishmen found satisfactory was unacceptable to Jewel. To admit the unqualified authority of the state in doctrinal matters would mean that he must renounce his fundamental conviction concerning the objective nature of divine truth. Concessions would have to be made that the more devout of the early Elizabethan churchmen were unprepared to make in the realm of theory, no matter how many they were forced by the pressure of circumstances to accept in fact. On the other hand, a solution that ignored the civil power would have little relation to reality and would be wholly unacceptable to the Queen.

Jewel expressed a thoroughly conventional theory of the origin and continuing source of the civil authority itself. "Touching the prince's power, we are certainly assured by God's holy word it is from God."[28] He dissociated himself altogether from any concept of popular consent, expressing abhorrence of the view that "kings have none other right of government than it has pleased their subjects by composition to allow unto them." As if God had never said "'By me and my authority kings bear rule over their subjects;'" as if "St Paul had not said, *Non est potestas nisi a Deo.*"[29] He rejected with equal vigor the view "that kings and emperors have their authority by the positive law of nations" rather than from God.[30]

[28] Jewel, *Defence, Works*, IV, 1037.
[29] *Ibid.*, III, 117.
[30] *Ibid.*, IV, 1037.

In these statements Jewel has not diverged in the least from the point of view almost universally held both on the continent and in England during the first half of the century. In Professor Allen's words, "it was really almost unnecessary to say that magistracy was an ordinance of God, . . . if everyone did not really believe these things, at least no one denied them."[31] Jewel simply restated them and heavily underlined them to strengthen his case against Rome. His extreme position stemmed, as did that of other sixteenth-century theorists, on the one hand from the challenge of the Roman assumption of divine authority and on the other from the availability of a practical answer, the civil magistrate in the person of the prince. The political developments of the sixteenth century rather than any logical philosophic evolution was responsible. While the claim of papal theorists in the fourteenth century had produced a variety of counter theories, the papal challenge of the sixteenth century was uniformly met, at least until later in the century, by recourse to the divine origin of the secular power.

As a result of his study of the early Church and interest in the precedents provided by the early Christian centuries Jewel had a wealth of evidence available to support his view of the secular power. Time and again he noted the striking contrast between contemporary papal actions and the relation of the early Church to the emperor, always with the conclusion that imperial power over patriarch, pope, and council had been complete and unquestioned.[32]

In view of the characters and motives of the early Christian emperors such an argument has little appeal to the modern student, even when he admits the validity of Jewel's evidence. But to the sixteenth-century princes the precedents would doubtless be of considerable interest, suspicious as the most professedly orthodox of them were of the papal threat to their own power. The community of interest amongst princes was a basic reality of sixteenth-century politics. A challenge to one of them, whether from peasantry, feudal nobility, or the Church, was regarded uneasily by the others, how-

---

[31] Allen, *History of Political Thought*, p. 127.
[32] Jewel, *Apology, Works*, III, 98–99; *Reply, Works*, I, 396, 415; *Defence, Works*, III, 167; *Ibid.*, IV, 992, 1009, 1027, 1033.

ever tempted they might be to cultivate the challenge in their own interest. Although the unfavorable reaction of Philip II and the Emperor Ferdinand to the Bull of Excommunication against Elizabeth may have stemmed more from their embarrassing impotence in 1570, neither had cause to welcome papal interference in the affairs of princes, unless of course, it came at his own behest and under his own control.

Whenever Jewel refers to contemporary continental rulers, without exception it is with the most profound respect. His regard for duly constituted authority appears to have been quite genuine— there is certainly no trace of the revolutionary in his make-up. But his firm grasp of the realities of European politics doubtless influenced him to as great an extent. He was as jealous as the Queen herself, not only of the rights of duly constituted magistrates but also of the reputation of England and the English in the matter of sedition and rebellion. Furthermore, as he discussed princely rights doubtless with an eye to princely reactions, so he made every effort to associate political conservatism and loyalty to the duly constituted magistrate with the opponents of Rome, English and continental alike, and conversely to associate the papal Church with sedition and rebellion. As a result, the whole question of the relation of the temporal power both to the Church of Rome and to the Protestant groups received a thorough review in his controversial works. Harding, with his eye also upon the civil ruler and with a full awareness of the sixteenth-century reverence for civil order, charged Protestantism with sedition both in its teaching and in its actions. Jewel, aware of the danger inherent in Harding's attack, reviewed in detail each instance which Harding cited and in every case absolved official Protestantism from the charge; noting Luther's action against the peasants, defending the right the "free" German princes "had possessed to draw their sword in their own defence," ruling out the example of the Munster Anabaptists on the ground that they were heretics rather than "Gospellers," and pointing out that in the case of the *Monstrous Regiment of Women* the Churches took no responsibility for the errors of individual men,—the heads of the

Churches, Calvin, Bullinger, and others, had written with authority against that work.[33]

In contrast, Jewel cited a wealth of evidence condemning the papacy as in inciter to rebellion. The long record of papal interference in imperial politics in the middle ages of course provided a splendid series of examples.[34] Nearer home were the cases of papal action against Henry II and King John, together with the more recent instance of Henry VIII. To Harding's righteous and scathing rejections of these examples Jewel replied as vigorously, though in general terms.

Notwithstanding the pope, as his manner hath been, raise commotion within the realm, and arm the subjects against their sovereign, and pull the crown imperial from his head, yet, by your doctrine, whosoever dare speak in his prince's right, is a fool, and killeth himself; as if there were no life or salvation but only under the frantic government of the pope. Such obedience and loyalty the pope hath taught you towards your prince.[35]

Harsh words, and the examples they defend arguable, to say the least. It remained for Rome herself, beginning with the Bull of Excommunication and increasingly in the years that followed its publication, to supply the evidence which would convince Englishmen of many shades of opinion that Jewel was right.

From a belief in the divine nature of the secular power a theory of popular obedience to the civil magistrate follows inevitably. And so with Jewel. "The word of God," he declared in a sermon, "chargeth all estates to be subject to their prince or higher power." The subject "must thus think with himself; I owe obedience to my sovereign; I must be subject, not because of wrath only, but also for conscience sake. If I resist, I resist the ordinance of God, and shall receive to myself damnation."[36] In the *Apology* Jewel asserted that the Church of England had always sought to "put the people in

[33] *Ibid.,* IV, 665.
[34] Jewel, *Apology, Works,* III, 76; *Defence, Works,* IV, 698.
[35] Jewel, *Defence, Works,* IV, 1076–1077.
[36] Jewel, *Thessalonians, Works,* II, 831, 862.

mind of their duty to obey their princes and magistrates, yea, though they be wicked."[37] We teach the people "to be subject to the higher powers, not only for fear, but also for conscience. We teach them that whoso striketh with the sword by private authority shall perish with the sword. If the prince happen to be wicked, or cruel, or burdenous, we teach them to say: . . . 'Tears and prayers be our weapons.'"[38]

There could be no serious dispute over the power of the prince as the source of civil order. No practical alternative was available. But the extension of princely authority in the ecclesiastical and spiritual spheres was an altogether different matter. Since the reformers exalted the princely power primarily to oppose the Church of Rome and since their basic concern, after all, was with the ecclesiastical and spiritual power of Rome, not its secular manifestations, they had no choice but to accept the extension of princely power well beyond the limits of secular affairs. How far it should extend and whether or not it could be confined once it broke the older limitations, were grave questions which eventually confronted every reformer and reform group.

Jewel's treatment of obedience reflected an implicit acceptance of the ideal of the one commonweal. There could be no division of power in the state. Obedience is owed to the prince by spirituality as well as by the laity. The prince "is the head of the people, not only of commons and laity, but also of the ministers and clergy."[39] He has the right and duty therefore to judge in causes ecclesiastical.[40] Furthermore, and here Jewel turned to what for the reformer was really the crux of the matter, "every prince is bound in the whole to see the reformation of his own church and country."[41] God has raised up "faithful magistrates and Godly princes, not to do the priests' or bishops' duties, but to force the priests and bishops to do their duties."[42] In this last statement, in the negative qualifying

---

[37] Jewel, *Apology, Works*, III, 74.   [38] Jewel, *Defence, Works*, III, 171.

[39] Jewel, *Sermons, Works*, II, 997.   [40] Jewel, *Defence, Works*, IV, 963–69.

[41] Jewel, *Reply, Works*, I, 323.

[42] Jewel, *Defence, Works*, IV, 959; *cf.* Peter Martyr's letter to Elizabeth (Dec. 22, 1558): "If Bishops and Ministers of Churches will not do their duty, if in handling doctrine and administering of sacraments they forsake the just rules of Holy Scripture—who but a godly Prince shall recall them into the right way?" (McLelland, *Visible Words*, p. 56).

phrase, is a specific limitation upon the prince's power, one to which Jewel recurred when Harding produced the argument that the English king, in replacing the pope, had taken over the pope's priestly functions. These functions, Jewel insisted, remained, as in the past, in the hands of the qualified priest. The bishop and the prince, he explained, "have not both one kind of charge." While the duty of the bishop is to preach, to administer the sacraments and the other offices of the Church, the charge of the prince is "not to do any of these things himself," but to see that they are done by the bishops.[43] Furthermore, while the priest must "be authorized by his prince by outward and civil calling," in order to be a proper minister he must be inwardly called by God.[44] The prince cannot "bind and loose, or minister sacraments, or preach the gospel, or sit down and hear confessions."[45] Jewel noted with satisfaction that the English kings had never attempted to take upon themselves the office of priest or bishop. However, while the king may not in "any wise execute the bishop's office"; he "may lawfully correct and chastise the negligence and falsehood of the bishop; ... in so doing, he doth only his own office and not the bishop's."[46]

Such a limitation upon the prince's power is not only obvious and simple: it can be reconciled with the most exalted views of sixteenth-century kingship. No ruler or royal apologist, not even Henry VIII himself, had suggested that the king might perform the sacramental functions of the priest.[47] No final sanction existed to prevent it simply because none was needed. In the realm of doctrine, however, the situation was far otherwise. The same Henry VIII, though he might respect the priest in the performance of his sacramental duties, did not hesitate to pronounce with authority upon the meaning of the performance.[48] Jewel's views presented so far suggest nothing

[43] Jewel, *Defence, Works*, IV, 959.

[44] Jewel, *Sermons, Works*, II, 1022; *Thessalonians, Works*, II, 831–832.

[45] Jewel, *Defence, Works*, IV, 976.

[46] *Ibid.*, IV, 985.

[47] See E. T. Davies, *Episcopacy and the Royal Supremacy* (Oxford, 1950), pp. 64, 82, 107.

[48] Frere and Kennedy, *Visitation Articles*, II, 34–43. The Injunctions of 1538 clearly trespassed beyond administrative matters into the realm of doctrine: see Davies, *Episcopacy*, pp. 72–73.

to indicate disagreement with the Henrician precedent—the priest as a specially trained servant of the prince. Such, however, was not his view. At one point in his debate with Harding on the subject, he suggested a limitation on the prince more basic and far-reaching. While "it is a great arrogancy," he wrote,

to advance a bishop above a king; notwithstanding in some good meaning it may be true. So a judge, in knowledge of the law; . . . so a pilot, in knowledge of the sea, and guiding of a ship; so a captain, in martial affairs, is above any king; and it behoveth a king, be he never so wise or mighty, in every of these several faculties to be guided by them. And thus is the king inferior, not only to a bishop, as you say, but also to every inferior priest. . . .

For the prince is bound to the obedience of God's word no less than if he were a private subject. And if he refuse to hear and reverence the same, as the declaration of God's holy will, he is accursed.[49]

Despite the harsh qualifications of the bishop's power in relation to royal power (the passage occurs in a refutation of the papal claim to power over kings and magistrates), the relation that finally emerges is different indeed from the one we normally associate with Henry and the Church during his lifetime. While it might be argued on the basis of the wording of the first paragraph that the king has the right to overrule the bishop in spiritual matters to the same extent he can overrule the judge, the pilot, or the captain, each in his field, the very nature of the area of priestly knowledge, in contrast to that of the others, indicates a difference in kind rather than degree. No one could question the *right* of the king, as opposed to his wisdom, in overruling pilot or captain. Few would question his *right,* as the final source of justice in the land, to overrule the judge, since the more exalted the level of the law, as one approaches the law of nature and the law of God, the less the difference between the knowledge of the king and the knowledge of his judges. But it would be difficult indeed to make a case for the *right* of the king to overrule God's Word. And Jewel had no doubt concerning the superior knowledge of priest and bishop at this point. "Touching

⁴⁹ Jewel, *Defence, Works,* IV, 674.

the knowledge of God's word and cases of religion, certain it is the king is inferior to a bishop."[50]

As in the case of the less likely possibility of the prince's attempting to perform the priestly office, so here in the more controversial area of the declaration of doctrine there is no sanction to protect the Church from the encroachment of the civil power. "It *behoveth* a king, . . . to be guided by" the priest! Since Jewel was fully aware that no such sanction existed in the English Church, it was perhaps the better part of wisdom not to create one in theory. The sovereign had shown in word and deed that she had no intention of violating the priestly office,[51] however vigorous she might be in seeing to it that the episcopal and priestly functions were properly performed.

On the right of the prince to interfere in matters of faith and doctrine, an area where Elizabeth's position could not be so easily determined, Jewel is silent. Fortunately for him, as for his fellow bishops, there seems to have been no conflict on the fundamentals of doctrine, the result perhaps of the skill with which the episcopal bench had been selected—or royal indifference. Since Archbishop Parker and his colleagues were more anxious for support from the crown than for protection against it, whatever influence Elizabeth exerted did not appear to them to be interference. The relation between the actual situation and the theory, or rather the absence of theory, is very intimate. The major problem, the existence of which Jewel tacitly admitted, he wisely did not attempt to solve.

If the state of affairs in England allowed Jewel to bypass the question, affairs in Scotland did not. Nemesis, in the person of the Scottish Queen, forced him to a positive practical answer as it had forced Elizabeth to positive action, the implications of both being unavoidable and far-reaching. The Scots had justified their rebellion against their duly constituted sovereign on the grounds of her persecution of the true religion. Jewel, aware of the direction in which Harding, with his identification of the Scottish rebels and "your gospel" sought to drive him, at first took refuge in the claim that

[50] *Ibid.*, IV, 675.
[51] See Elizabeth's "Admonition, in explanation of her supremacy" (1559), in Jordan, *Toleration,* I, 92, n. 1.

the Scottish lords had armed originally against the foreign invader rather than against their Queen. In short, the war was foreign and political rather than internal and religious. But Jewel knew Scottish affairs too well not to recognize the weakness of his position and stated frankly that "the subject is bound to obey his prince," but "not in all things without exception"; only insofar "as God's glory is not touched." The Scottish leaders had learned that it was better to obey God than man. Furthermore, a godly prince should not "take it as any dishonour to his estate to see God obeyed before him." In conclusion, "the queen of Scotland . . . is obeyed of her subjects, so far as is convenient for godly people to obey their prince."[52]

Jewel has replaced his theory of obedience with its opposite. Rebellion can provide the sanction necessary to guarantee the prince's support of the true religion. Small wonder that Elizabeth hesitated so long and protested so much as she faced the issue of aiding Mary's rebellious subjects when the action finally taken evoked a defense of such nature from her conservative bishop and apologist.

Jewel obviously presents conflicting views on the subject of obedience and rebellion. On the one hand subjects should obey in religious matters and trust to God. On the other hand they might have good cause in the future to rejoice that rebellion has occurred and that true religion has thereby been maintained. How such a rebellion is to be reconciled with a doctrine of obedience, Jewel does not say. He appears to have been ready to discard obedience in actual cases where the prince did not maintain the true religion.[53] His belief in the necessity of obedience was almost entirely a matter of theory. That such a contradiction did not result in great embarrassment to him is due to the coincidence of theory and fact in the case of his own prince and Church. His prince supported the true religion. Hence, in the only case that really mattered to him, he was able to preach a practical obedience in keeping with his theory. One is forced to conclude that Jewel, like many of his contemporaries, would have adopted a very different attitude had religious conditions in his own country been less favorable, had the temporal power

[52] Jewel, *Defence*, III, 172–173.
[53] Jewel, *Apology, Works*, III, 55; *Sermons, Works*, II, 973, 976–977, 1005.

maintained a religion that he could not reconcile with his own beliefs. Certainly there were significant elements in his thought which later might be used most effectively in defense of rebellion and tyrannicide.

Jewel qualified the theory of obedience in a somewhat different direction when he maintained that the prince could not control the inward faith of his subjects, that he had no power over those things which a man considers essential to salvation. However, the subject has no recourse in such a case save to nonresistance. He owes obedience to the prince in all things; if the prince demand that he deny the Word his only recourse is martyrdom. This belief is clearly stated in a hypothetical speech of a martyr to the ruler who has condemned him:

> O my gracious lord, I would fain do your commandment: I am your subject: I have done faithful service with my body, and with my goods; but I cannot serve you against God: . . . I may not bear false witness against the Lord. My life is not dear unto me in respect to the truth. I know, if I should deny him to save my life, I should lose it; and, if I lose my life for his sake, I shall find it. . . . I owe you obedience; I will not resist your power; for, if I should resist, I should resist the ordinance of God. I am subject to you for conscience' sake. . . . This is the only thing wherein I cannot yield. . . . there is no creature in heaven or earth that can carry me from that blessed hope I have conceived by his word.[54]

In the *Defence,* Jewel stated the principle that underlay the martyr's action. "In civil government a king is a king; and so hath God commanded him to be known; but, after that we be once come to the reverence and obedience of God's will, there God only is the king; and the king, be he never so mighty, is but a subject."[55] To this principle Jewel recurred many times. He admitted that while princes could be, and indeed had been, most helpful to the protecting and promulgating of the gospel, as was their duty, nevertheless, "the gospel came not first from them."[56] The Word of God had existed through all time: everyone, princes, magistrates, subjects, should live under it

---

[54] Jewel, *Holy Scriptures, Works,* IV, 1172.

[55] Jewel, *Defence, Works,* IV, 670.

[56] *Ibid.,* III, 194.

and according to it. The Word is the law by which kings should rule. If the king disregard the law, if his actions contradict the law, even if he attempt to destroy the law, the people have no legal recourse. Jewel makes no provision for resistance to the prince, not even the legal or constitutional resistance of the duly constituted magistracy which John Ponet and Calvin had allowed and which his friend Humphrey and the Puritan leaders supported.[57] For Jewel it was not practical, and in his own case and for his own country it did not seem necessary.

A final and basic question remains: who is to interpret the law of God, who is to have responsibility for the formulation of doctrine? In developing his answer Jewel was hardly a free agent, since he wrote in the face of events which had already taken place. His task would have been relatively easy had he been able to posit a completely independent convocation of the Church of England as the agency responsible. Such a convocation, as the true successor to the councils of the early Church, would have provided an admirable answer to the "false councils" of the late middle ages. However, in the early years of Elizabeth's reign, it was only too obvious that, whatever action convocation might eventually take, it was not convocation but prince and Parliament who had the final authority in the constitutional and doctrinal organization of the English Church. Jewel therefore faced the issue squarely and accepted the authority of the civil power. In a sermon delivered before the Queen, he declared that "your grace hath already redressed the doctrine."[58] At another time he stated that the people "are commanded to change their religion."[59] That the Roman Catholic critic of Anglicanism should cite these passages with such gusto is as incomprehensible to the historian as it is for the Anglican apologist to deplore them.[60]

---

[57] W. S. Hudson, *John Ponet (1516?–1556): Advocate of Limited Monarchy* (Chicago, 1942), pp. 160–161, 192–194, 189, 201–203; Davies, *Problem of Authority,* pp. 135–136.

[58] Jewel, *Sermons, Works,* II, 1015, cited by Hughes, *Reformation,* III, 72.

[59] *Ibid.,* II, 1024, cited by Hughes, *Reformation,* III, 59.

[60] Professor Dawley's comment is very much to the point: "Hooker's famous remark, 'By the goodness of Almighty God and his servant Elizabeth, we are,' is only an embarrassment to those who fail to grasp the sixteenth-century conception of the proper functions of the 'Godly Prince' and the 'True Obedience' owed him" (Dawley, *John Whitgift,* pp. ix–x).

Jewel was simply accepting what was to him a simple fact. The official doctrine had been changed under Elizabeth's authority just as a few years previously official doctrine had been changed in the other direction under Mary's authority. Surely, to the Roman Catholic, the rightness of doctrine authorized under Mary had been in no way affected by Mary's action. Nor to the Anglican could the rightness of the teachings of the Prayer Book and the Articles be affected in the least by Elizabeth's willingness to have them made official. The historian must observe, however, that doctrine in each case was *made official* by authority of the civil magistrate. So it was with Lutheranism in the German states, with Calvinism in Geneva, and with Roman Catholicism in the France of Henry II and Louis XIV.

In answer to his own rhetorical query in the *Apology* whether it were treason to attempt the settlement of religious matters without a "sacred general council," he wrote that "truly we do not despise councils, assemblies, and conferences of bishops and learned men; neither have we done that we have done altogether without bishops or without a council. The matter hath been treated in open parliament, with long consultation, and before a notable synod and convocation."[61] His answer to a similar questioning of his authority by Cole in the early controversy was worded somewhat differently and in a sense gives further meaning to the one above. The doctrine that is called into question, he stated, "was grounded upon God's word, and authorized and set forth by the queen's majesty, and by the assent of the whole realm."[62] In his final reply to Cole, Jewel paraphrased the above passage to read: "the doctrine . . . which I knew to be established by God's word, and by *sufficient* authority throughout this realm."[63] The ideas are expanded further in the *Reply* where Jewel declared that

in these cases of religion there was nothing at any time done either hastily and upon the sudden, or by any small assembly; but in the open parliament of the whole realm, with great and sober deliberation, with indifferent and patient hearing what might be said and answered and

[61] Jewel, *Apology, Works,* III, 93.
[62] Jewel, *Answer to D. Cole's Second Letter, Works,* I, 31.
[63] Jewel, *Reply to Cole, Works,* I, 44. The italics are mine.

replied of both sides, and at last concluded with public authority, and consent of all states and orders of this most noble kingdom.[64]

What has appeared to be unqualified Erastianism in regard to doctrine as well as to church government takes on a different color in this passage. Jewel throughout his works had placed great emphasis upon the full presentation of evidence concerning a question—the original biblical authority or authorities, and all the evidence relevant to the point in question from the early Church, the councils, and the fathers. With this before them, ordinary men with the aid of grace and the use of reason were capable of reaching a valid conclusion. In theory, if not in fact, such had been the procedure in the English assemblies of the early years of the reign. Obviously the power of Parliament in religious matters could not affect in any way the fundamental truth of religion. Parliament was a human agency in divine matters and nothing more. It possessed the faults of a human agency, but it possessed greater virtues than most human agencies. It was a body of baptized Christians representing the Christian commonweal of England.

In answer to Harding's assertion that the English possessed a "parliament-religion," Jewel declared: "We will not discuss the right and interest of the parliaments of England. As much as concerneth God's everlasting truth, we hold not by parliament, but by God." Parliaments, he pointed out, had shown themselves but uncertain authorities in these matters, in the time of Queen Mary for example, but they remain on the whole the best representative of the realm. Parliament, indeed, is the only body which speaks for the whole, and, he insisted, it may speak for the whole, spiritual as well as temporal, though the spirituality do not subscribe. As for its being a "parliament-religion," he reminded Harding, every change in religious matters in times past had been by the authority of the King and Parliament. By this authority the pope was brought back into England in the previous reign and by this authority he has been sent away.[65]

[64] Jewel, *Reply, Works*, II, 629.
[65] Jewel, *Defence, Works*, IV, 903–904.

From these admissions it is clear that Jewel regarded parliamentary authority in religious matters as no more than a practical working solution. The problem arising from the possibility of Parliament's pronouncing in favor of that which was contrary to God's law he did not consider. The explanation, as we have noted before, probably lies in the practical situation which he faced. The Parliament and the Queen had given support to a doctrinal structure of which he approved. Since he was not considering the theoretical basis of the Establishment, since indeed he saw no need of considering it, he was able to ignore the problem.

Satisfied as he was with the course of events, it was natural that he should defend that authority which he held responsible for them. Parliament, he maintained, had debated and considered religious problems since early times. It had always been the duty of Catholic princes, "and that even by the parliaments of the realm," to attend to matters of religion "before all other affairs of the common weal." He admitted the imperfections of past Parliaments, and therefore by implication the fallibility of present Parliaments, but he accepted the prince in Parliament as a practical authority in the Church. In frank recognition of the weakness of his position he could only conclude that "the hearts of princes and determinations of parliaments are in God's hand."[66]

There remain then two propositions that in theory cannot be reconciled. First, there is a body of divine truth independent of all human authority. This body of truth can be known and its rightness can be demonstrated. Secondly, the rightful authority of the realm in spiritual affairs as well as in temporal affairs is the prince in Parliament. This authority in no way affects the nature of the divine truth. Jewel was able to overlook the possibility of contradiction. In his eyes the prince in Parliament had declared that to be right doctrine which actually was in the final sense right doctrine; perhaps more correctly, had accepted right doctrine. The English Church did not give authority to doctrine as the Church of Rome gave authority, without further question of proof. The rightness of English doctrine had to be proved. Jewel assumed without question

[66] *Ibid.*, IV, 905.

that it was proved. After proper consideration of the Scriptures, and the teachings of the early Church and the fathers concerning them, men had come to agreement upon the essentials of doctrine. With Rome the proof was incidental, the authority of the Church was final. In Jewel's conception of Anglicanism the proof was essential and the authority of the Church only a practical necessity.

Conclusion

Jewel did not present a final solution to the problem of authority for doctrine. His contribution lay not in the establishing of a declarative authority but rather in the setting up of a method by which doctrine was to be found, a method fundamentally incompatible with an absolute declarative authority. As a practical matter he accepted the government of the Church of England, but he never admitted that it possessed absolute authority in the determining and declaring of doctrine. It is doubtful if there could have been a complete solution to the problem short of claiming for the English Church a power comparable to that claimed by the Church of Rome. Had Jewel been willing to admit the perfect clarity of the meaning of divine revelation concerning all matters, there would have been no need of interpretation and consequently no problem. The Elizabethan settlement and its early defenders neither proclaimed the institution absolute nor did away with it as a true *ecclesia*. The Elizabethan Anglicans occupied a delicate position. The only sanction for their system of doctrinal authority they could logically cite was the sanction supplied by the force of truth itself, an exalted sanction certainly, but not an effective practical sanction. The practical sanction they had to depend on was the political authority of the government—merely an enforcing authority. As a guarantee of the truth of doctrine, it was no sanction at all.

This enforcing authority, as we know, was given for reasons that were other than religious. The moderate group, weak in popular support because it could not claim absolute certainty and finality for its teachings, was kept in control by the civil government for political reasons. But because this moderate group could not have survived without the aid of the civil power it does not follow that it lacked integrity and spiritual depth. Although it was dependent upon the state, and hence, from a spiritual point of view, artificially supported, its thought was neither artificial nor weak. There were many devout men who sincerely desired to break with Roman absolutism and yet not deliver themselves into the hands of another absolute institution or an absolutism of the letter of the Word equally severe. These men, of whom Jewel was one of the most outstanding, achieved a working solution which satisfied them and many others. That their labor would have been in vain without the aid of the civil power, does not invalidate its sincerity and its true greatness.

Jewel's solution, I repeat, is incomplete. It has an almost tentative quality. The civil government might posses legal power over religious matters. If it went no further than it had gone, if it did not interfere in essentials, then study and proof and discussion among reasonable men might lead towards a further understanding of divine truth. As to non-essentials, someone must deal with them. The Church by the authority of the civil power was the obvious choice. There is something very English in this. There is no attempt to deal in absolutes, no attempt to answer fully the unanswerable.[1] The system, quite divorced from the political forces which had made it possible, could and did satisfy the religious aspirations of many.

But there were those who preferred absolutes, who dealt in certainties. The Puritans by their attack upon the distinction drawn between non-essentials and essentials, struck at the system's weakest point and drove its defenders eventually to extend the authority of the crown in Parliament to essentials of doctrine as well as to non-essentials.[2] Hooker, as Professor Jordan has pointed out,[3] would not

---

[1] *Cf.* McNeill, *Unitive Protestantism*, p. 222: "The Israel of which (Cranmer) was the Moses has like him exhibited more moderation than zeal, more breadth of view than depth of conviction, and has often been content with temporizing measures. But there is a kind of greatness in the spirit of the Anglican communion of which these qualities are the natural accompaniment and, we might say, the condition. Its catholicity, comprehensiveness, and variety of spontaneous religious expression have been made possible by the very elasticity and indeterminateness which are found exemplified in the psychology of its chief reformer."

[2] Whitgift declared: "The continual practice of Christian Churches, in the time of Christian magistrates, before the usurpation of the Bishop of Rome, hath been to give to Christian princes supreme authority in making ecclesiastical orders and laws, *yea, and that which is more, in deciding of matters of religion, even in the chief and principal points*" (Whitgift, *Defence of the Answer, Works*, I, 184, quoted by Allen, *History of Political Thought*, p. 174. The italics are mine).

[3] Jordan, *Toleration*, I, 231.

face the problem as clearly as did Whitgift. But his failure to do so was not a mere lack of frankness. He differed fundamentally from Whitgift. While the latter tended to settle the problem by a complete surrender to Erastianism, Hooker endeavored to indicate a solution on the basis of reason and tradition. By its very nature such a solution, like Jewel's, could not be final. That is not to say that Hooker's work is as incomplete as Jewel's. With his development of the appeal to reason he provided, it might be said, a justification for the lack of a final solution. His thought differs in degree, in marked degree from that of Jewel, but it remains a difference in degree. Hooker's work, depite its much greater emphasis upon reason, is consonant with and indeed complementary to the work of his patron. Jewel's reasonable appeal to a demonstrable authority is developed by Hooker to a point where reason itself becomes the chief authority.

Jewel's work was a successful defense of the Church of England in the early years of Elizabeth, years that were not ready for the solution of Hooker. It served to strengthen the Church in the eyes of men outside, and, far more important, it gave Englishmen confidence and even faith in their Church. It was thus a major contribution to the strengthening of the Establishment that Hooker was to defend, and at the same time it served as a basis upon which Hooker could construct his greater work.

BIBLIOGRAPHY

INDEX

Bibliography

Abbott, E. S., et al., *Catholicity: A Study in the Conflict of Christian Traditions in the West.* Westminster, 1947.

Allen, J. W., *A History of Political Thought in the Sixteenth Century.* London, 1928.

Allison, S. F., et al., *The Fulness of Christ: The Church's Growth into Catholicity.* London, 1950.

Bainton, R. H., *Here I Stand.* New York, 1950.

Baird, H. M., *Theodore Beza.* New York, 1899.

Bateson, Mary, *Collection of Original Letters,* etc. Camden Society Miscellany IX. London, 1893.

Bayne, C. G., "Visitation of the Province of Canterbury, 1559," *English Historical Review 28* (1913).

Beard, Charles, *The Reformation of the Sixteenth Century.* London, 1907.

Becon, Thomas, *Works,* ed. John Ayre. 3 vols. Cambridge: Parker Society, 1843–1844.

Bindoff, S. T., *Tudor England.* Harmondsworth, 1950.

Birt, H. N., *The Elizabethan Religious Settlement.* London, 1907.

Black, J. B., *The Reign of Elizabeth, 1558–1603.* Oxford, 1936.

Bosanquet, E. F., "The Destruction of Monuments at Salisbury Cathedral," *Wiltshire Archaeological and Natural History Magazine 40* (1918).

Brodrick, G. C., *Memorials of Merton College.* Oxford, 1885.

Bromiley, G. W., *Baptism and the Anglican Reformers.* London, 1953.

—— *Thomas Cranmer: Theologian.* London, 1956.

—— *Zwingli and Bullinger.* Philadelphia, 1953.

Buckle, H. T., *History of Civilization in England.* 2 vols. London, 1857–1861.

Burnet, Gilbert, *History of the Reformation of the Church of England,* ed. E. Nares. 4 vols. London, 1839.

Calvin, John, *Commentaries,* trans. and ed. Joseph Haroutunian and L. P. Smith. Philadelphia, 1958.

—— *Institutes of the Christian Religion,* trans. John Allen; ed. B. B. Warfield. 2 vols. Philadelphia, 1936.

—— *Theological Treatises,* trans. J. K. S. Reid. Philadelphia, 1954.

Calendar of State Papers Domestic, 1547–1625. London, 1856–1872.

Calendar of State Papers Foreign, 1558–1589. London, 1863–1950.

Calendar of State Papers Roman, 1558–1578. London, 1916–1926.

Calendar of State Papers Spanish, Elizabeth. London, 1892–1899.

Catholic Encyclopedia. 16 vols. New York, 1907–1914.

Churton, Ralph, *Life of Alexander Nowell.* Oxford, 1809.

Constant, Gustave, *La réforme en Angleterre.* 2 vols. Paris, 1930–1939.

Cranmer, Thomas, *Remains,* ed. Henry Jenkyns. 4 vols. Oxford, 1833.

—— *Works,* ed. J. E. Cox. 2 vols. Cambridge: Parker Society, 1844–1846.

Dakin, A., *Calvinism.* Philadelphia, 1946.

Davies, E. T., *Episcopacy and the Royal Supremacy.* Oxford, 1950.

Davies, Horton, *The Worship of the English Puritans.* Westminster, 1948.

Davies, R. E., *The Problem of Authority in the Continental Reformers.* London, 1946.

Dawley, P. M., *John Whitgift and the English Reformation.* New York, 1954.

DeVocht, H., "Thomas Harding," *English Historical Review* 35 (1920).

D'Ewes, Simonds, *The journals of all the Parliaments during the reign of Queen Elizabeth.* London, 1682.

Diocesis Cantuariensis: Registrum Matthei Parker, 1559–75, ed. W. H. Frere. Oxford: Canterbury and York Society, 1907–1935.

Dixon, R. W., *History of the Church of England from the Abolition of the Roman Jurisdiction.* 6 vols. Oxford, 1895–1902.

Dowey, E. A., Jr., *The Knowledge of God in Calvin's Theology.* New York, 1952.

Dugmore, C. W., *The Mass and the English Reformers.* London, 1958.

Eells, Hastings, *Martin Bucer.* New Haven, 1931.

Elton, G. R., *England under the Tudors.* London, 1955.

Fife, R. H., *The Revolt of Martin Luther.* New York, 1957.

Figgis, J. N., *The Divine Right of Kings.* Cambridge, 1914.

Fletcher, J. M. J., "Note on the Stained Glass in Salisbury Cathedral," *Wiltshire Archaeological and Natural History Magazine* 45 (1930).

Flew, R. N., and R. E. Davies, *The Catholicity of Protestantism.* London, 1951.

Fowler, Thomas, *The History of Corpus Christi College.* Oxford, 1893.

Foxe, John, *Actes and Monuments,* ed. Josiah Pratt. 8 vols. London, 1877.

Frere, W. H., *The English Church in the Reigns of Elizabeth and James I.* London, 1904.

Frere, W. H., and W. M. Kennedy, *Visitation Articles and Injunctions of the Period of the Reformation.* 3 vols. London, 1910.

Froude, J. A., *History of England from the Fall of Wolsey to the Defeat of the Spanish Armada: The Reign of Elizabeth.* 5 vols. New York, 1912.

Fuller, Thomas, *Abel Redivivvs.* London, 1651.

Garrett, C. H., *The Marian Exiles.* Cambridge, 1938.

Gasquet, F. A., *The Old English Bible and Other Essays.* London, 1897.

Gee, Henry, *The Elizabethan Clergy, and the Settlement of Religion, 1558–64.* Oxford, 1898.

Gorham, G. C., *Gleanings of a Few Scattered Ears during the Period of the Reformation in England*. London, 1857.

Grimm, Harold, *The Reformation Era*. New York, 1954.

Grindal, Edmund, *Remains,* ed. William Nicholson. Cambridge: Parker Society, 1843.

Gwatkin, H. M., *Church and State in England to the Death of Queen Anne*. London, 1917.

Harding, Thomas, *An answere to maister Juelles chalenge*. Louvain, 1564.

―――― *A confutation of a book intituled An apologie of the Church of England*. Antwerp, 1565.

―――― *A detection of sundrie and foule errours uttered by M. Jewel*. Louvain, 1568.

―――― *A reioindre to M. Jewels Replie. By perusing whereof the reader may see the answer to parte of his Chalenge iustified,* etc. Antwerp, 1566.

―――― *A reioindre to M. Jewels replie against the sacrifice of the Masse*. Louvain, 1567.

Hardwick, Charles, *A History of the Articles of Religion*. Cambridge, 1851.

Hardy, T. D., *Syllabus of Documents in Rymer's Foedera*. 3 vols. London, 1869–1885.

Harington, John, *Nugae Antiquae; being a miscellaneous collection of original papers,* etc., ed. Henry Harington. 2 vols. London, 1769.

Harkness, Georgia, *John Calvin: The Man and His Ethics*. New York, 1931.

Harnack, Adolph, *History of Dogma,* trans. Neil Buchanan, et al. 7 vols. London, 1896–1899.

Historical Manuscripts Commission, *Calendar of the Manuscripts of the most Hon. the Marquis of Salisbury, preserved at Hatfield House, Hertfordshire*. Part I, London, 1883.

Hoare, H. W., *The Evolution of the English Bible*. London, 1902.

Hobhouse, Charles, "Some Accounts of the Parish of Monkton Farleigh," *Wiltshire Archaeological and Natural History Magazine 20* (1881).

Hooker, Richard, *Works.* ed. John Keble; 7th ed. rev. W. Church and F. Paget. 3 vols. Oxford, 1888.

Hopf, Constantin, *Martin Bucer and the English Reformation*. Oxford, 1946.

Hudson, W. S., *John Ponet (1516?–1556): Advocate of Limited Monarchy*. Chicago, 1942.

Hughes, Philip, *The Reformation in England*. 3 vols. London, 1950–1954.

Humphrey, Laurence, *J. Juelli, Episcopi Sarisburiensis, vita*. London, 1573.

Hunter, A., *The Teaching of Calvin*. London, 1950.

Hyma, A., *The Christian Renaissance*. New York, 1925.

The Interpreters' Bible, ed. G. A. Buttrick, et al. 12 vols. New York, 1951–1957.

Jewel, John, *Works,* ed. John Ayre. 4 vols. Cambridge: Parker Society, 1845–1850.

—— *The works of J. Jewell; and a briefe discourse of his life* [by D. Featley]. London, 1609, 1611.

—— *An apologie or aunswer in defence of the Church of England.* [Trans. Ann, Lady Bacon]. London, 1562.

—— *Certaine sermons preached before the Queenes Maiestie and at Paules crosse,* etc. London, 1583.

—— *The copie of a sermon wherupon D. Cole first sought occasion to encounter,* etc. London, 1560.

—— *A defence of the Apologie of the Churche of Englande, an answeare to a certaine booke by M. Hardinge.* London, 1567.

—— *A defence of the Apologie, etc., whereunto there is also newly added an Answeare unto other like booke, written by the saide M. Hardinge, entituled, A Detection of sundrie foule Errours etc., Printed at Louaine, . . . 1568, and inserted into the foremer Answeare, as occasion, and place required, as by special notes added to the Margine it maie appeare.* London, 1570.

—— *An exposition upon the two Epistles to the Thessalonians.* London, 1583.

—— *A replie vnto M. Hardinges answeare.* London, 1565, 1566.

—— *The true copies of the letters betwene John Bisshop of Sarum and D. Cole vpon occasion of a sermon.* London, 1560.

—— *A viewe of a seditious bul sent into Englande, 1569.* London, 1582.

Jones, W. H., "Aldhelm," *Wiltshire Archaeological and Natural History Magazine 3* (1863).

—— *Fasti Ecclesiae Sarisberiensis.* 2 vols. Salisbury, 1879–1881.

Jordan, W. K., *The Development of Religious Toleration in England.* 4 vols. Cambridge, 1932–1940.

Jung, Rudolph, *Die englische Flüchtlingsgemeinde in Frankfurt am Main, 1554–9.* Frankfort, 1910.

Knappen, M. M., *Tudor Puritanism.* Chicago, 1939.

Knox, John, *Works,* ed. David Laing. 6 vols. Edinburgh, 1846–1864.

Kraeling, Emil, *The Old Testament since the Reformation.* New York, 1955.

Kressner, Helmut, *Schweizer Ursprünge des anglikanischen Staatskirchentums.* Gütersloh, 1953.

Le Bas, C. W., *The Life of Bishop Jewel.* London, 1835.

Lindsay, T. M., *A History of the Reformation.* 2 vols. New York, 1906–1907.

Luther, Martin, *Letters of Spiritual Counsel,* ed. T. G. Tappert. Philadelphia, 1955.

—— *Works.* 6 vols. Philadelphia, 1915–1932.

McGovern, J. B., et al., "Notes on Jewel's Library," *Notes and Queries 9* (1914), 401–403, 441–443, 475.

Machyn, Henry, *The Diary of Henry Machyn, Citizen and Merchant-Taylor of London, 1550–63,* ed. J. G. Nichols. London: Camden Society, 1848.

McLelland, J. C., *The Visible Words of God*. Grand Rapids, 1957.

McNeill, J. T., *The History and Character of Calvinism*. New York, 1954.

—— "The Significance of the Word of God for Calvin," *Church History 28* (1959).

—— *Unitive Protestantism*. New York, 1930.

Makower, Felix, *Constitutional History and Constitution of the Church of England*. New York, 1895.

Mallet, C. E., *A History of the University of Oxford*. 3 vols. London, 1924–1927.

Meyer, A. O., *England and the Catholic Church under Elizabeth and the Stuarts,* trans. J. R. McKee. London, 1916.

Mueller, W. A., *Church and State in Luther and Calvin*. Nashville, 1954.

Muller, J. A., *Stephen Gardiner and the Tudor Reaction*. New York, 1926.

Neale, J. E., *Elizabeth I and Her Parliaments, 1559–1581*. London, 1953.

—— "The Elizabethan Acts of Supremacy and Uniformity," *English Historical Review 65* (1950).

—— *The Elizabethan House of Commons*. London, 1949.

—— "Parliament and the Articles of Religion, 1571," *English Historical Review 67* (1952).

Original Letters Relative to the English Reformation 1531–58, chiefly from the Archives of Zurich, ed. Hastings Robinson. 2 vols. Cambridge: Parker Society, 1846–1847.

Parker, Matthew, *Correspondence, 1535–1575, eds. John Bruce and T. T. Perrowne.* Cambridge: Parker Society, 1853.

Parker, T. H. L., *The Doctrine of the Knowledge of God: A Study in the Theology of John Calvin*. Edinburgh, 1952.

—— *The Oracles of God: An Introduction to the Preaching of John Calvin*. London, 1947.

Parsons, Robert, *The Memoirs of Father Robert Parsons, ed. J. H. Pollen.* Catholic Record Society Miscellany, II (1905); IV (1907).

Pearson, A. F. S., *Thomas Cartwright and Elizabethan Puritanism*. Cambridge, 1925.

Pollard, A. W., *Records of the English Bible*. London, 1911.

Pollard, A. W., and G. R. Redgrave, et al., *A Short Title Catalogue of Books printed in England, Scotland, and Ireland, and of English Books printed abroad, 1475–1640*. London, 1926.

Pollen, J. H., *The English Catholics in the Reign of Queen Elizabeth*. London, 1920.

Powicke, F. M., *The Reformation in England*. Oxford, 1941.

Read, Conyers, ed. *Bibliography of British History: Tudor Period, 1485–1603*. 2nd ed., Oxford, 1959.

—— *Mr. Secretary Cecil and Queen Elizabeth*. London, 1955.

Richardson, Alan, and W. Schweitzer, *Biblical Authority for Today*. Philadelphia, 1951.

Richardson, C. C., *Zwingli and Cranmer on the Eucharist*. Evanston, 1949.

Ridley, Nicholas, *Works,* ed. Henry Christmas. Cambridge: Parker Society, 1841.

Rowse, A. L., *The England of Elizabeth*. London, 1950.

Rupp, E. G., *Studies in the Making of the English Protestant Tradition*. London, 1947.

Ryan, L. V., "The Haddon-Osorio Controversy (1563–1583)," *Church History* 22 (1953).

Sanders, Nicholas, *Report to Cardinal Moroni on the Change of Religion in 1558-9,* ed. J. H. Pollen. Catholic Record Society, Miscellany I, London, 1905.

Schaff, Philip, *The Creeds of Christendom*. 3 vols. New York, 1919.

Schwiebert, E. G., *Luther and His Times*. St. Louis, 1950.

The Seconde Parte of a Register, ed. Albert Peel. 2 vols. Cambridge, 1915.

Seebohm, Frederic, *The Oxford Reformers*. London, 1911.

Solt, L. F., "Revolutionary Calvinist Parties in England, etc.," *Church History* 27 (1918).

Southgate, W. M., "The Marian Exiles and the Influence of John Calvin," *History* 27 (1942).

Smith, H. M., *Henry VIII and the Reformation*. London, 1948.

Smith, L. B., *Tudor Prelates and Politics*. Princeton, 1953.

Smits, Luchesius, *Saint Augustin dans l'oeuvre de Jean Calvin*. Vols. I and II, Assen, 1957–1958.

Smyth, C. H., *Cranmer and the Reformation under Edward VI*. Cambridge, 1926.

Statutes of the Cathedral Church of Sarum, eds. E. A. Dayman and W. R. H. Jones. Bath, 1883.

Strype, John, *Annals of the Reformation,* etc. 4 vols., Oxford, 1824.

—— *Ecclesiastical memorials,* etc. 3 vols., Oxford, 1822.

—— *Historical Collections of the Life and Acts of . . . John Aylmer,* etc. Oxford, 1821.

—— *History of the Life and Acts of . . . Edmund Grindal,* etc. Oxford, 1821.

—— *The Life and Acts of John Whitgift,* etc. 3 vols., Oxford, 1822.

—— *The Life and Acts of Matthew Parker,* etc. 3 vols., Oxford, 1821.

—— *Memorials of . . . Thomas Cranmer,* etc. 2 vols., Oxford, 1840.

Stubbs, William, *Registrum Sacrum Anglicanum*. Oxford, 1858.

Sykes, Norman, *Old Priest and New Presbyter*. Cambridge, 1957.

Symonds, Richard, *Diary of the Marches of the Royal Army during the Great Civil War,* etc., ed. C. E. Long. London: Camden Society, 1859.

Synodalia, ed. Edward Cardwell. 2 vols. Oxford, 1842.

Thompson, J. V. P., *Supreme Governor*. London, 1940.

Trésal, J., *Les Origines du schisme Anglican, 1509–71*. Paris, 1908.

Wallace, R. S., *Calvin's Doctrine of the Word and Sacraments*. Edinburgh, 1953.

Whitgift, John, *Works*, ed. John Ayre. 3 vols. Cambridge: Parker Society, 1851–1853.

Whitney, E. A., "Erastianism and Divine Right," *Huntington Library Quarterly* 2 (1939).

Whittingham, William, *A brieff discours off the troubles begonne at Franckford A.D. 1554*. Zurich[?], 1575.

Wilkins, David, *Concilia Magnae Britanniae,* etc. 4 vols. London, 1737.

Wiltshire Bibliography: A Catalogue of Printed Books, etc., ed. E. H. Goddard. Wilts Education Committee, 1929.

Wood, Anthony À., *Athenae Oxonienses*. 4 vols. London, 1813–1820.

Woodhouse, H. F., *The Doctrine of the Church in Anglican Theology, 1547–1603*. London, 1954.

Wordsworth, Christopher, "Elias de Durham's Leadenhall in Salisbury Close," *Wiltshire Archaeological and Natural History Magazine* 39 (1917).

———*Statutes and Customs of the Cathedral Church . . . of Salisbury*. London, 1915.

The Zurich Letters, ed. H. Robinson. 2 vols. Cambridge: Parker Society, 1842–1845.

Index

Index

Harvard Historical Monographs

*Out of print